THE POLITICS OF COURTLY DANCING
IN EARLY MODERN ENGLAND

The Politics of Courtly Dancing
in Early Modern England

SKILES HOWARD

UNIVERSITY OF MASSACHUSETTS PRESS
Amherst

Copyright © 1998 by
University of Massachusetts Press
All rights reserved
Printed in the United States of America
LC 97-32623
ISBN 1-55849-144-9
Designed by Sally Nichols
Set in Garamond No. 3 by Graphic Composition, Inc.
Printed and bound by Braun-Brumfield, Inc.

Library of Congress Cataloging-in-Publication Data

Howard, Skiles.
The politics of courtly dancing in early modern England / Skiles Howard.
p.   cm. — (Massachusetts studies in early modern culture)
Includes bibliographical references (p.) and index.
ISBN 1-55849-144-9 (alk. paper)
1. Dance—England—History—16th century.   2. Dance—England—History—
17th century.   3. Dance—Social aspects—England—History—16th century.
4. Dance—Social aspects—England—History—17th century.   5. Dance in
literature—History—16th century.   6. Dance in literature—History—17th
century.   I. Title.   II. Series.
GV1646.E6H69   1998
394'.3—dc21   97-32623
                                                                                 CIP

British Library Cataloguing in Publication data are available.

For Rudi

Contents

Illustrations

Acknowledgments

Finally, a chance to thank those who contributed to this endeavor in so many ways. The writing of the earlier drafts of this book was generously supported by a Charlotte E. Newcombe Fellowship, and the revision for publication by a J. Paul Getty Postdoctoral Fellowship in Art History and the Humanities. William Burdick taught me Renaissance dances and kindly shared his considerable knowledge both historical and practical. The late Bernard Beckerman encouraged me while I was still a dancer to pursue my scholarly interests. Teachers and colleagues at Columbia offered helpful suggestions as I worked on this project, especially Mario diGangi, Martin Meisel, James Mirollo, Ian Frederick Moulton, Anne Lake Prescott, James Shapiro, and Edward Tayler. I was fortunate to have had two splendid advisers in David Scott Kastan and Jean E. Howard, who is the most acute and certainly the most tireless reader imaginable. I am grateful to Arthur Kinney at the University of Massachusetts Press, to the astute and constructive readers who responded to the manuscript, and for the editorial support of Chris Hammel, Pam Wilkinson, and Betty Waterhouse.

For permission to reprint works in their collections, I thank the Folger Shakespeare Library; the Bibliothèque Nationale, Paris; the British Library and British Museum; the Devonshire Collection, Chatsworth; the Historic Royal Palaces; the National Gallery of Art, Washington, D.C.; the Cia Fornaroli and Spenser Collections of the New York Public Library; and the Pierpont Morgan Library, New York. I am grateful to the staff at these institutions for their assistance, especially to Madeleine Nichols and Charles Perrier of the Dance Collection of the Library for the Performing Arts, Charles E. Pierce Jr., of the Morgan, Theresa Helein at the Folger, Sarah Winbush of the Courtauld Institute, Peter Day of the Devonshire Collections, and Clare Murphy of the Historic Royal Palaces.

Portions of this book appeared in *Shakespeare Quarterly, SEL,* and Peter Herman's *Rethinking the Henrician Era,* and I benefited immeasurably from the stimulating responses I received from their readers, and from those who offered comments at conferences of the Shakespeare Association of America, the Group for Early Modern Cultural Studies, the Center for Medieval and Renaissance Studies, and the

American Society for Theatre Research. Many other people offered help and support in one way or another; I especially thank A. R. Braunmuller, Mark Franko, Kim Hall, Coppélia Kahn, Carole Levin, Lena Cowen Orlin, Andrew Sabol, and Bruce Smith. Most of all, I thank two whose encouragement both professional and personal has been extravagant, indispensable, and much valued: Peter Herman and Gail Kern Paster. None of these kind people is responsible, of course, for the indiscretions and imperfections in this book, which are completely my own. Last, but certainly not least, I thank my husband and best friend, Howard, for his example, strength, and love, our neighbor Rose Gima for her warm assistance, Marjorie Carsen for her patience and insight, and Adam and Caitlin for being themselves.

THE POLITICS OF COURTLY DANCING
IN EARLY MODERN ENGLAND

Introduction

An engraving of "Court and Country Dancers" printed by
Thomas De Bry in the late sixteenth century (Fig. 1) illustrates
with dramatic clarity the opposition of two traditions of dancing, as
well as their contrasting bodily paradigms.[1] The Lady and Gentleman of the Court are elongated emblems of heavenly aspiration;[2] at
the same time, the tranquil alignment of their bodies conveys an

1. Court and Country Dancers. J. Th. DeBry, after H. S. Beham,
sixteenth century. The Mansell Collection/Time, Inc.

effortless earthly rapport. Yet their harmony is patently hierarchical.
The Gentleman leads the Lady with his strong right arm, enfolding
her hand, his muscular legs and prominent sword confirming his
power and agency. The Lady, represented as more diminutive to signify her subordinate status, is conveyed by her left hand while the
right hovers pliantly over the weighty gown, a visible restraint. Her
head and body incline deferentially toward the Gentleman; her eyes
are modestly averted from onlookers and away from the direction
in which she moves, emphasizing her dependence on gentlemanly

1

navigation. The Gentleman, in contrast, expectantly scans the distance as if for approval from king, rival, or lover—except when he is impressing the Lady with an ardent yet proprietary kiss.

Where the Lady and Gentleman stand erect and parallel to one another, sleek, isolated, and self-contained, the country folk, bulky and bottom-heavy, overlap and embrace above and below, arms and legs entwined, everywhere in contact. Their bodies do not ascend toward heaven, but parallel the earth on which they dance; their stance is wide, their positions asymmetrical, their bodies and heads turned to one another in a variety of attitudes that reflect permutations of mutual interest and involvement. The women, visibly endowed with legs, are the ambulatory equal of men, and are shown in movements of comparable freedom. The irregularity of the country dancers' positions conveys a spontaneity that underscores the restraint of the courtly dancers and the constructedness of their relations. But lest country liveliness and freedom hold excessive appeal, the superior charm and grace of the courtly dancers are proclaimed in a homiletic caption that bears witness to the politics of dancing: "Here flourish integrity of behavior, courtly charm, both grace and well-bred decorum. What wonder if divine qualities naturally follow divine beings. The bumpkin is as far from the courtier as the sheep-cote from the palace—so much the dancing before you will show. But . . . let the differences between the different kinds of life appear as they are."[3]

The dancing of early modern England has long been supposed to signify heavenly concord and little else; sixteenth-century defenders of dancing from Thomas Elyot to John Davies, reviving the classical trope of the cosmic dance, vigorously promoted elite social dances on the basis of their heavenly lineage. Thereafter, the identity of *cosmos* and *orchestra* was so successfully propagated in E. M. W. Tillyard's "Elizabethan World Picture" that, until recently, dancing on the public stage as well as in court masque has been understood primarily as a celebration of the transcendent order and perpetual harmony of the firmament.[4] The critical equation of dancing and celestial harmony was further fortified by the subsequent tendency to sentimentalize dancing as a transcendent expression of human emotion in which historical specificity and ideological intent were eclipsed by "essential human truth" or exemplary form. However, in early modern England, dancing was becoming increasingly diverse, socially linked, and controversial. As the Middle Ages waned, the dancing of the elite began a separate development, evolving into a means of courtly self-fashioning,[5] an instrument for the acquisition and exercise of social power.

As an important cultural practice, dancing reflected and participated in the broad social and political changes of early modern England: the rise of the centralized state, the emergence of the patriarchal family, the polarization of religious factions, and the acceleration of exploration and colonization. A visual and kinetic discourse by which social norms were circulated, dancing became a site of contestation—variously recommended and regulated, compulsory and forbidden, discursively plundered and stockpiled as ordnance in a variety of religious and social conflicts. Countervailing forces soon found expression through the medium of dancing as elite and popular practices collided, interacted, and were transformed. Courtly dances changed throughout the early modern era, and signified differently in different settings: at the social events of the elite, performed by ladies and gentlemen, they were a display of aristocratic entitlement, but on the popular stage, performed by artisan players and framed by popular jigs, they often served to comment on elite assumptions. In the Henrician masque, dancing was one of a constellation of visual practices that circulated paradigms of rank and gender to stabilize a reforming governing class. However, in the early Jonsonian masque, dancing also functioned to manage space and difference in the service of English expansion. On the public stage, the interaction of popular and courtly dancing in Shakespearean comedy was a metonym of urban social relations, but in Middleton's later plays, the satirical representation of elite dances embodied an anticourt resistance. Even in its absence, as in Elizabeth Cary's *The Tragedy of Mariam,* dancing was a discursive practice that circulated and interrogated the bodily paradigms of the age.

Nevertheless, until recently, the gentlemanly equation of dancing and heavenly concord has been perpetuated, the role of this important practice in the construction of social difference and national identity has gone largely unexplored, and though courtly dancing was obviously a patriarchal practice, it has not been examined as such. The dancing of the early modern era has much to offer in terms of current interests in gender, rank, and nationality; it is also, not incidentally, relevant to contemporary codes of physicality, since courtly dancing represents a first elaboration of the system of bodily aesthetics that privileges the elongated and enclosed aristocratic form, and endows it with magical powers. This system has lately enjoyed quite a renaissance of its own—witness the prosperous market in fitness regimens based on the assumption that one can shape one's destiny by trimming one's thighs.

But dancing is an evanescent practice that leaves no trace of itself; we cannot go to the Folger Shakespeare Library and study a caper. And as there is no "body" that is not shaped by historical forces,[6] so there is no universal dance accessible over time, only individual dances that ceased to exist when they ended. How can we imagine, theorize, and write about the ephemeral movements of the past? Conceptual frameworks, none wholly unproblematic, must be enlisted to organize the minutiae found in civility treatises, dancing manuals, chronicles, and criticism—specifically an opposition of "elite" and "popular" dancing, and the extrapolation of "English dancing" from Continental texts, and other forms directed to the elite.

Objections to the opposition of "high" and "low" dancing may rightly be raised on the grounds that it is a monolithic model in its own right that merely replaces the monolith of "concord" with another. Moreover, "elite" and "popular" as categories are difficult to define as each embraces a wide range of attitudes and practices, and as cultural formations were mutually influential.[7] Furthermore, as de Bry's caption suggests, both the opposition of court and country and the category of the popular were themselves the textual traditions of the elite. However, the coexistence in early modern Europe of two socially linked cultures has been widely recognized although these cultures did not correspond exactly to the social division of gentle and common, since the gentle shared in the "popular" culture that was transmitted in traditional observances, but the common people were excluded from the refinements of "elite" practices transmitted by formal instruction.[8] While the separation of dancing into "elite" and "popular" does not begin to convey the variety or complexity of early modern practices, it does provide an avenue to their diversity.

As we assume a model of civility, we must for critical purposes assume a model of dancing; this model, however, is necessarily based on documents that may not record actual practice so much as an "utopian ideal of what the dance should have been."[9] Furthermore,

4

in the absence of dancing manuals in English, notions of English courtly dances are derived primarily from French and Italian texts directed to the aristocracy and urban gentry, and the social formations of sixteenth-century London differed considerably from those of a fifteenth-century Tuscan court or a sixteenth-century French one. Likewise, ideas of "popular" dances have been based primarily on anecdotal or iconographic evidence, most of which was produced for or by the elite,[10] or on more recent work whose assumptions were fundamentally ahistorical.[11] Inconveniently, in England, many of the written records of popular dancing involve its prosecution, and iconography is frequently of Continental origin.

Until Playford printed English "country" dances in 1651, dancing in England was not dignified by detailed efforts at transcription, and there is no English treatise on elite dancing comparable to the Continental instruction books.[12] Descriptions of courtly dancing in England are effectively limited to Elyot's *Governour,* Coplande's *maner of dancing,* some private papers, and Sir John Davies' poem *"Orchestra."*[13] However, court festivity throughout Europe, it is generally agreed, was informed by the same images, assumptions, and practices. Cultural trends that emerged in Italy and France in the fifteenth century, including fashions in dancing, manifested themselves in England in the sixteenth, when Henry VII returned from exile and introduced the customs of the Burgundian court to dignify his reign.[14] Later, the "common going of Englishmen into Italy"[15] and the immigration of dancing masters from the Continent ensured a continuing fertilization of "lavoltas high and swift corantos."[16]

The reticence of dancing masters in England is remarkable in comparison with their Continental peers who recorded their dances in excruciating detail, and the reasons may only be guessed at. If some were of French and Italian origin, perhaps they were not fully literate in English; some may have been Jews, and wished to remain anonymous.[17] But even the patented dancing masters Richard Frythe and Robert and William Warren, appointed by the queen for twenty-one years "to be the only teachers of dancing within the City of London and suburbs" neglected to record the dances they taught with evident success.[18] Perhaps the explanation may be found in the relative mobility of English dancing masters: "Why should the leaden-heeled plumber have his hall," asks Middleton's Sinquapace plaintively, "And the light-footed dancer have none at all? / . . .

We're born to teach in back-houses and nooks, / Garrets sometimes, where it rains on our books." Moving between city craft and courtly service, between music and dancing, self-employed purveyors of courtly refinements rather than members of a royal household, they may not have had sufficient leisure to record their accomplishments.[19] Whatever the reason for the lamentable silence of the English dancing master, English references to dancing confirm the adoption of French and Italian styles, and support the relevance of Continental manuals.

THE COURTLY DANCES OF THE RENAISSANCE

In the late Middle Ages, so the story goes, singing and dancing were an important part of feast-day processions and secular celebrations, when gentle and common met in open spaces, linked hands, and danced to their own songs. But on the Continent, toward the end of the fourteenth century, the elite began to withdraw and develop a festival of exclusivity: we remember messer Federigo's fastidious objection: "This dancing in the [sun] . . . can I in no [way approve] withal, and I can not see what a man shall gain by it."[20] The elite retreat and the subordination of the popular are shown in an early sixteenth-century Flemish Calendar with a richly attired couple preparing to dance before a feasting assembly and a household of entertainers: torchbearers, musicians, and a fool. The common people are strictly contained: through one door, men peer enviously; in another, a woman serves; and in the bottom margin, boys and men roll hoops, a popular pastime (Fig. 2).[21] John Stow reports a parallel withdrawal in England, attributed to the religious repression of popular festivals:

In the holidays all the summer, the youths are exercised in leaping, dancing, shooting, wrestling, casting the stone, and practicing their shields; the maidens tip in their timbrels, and dance as long as they can well see . . . [and] on holy days after evening prayer . . . maidens, one of them playing the timbrel, in sight of their masters and dames . . . dance [beneath] garlands hung athwart the streets; which open pastimes of my youth being now suppressed, worse practices within doors are to be feared.[22]

As the elite moved their entertainments into halls or formal gardens, dancing assumed discrete forms: "country" or popular dancing,

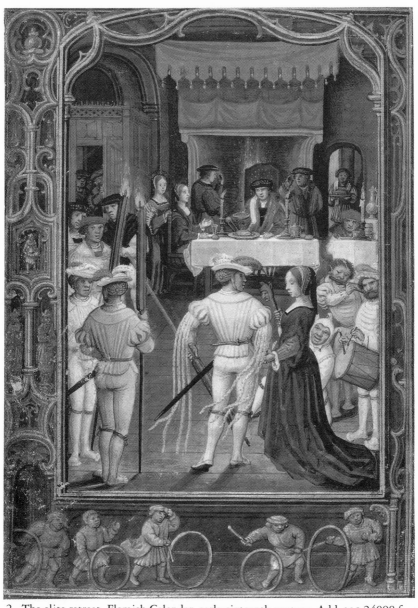

2. The elite retreat. Flemish Calendar, early sixteenth century. Add. M S 24098 f. 19b. By permission of the British Library.

still improvised outdoors in mixed groups; and "courtly" dancing, taught by a dancing master and performed indoors in couples to the accompaniment of professional musicians. Among the gentility, the circumstances and forms of social dancing changed profoundly as dancing moved out of the oral tradition and, progressively codified, designed, theorized, taught, and transcribed, into literate culture. Popular and courtly dancing embodied the fundamental social distinction between those who worked with their hands and those who did not.[23] While the dances of the working people often mimed their occupations, the gestures of the elite were suppressed[24] and dancing masters derided ladies who flung their arms about like peasants sowing seeds. Dancing also afforded a genial occasion for the rehearsal of social mobility: a barrister gallant strongly advised his pupils to maintain a discreet distance from those ahead, to advance deliberately with measured steps, and not to pile atop one another like nursing piglets.

Around the beginning of the fifteenth century, the dancing masters of the Lombard courts began to record their dances in manuals that included theoretical material, details of social deportment, the steps of fashionable dances, and a rudimentary notation of musical accompaniment. Within the private spaces of the Continental elite, social dancing developed in a trajectory that began with the gendering of the round dance, evolved through processional couple dances like the *basse* dance or measures, was elaborated in choreographed dances such as the *galliard* and the *coranto,* and culminated in ornate theatrical figured dances. This, at least, is a familiar narrative, most fully explicated in (and perhaps originating with) Davies' "*Orchestra,*" but French and Italian treatises do tend to support it.[25]

The round is a choral dance known in nearly every human society, and reputedly is also enjoyed by chimpanzees. Originally performed around a symbol of power such as a fire or a tree, circle dances were part of religious celebrations during the Middle Ages, and were often used in iconography of the Annunciation or the Nativity (Fig. 3).[26] Gradually, rounds, though still performed by the elite, became associated with fairies, witches, and the lower classes, an emblem of incivility. Round dances functioned not only as a marker of difference, though, but as one of national unity. In England, they were part of the old seasonal festivals like May Day or Midsummer's Eve and were associated with Queen Elizabeth as traditional rural customs became an important element in the entertainments given for her on her summer progresses, and in her mythology.[27] An engraving in Spenser's *Shepheardes Calendar* (1581) portrays a Maying dance of bouncing couples around a horse-drawn vehicle that may contain the queen (Fig. 4). However, poem and print articulate conflicting social attitudes toward festivity: in the verses, Piers puritanically reminds Palinode that the dancing shepherds are delinquent and "play while

3. Round. French Book of Hours, c. 1445. The Pierpont Morgan Library, New York. M. 287, f. 64v. Photography: David A. Loggie.

4. Round. Edmund Spenser, *The Shepheardes Calendar.* London, 1581. Folio 16r, "Maye" plate. The Pierpont Morgan Library, New York. PML 78109. Photography: David A. Loggie.

their flocks be unfed" (fol.17r), but in the woodcut the animals appear satisfied, almost rapturous.[28]

In the round, or *carole,* the dancers joined hands and, often singing their own accompaniment, faced inward toward one another and moved together in unity. Early dances also took a processional form: in the hay, or *farandole,* the line of dancers wound through field, village, or town. A fifteenth-century French book of hours shows dancing in transition: in the foreground of a public square, five well-attired and regulated couples dance a protocourtly round accompanied

10

5. Round and *Farandole*. "Dance Scene in a Public Square." French Book of Hours, c. 1473. The Pierpont Morgan Library, New York. M. 677, f. 137. Photography: David A. Loggie.

by piper and directed by an elderly man, as a comparatively amorphous *farandole* recedes in the distance (Fig. 5).[29] Of course, early dances were performed in couples as well as chains, but gender roles were not so strictly codified as they were in the later dances. In addition to linked dances, there were individual theatrical or "spectacular" dances and linear group ones, usually performed by males: the Morris, of uncertain origin but danced throughout the Continent, took both of these forms, and in England, the familiar pantomime featuring the hobby-horse and Maid Marian as well (Fig. 6).[30] These early dances had certain characteristics in common: their transmission was participatory and informal, their performance was improvisational, their length was undetermined, and they were danced outdoors or in public spaces.

The separate development of courtly dancing is believed to have begun with the *estampie,* a couple dance favored by the poet-musicians of the late Middle Ages, under whose influence the male and female dancers, formerly dispersed randomly around the communal circle, were reorganized into heterosexual pairs to reflect the Provençal songs of romantic love.[31] The emergence of recognizably

11

6. Morris Dance. Window in the House of George Tollet, Esq., sixteenth century. Art File M875#1. By permission of The Folger Shakespeare Library.

courtly and popular ways of dancing in the early modern era is recorded in the manuscript illustrations of the elite, some of the earliest modern dancers found on a fourteenth-century century manuscript of secular poetry celebrating courtly love, Machaut's *La Remède de Fortune* (Fig. 7).[32] With elongated bodies, rigid postures, and impassive countenances, these dancers articulate the "upward training" and emotional containment of the courtier. Elite withdrawal is emphasized in the compression of their circle, which, with the elemental object removed from its center, appears to have become the totem. Within the ring of dancers, the gentlemen and ladies are sartorially differentiated and alternated in couples, a spare lady installed opposite the bearded "Machaut" and his beloved who enact romantic love with audacious glances. Although they dance outside the castle walls amid grass, flowers, and trees, this is no pastoral; their garden, with a neatly constructed pool of flowing water, is, like their dance, patently cultivated.

In contrast, a fifteenth-century manuscript illustration of an open round dance (Fig. 8)[33] emphasizes rural amorphity. Surrounded by barnyard animals, accompanied by the music of shawms, the dancers, in the variety of positions and shapes that signify rudeness, seem impatient to move in conflicting directions. The courtiers of the French *carole* maintain a measured distance from one another and link hands well below waist-level as though in secret, but the peasants invade each others' space and clasp each other firmly and boldly. Where the progress of the courtly dancers promises to be smooth and predictable, in the country, collisions between dancers and domestic animals seem imminent, and one looks ready to trip over his foot. Where the faces of the carolers are composed in a pleasant, impersonal restraint, the peasant man and woman in the foreground appear to be engaged in a highly charged dalliance or dispute. That the joviality of this bucolic scene is a representation of an elite perspective is articulated by a design that visually subordinates the dancing bumpkins below an ornately designed caption and a well-cultivated tree.

For the elite, the paradigm of early Renaissance dancing became the *bassadanza,* known in France as the *basse* dance, and in England as the measures.[34] Fashionable for more than a hundred years, this dance reigned on the Continent at the beginning of the fifteenth century, and in England in the sixteenth; a fifteenth-century illustra-

7. *Carole. La Remède de Fortune,* fourteenth century. M S Fr. 1586, fol. 51v. By permission of the Bibliothèque Nationale, Paris.

tion from the *Livre de Roi Modus* represents this processional dance in all its conscious dignity, with ladies clasped tightly on the gentleman's right and appended firmly to the ground by the trains of their gowns (Fig. 9).[35] The relationship of the Italian and French versions to each other and to the English measures is still unclear. However, the assortment of Continental treatises and English writing reveals common features, including an increasing formalization of all aspects of the practice, a theorization that presupposed human control over space and time, and the performance of social difference. The most fundamental link between the various manifestations of the *basse* dance, though, was a common vocabulary of movements that rendered it a kind of universal kinetic language of the European elite.

The *basse* dance was a slow, sedate procession into or around the banquet hall, usually performed in gendered couples, in which the gentleman led and the lady followed. To begin the dance, the gentleman is instructed by Toinot Arbeau, the French cleric whose *Orchesography* (1581) is regarded as the authority on Renaissance dancing,

to "choose some comely dansel who takes your fancy, and, removing your hat or bonnet with your left hand, proffer her your right to lead her out to dance. She, being sensible and well brought up, will offer you her left hand and rise to accompany you."[36] The *basse* dance consisted of five steps: it began and

8. Round. French-Flemish manuscript, fifteenth century. M S Lat. 1173, fol. 20v. By permission of the Bibliothèque Nationale, Paris.

ended with a *révérence* or *honor,* and progressed at a deliberate and dignified pace, with the *simple* (single) and *double* moving forward by one and three steps, the *réprise* retreating diagonally back, and the *branle* swaying from side to side. These five steps were repeated in different sequences until the procession either returned to its original position, to its destination, or until the music ended. Outside the hall, the *basse* dance traveled well and lived long; some of the same versions were recorded in both fifteenth- and sixteenth-century treatises, of French as well as Italian origin.[37] Their extensive transmission was facilitated by a common tabulature that represented each step by its first letter—"b" for *branle,* "ff" for *"simples,"* "d" for *double,* "z" for *réprise*—a conventional notation that served to latinize the practice and to move dancing into the realm of literate culture.[38]

In the medieval round and *farandole,* dancers covered the same ground repeatedly and collectively, but as the ideal of a universal elite dancing took hold, the community of dancers itself began to break apart. In the early Renaissance, when the linked circle broke into separate couples, the spatial options of dancing were apparently extended: detached, the pairs might move or turn in any of the four directions, singly or together. In the *basse* dance as in the round, the dancers moved in concert in a circle or oval, but the gendered couples, while moving in the same direction, were disconnected; revolving on their own axes, they

9. *Basse* dance. *Livre de Roi Modus,* c. 1465. The Pierpont Morgan Library, New York. M. 820, f. 105.

were—as the slight variation in the directional orientation of the three couples in the *Livre de Roi Modus* suggests—effectively privatized. While the couples gained an illusory independence from the group, in fact they were increasingly controlled by clearly defined norms, elaborated and recorded by their dancing masters, governing the parameters of the dance and the movements of the assembly.

The Continental treatises that identify the common features of the *basse* dance also reveal local preoccupations that may be generalized as spatial for the Italians, metrical for the French. The fifteenth-century Italian masters were overwhelmingly concerned with the management of space, repositioning the dancer at the center of a circumscribed territory and propelling him across it on a linear current. Where rounds and hays were usually danced in open spaces over bumpy tufts and hillocks, the *bassadanza* was danced indoors on a smooth floor that facilitated the refinement of an imperturbable advance. The dance was fixed and framed by the interior walls of the *palazzo* as an aesthetic emblem of containment; simultaneously, the space cleared for elite celebration was a metonym of spatial entitlement. The movements of the dancer within space were first theorized by the dancing masters Domenico di Piacenza and his pupils Guglielmo Ebreo and Antonio Cornazano as the six "primary requisites" of the dancer: *misura, memoria, aeire, maniera, partire del terreno,* and *movimento corporeo.*[39] The first two of these are both spatial and temporal: *misura,* measure, refers to the dancer's relationship to the music, and to the spatial extremes (high and low, movement and stillness) that music evokes; *memoria,* memory, refers to sequence in time as well as space. The other four, however, are exclusively spatial paradigms: *aeire,* is the gentle rise and fall inherent in vertical movement, and *maniera* the opposition of upper and lower body that inflects the horizontal. *Partire del terreno* governs the dancer's relation to the space he occupies, the space of the dance and its apportionment in dancing; *movimento corporeo* is a dynamics of motion achieved by variations in all of the above.[40]

If the aestheticized sweep of the dance was the primary concern of the Italians, the French were occupied with intervals, segmentation, and the classification of "measures," an emphasis that perhaps reflected the growing importance of clock time in early modern culture.[41] The focus of French treatises is formal rather than aesthetic, temporal rather than spatial, and the persistent "enigma" of the *basse* dance concerns the relation of the dance to the music that the dancers no longer made. On Burgundian manuscripts, the visual juxtaposition of dance steps and musical notes is pictorial rather than choreographic, and with dance steps adjacent to but not paired with musical notes, they are perplexing to generations accustomed to a tradition wherein the dance is choreographed to a set piece of music.[42] The relation of the *basse* dance to its music is unclear. Perhaps music and dance were aligned, or perhaps they unfolded on parallel but ancillary courses—monophonic, polyphonic, or somewhere in between. Perhaps the printed music was a tenor upon which the musicians improvised as they followed the dance, or, alternatively, a melodic aide-mémoire for the dancers. The still-unresolved relationship between music and dance locates the *basse* dance on the boundaries between an oral, improvisatory culture and a written, replicable one, a "bridge and border between two eras."[43]

The English authorities on the measures are Coplande's *maner of dancing* (which titularly acknowledges its debt to France and replicates the French preoccupation with lists) and Thomas Elyot's defense in *The Boke named the Governour.* Not a dancing master himself, Elyot abstains from the Continental custom of privileging aesthetic or formal qualities and emphasizes instead the social utility of dancing practice. Where in the Italian treatises, the issue of social dominance is implied in the organization of space and time around the elite dancer, Elyot is magnificently explicit concerning the political uses of dancing. The unison steps of the measures, he argues, serve to train the rising governors and ladies in the physical and social requisites of high society, and entitle them to a secure place in courtly company. Moreover, Elyot specifically connects social hierarchy with gender difference, heretofore a minor theoretical consideration in dancing texts, by endorsing the measures as an image of ideal marriage between a dominant gentleman and a submissive lady.

Gradually, the Queen of Measures, as the *basse* dance was called, was dethroned by couple dances that elaborated the elementary gender distinction—the gentleman leads, the lady follows—established by the measures. The *pavane,* a solemn processional to "staid music ordained for grave dancing" continued the measures' horizontal flow. According to Arbeau, it was performed on ceremonial occasions, often as an entrée, to exhibit intense dignity and costly clothing (Fig. 10):

A cavalier may dance the pavan wearing his cloak and sword. . . . And the damsels with demure mien, their eyes lowered save to cast an occasional glance of virgin modesty at the onlookers. On solemn feast days the pavan is employed by kings, princes and great noblemen to display themselves in their fine mantles and ceremonial robes. They are accompanied by queens, princesses and great ladies, the long trains of their dresses loosened and sweeping behind them, sometimes borne by damsels. And it is the said pavans played by hautboys and sackbuts, that announce the great ball and are arranged to last until the dancers have circled the hall two or three times, unless they prefer to dance it by advancing and retreating. Pavans are also used in masquerades to herald the entrance of gods and goddesses in their triumphal chariots.[44]

The authority of Arbeau's descriptions of the dances, as the most detailed available, has not been questioned, but given his social position as a provincial middle-class canon, one cannot help wondering about the proportion of fantasy in his descriptions of court life. However, his account does convey the increasing importance of gendered

10. *Pavane.* Matthaus Zasinger, engraving, "The Ball," c. 1500. Rosenwald Collection. Copyright © 1997 Board of Trustees, National Gallery of Art, Washington, D.C.

behaviors (glances of virgin modesty) to the correct execution of the dance, and the progressive use of a dance "employed" by kings, princes, and great noblemen to encode economic dominance and mythic divinity.

On social occasions, the *pavane* was followed by the lively *galliard*—often the music of the latter was simply that of the *pavane* played faster, as Robert Morley writes in *A Plaine and Easie Introduction to Practicall Musick,* "a kind of music made out of the other."[45] This dance was not *basse* but *haut,* lightly sprung rather than walked, originally made up of five steps and sometimes known as the "sink-a-pace."[46] Unlike the *pavane,* the *galliard* was often elaborately choreographed to a set piece of music, and as a gendered performance piece was the epitome of sixteenth-century choreographed dancing: the gentleman resolutely penetrated the air with elaborate capers and mounted virtuosic displays for the delight of his damsel and other onlookers, "present[ing] himself before [his partner] to perform a few passages, turning at will now to the right, now to the left . . . pursu[ing] her . . . to execute more passages before her . . . displaying his skill until the musicians stopped playing."[47] The Italians developed numerous variations on each step, and meticulous regulations on deportment: the drawings in Cesare Negri's *Le Gratie d'Amore* (1602) show the variety of the gentleman's moves (see Fig. 16); significantly, none shows an unaccompanied woman, much less one turning to the right, to the left, or performing a few passages.[48] In the *basse* dance, all the willing and able might participate, but the *galliard* was often performed as a choreographed duet, as in "The Garden Festival in Venice" (Fig. 11), with one or more couples displaying the gentleman's virile capers and the lady's admiration.[49] These performances, therefore, not only separated men from women—privileging the former—they exhibited the gendered couple as the central spectacle.[50]

Other social dances, notably the "leaping" *lavolta* and the "traversing" *coranto,* became fashionable toward the end of the sixteenth century;[51] on the Continent, however, the centerpiece of court masque became the geometric "figured" dancing choreographed for court celebrations.[52] Dancing was always configured to some extent: popular dances formed circles and spirals, and courtly dances might move through elaborate patterns. But the figured dances of the French court of the 1580s were different, a form of bodily writing character-

11. *Galliard.* "The Garden Festival in Venice," 1539. Copyright © British Museum.

ized by symbolic images—geometric shapes and alphabetic sequences—achieved by the legible distribution of dancers over the surface of the hall (Fig. 12).[53] These dances, deliberately designed and exactingly staged to inspire aesthetic admiration, marked a clear break between social and theatrical courtly dancing. Furthermore, figured dancing complicated the opposition of popular community and elite individual by returning courtly dancing to a unity more characteristic of popular tradition, while reducing the self-fashioned courtier to an epistemic fragment in a collective message.[54] However, the collectivity of figured dancing, an alluring vision designed to appeal to the will of the monarch and the wit of the spectator, subordinated both the dancer's pleasure and his ambition to the celebration of monarchical power and courtly literacy.

THE POLITICS OF COURTLY DANCING

The figures of court festivity written on the dancing place embodied the alliance of humanist learning, dancing, and power. Courtly dancing, as its self-conscious legibility suggests, was a cultural inscription related to the material practices of writing and civility, one that regulated and socialized the activities of the nether limbs as writing transformed the signifying hand and civility re-presented the body.[55] The proliferation of Italian and French dancing manuals in the fifteenth and sixteenth centuries anticipated a proliferation of courtesy

12. Figured dancing. *Le Balet des Polonais,* 1573. Spencer Collection. New York Public Library. Photo: Robert D. Rubic.

books,[56] which in turn anticipated the flood of writing manuals in late sixteenth-century England. All three cultural practices were committed to the calibration of social difference, and to the mastery of techniques that promised stability and prosperity in a world of rapid and unpredictable change. Like courtesy books, dancing treatises instructed the would-be courtier in a "rhetoric of bodily demeanor,"[57] and like writing manuals, dancing manuals privileged and disseminated codes of social literacy.

21

In his collection of fashionable courtly dances, *Nobilità di Dame* (1600) the dancing master Fabritio Caroso includes a choreographed dance called the *"Contrapasso Nuovo,"* accompanied by an engraving that witnesses the political appropriation of the dancing place.[58] Decorative rather than technical, the figure provides an idealized image of the floor patterns followed by the dancers of Caroso's *balletto.* A superscription explains that the *Contrapasso* was made *con vera mathematica sopra i' versi d'Ovidio,* and the salient choreographic feature is pointedly noted within the design: newly devised steps, the *spondeo* and the *datille,* invented by Caroso to reproduce the metrics of the ancients. The humanist incursion into the territory of festivity is announced by a superscription that elevates the *balletto* from diversion to high culture, and steps that explicitly define dancing as an adjunct to classical letters.[59]

The connection of dancing with writing, realized in Caroso's deployment of the anatomical foot in the service of the poetical one, was a Renaissance commonplace. Thomas Morley explains the *galliard* by invoking the language of poetry, as a measure that "the learned call *trochaieam rationem,* consisting of a long and short stroke successively . . . as the foot *trochaeus* consists of one syllable of two times, and another of one."[60] Richard Sherry, in *A Treatise of Schemes and Tropes* (1550), implies that dancing is the origin of all the arts: "Scheme is a Greek word, and signifies properly the manner of gesture that dancers use to make . . . but by translation is taken for the form, fashion, and shape of any thing expressed in writing or painting."[61] While Caroso authorizes dancing by means of poetry, and Sherry, poetry by means of dancing, both insist that poetry and dancing are not only complementary but they are comparable. In his poem *"Orchestra,"* Sir John Davies, too, elaborates on this conceit, representing the literary arts posing in an elaborately choreographed *divertissement,* with Grammar as the steps, Rhetoric as the patterns, and Poetry, the dancing master.[62]

Courtly dancing was identified with formal speech as well as poetry, and was recruited to serve the same purposes. No longer a spontaneous response to sexual, seasonal, or religious impulse, dancing was conceived as a forensic oration whose purpose was to persuade,[63] "a kind of mute rhetoric by which the orator, without uttering a word, can make himself understood by his movements and persuade the spectators that he is gallant and worthy to be acclaimed, admired, and loved."[64] Like oratory, courtly dancing was classically authorized, codified, rehearsed, and devised to control response: the dancer could make himself understood as well as make himself believed. Thus, dancing was credited with the power both to circulate social norms and to negotiate new formations.

Therefore, courtly dancing was not only an aspect of elite culture related to linguistic forms, it was a discursive practice in its own right—a Foucauldian "lost discourse" that, like the practice of civility, both negotiated power relations and preserved a "knowledge of the structures, circulations, and struggles" within the social body.[65] The dancing of the elite was a fully framed political discourse, an elaborate system of kinetic, spatial, and visual terms and interrelated ideas that organized a view of the world and the body that vindicated itself and excluded others.[66] The discourse of dancing visually articulated the signs and structures of power and difference, reflecting social pressures, and managing social anxieties. Significantly, the word "discourse" etymologically derives from Latin *discurrere,* moving "back and forth," or "running to and fro,"[67] suggesting both the protean nature of dancing as cultural artifact, and the means by which it stimulated social change. Inherent in the meaning of "discourse" is the iconicity of movement, and the paradoxical materiality and evanescence of dancing.

While courtly dancing was no doubt pleasurable, as Elyot often acknowledged (fols. 82r and 83v), it was seldom recommended for the pleasures it afforded, but was more often acclaimed as instrumental in the attainment of power. The movements of courtly dancing were an important component of aristocratic self-fashioning that simultaneously transfigured the subject and positioned him or her within a social hierarchy.[68] A physical practice whose elements were invested with meaning, dancing was both an emblem of social aspiration and a means for its realization,[69] a manifestation of social anxiety, and a way to address it. In England, bodily structures replicated social shapes: the upward training of the dancing body mirrored a concern with upward mobility, its enclosure paralleled enclosures of property, the segmentation of the dancing place was a miniature likeness of the mapping of the realm, and the expansion of the dancer's control at the center of the hall a micrometonym of the centralized state.

In courtly dancing, the sense of physical agency derived from martial exertions in feudal days was redirected from an external foe toward the self, as the subject unsettled by inscrutable economic forces and religious turmoil sought to secure his body, at least, in a stable system that offered the illusion of control. The body of the courtly dancer was a "docile" body, "manipulated, shaped, trained, which obeys, responds, becomes skillful and increases its forces . . . [one that] may be subjected, used, transformed, and improved."[70] Foucault assumed that the docile body was an invention of the "classical age" and that "docility" was determined by parameters of class, with the bodies of the lower classes systematically transformed and used to maintain the control of the elite. However, the characteristics of and operations upon the body that he identified as manifestations of eighteenth-century institutional oppression of the underclass describe perfectly the characteristics of and operations upon the body that the Renaissance courtier inflicted upon himself.[71]

Yet the power derived from dancing was inherently unstable. Courtly dancing promoted a divided subjectivity, simultaneously demanding both agency and passivity from the dancer as he sought to control his destiny by dominating his body. Dancing fragmented the subject in the dual role undertaken by the dancer—at the same time the disciplining gentleman he wished to become, and the disciplined man he wished to cease to be. The dancer was forced to maintain a relationship of "constant coercion" with himself that inscribed a contradiction between self- and social empowerment. Furthermore, the fragmentation of the dancer was inherent in the process of learning to dance; the body of the dancer was not treated "as if it were an indissociable unity, but . . . [worked] at the level of the mechanism itself—movements, gestures, attitudes, rapidity: an infinitisimal power over the active body . . . [with an] uninterrupted, constant coercion, supervising the process of the activity rather than its result . . . according to a codification that partitions as closely as possible time, space, movement."[72] And finally, the power conferred by courtly dancing was unstable in the mechanism of its transmission; the techniques of aristocratic self-fashioning were furnished to the elite, and later purveyed to the new gentility, by their social inferiors (servants, itinerants, and other outcasts), raising the possibility that power exercised into one body might later be appropriated by anybody with access to the proper techniques and used against power[73]—as indeed occurred as courtly dances were disseminated into the city.

In sum, dancing changed in the early modern era from an improvised, seasonal activity of companions who danced to their own music to a regulated, private, secular endeavor, whose participants constructed and maintained social formations of difference by training "the mechanism itself," transforming and improving the "movements, gestures, attitudes, rapidity" of each would-be lady and gentleman who practiced it. The dancing place and its representations were truly a site for the production of "shaping fantasies"[74] as cultural ideals crystallized in and through practiced behavior, and physical repetitions individually performed refigured the society.

Ascending the Rich Mount:

Performing Rank and Gender
in Henrician Masque

The Henrician masque was a constellation of visual practices with dancing as its magnetic core, its riches of setting, dress, dancing, and gesture generously displayed in Hall's account of a masque celebrated in 1522. On the night of Shrove Tuesday, the king and the ambassadors of France were honored at a "great and costly" banquet given by the lord cardinal. After supper,

they came into a great chamber hanged with arras . . . and at the nether end of the same chamber was a castle, in which there was a principal tower [with] a cresset burning, and two other less towers stood on [either] side, warded and embattled. . . . [T]his castle was kept with ladies of strange names, the first *Beauty*, the second *Honor*, the third *Perseverance*, the fourth *Kindness*, the fifth *Constance*, the sixth *Bounty*, the seventh *Mercy*, the eighth *Pity;* these eight ladies had Milan gowns of white satin, every Lady had her name embroidered with gold. . . . Underneath the base fortress of the castle were [eight other] ladies, whose names were *Danger, Disdain, Jealousy, Unkindness, Scorn, Malebouche, Strangeness* . . . attired like to women of India. Then entered eight lords in cloth of gold caps and all, and great mantel cloaks of blue satin; these Lords were named *Amorous, Nobleness, Youth, Attendance, Loyalty, Pleasure, Gentleness,* and *Liberty*. The king was chief of this company [which was] led by one all in crimson satin with burning flames of gold, called *Ardent Desire*, which . . . moved the ladies to give over the castle, but *Scorn* and *Disdain* said they would hold the place. Then *Desire* said the ladies should be won, and came and encouraged the knights, then the lords ran to the castle (at which time without there was shot a great peal of guns). . . . The ladies defended the castle with rosewater and comfits, and the lords threw in dates and oranges, and other fruits made for pleasure, but at the last, the place was won . . . [and Lady *Scorn* and her company were] driven out of the place and fled. Then the Lords took the ladies of honor as prisoners by the hands and brought them down, and danced together very pleasantly.[1]

The entertainment seems a benign and trivial amusement. The gallant rescue of feminine virtues from a prison of Petrarchan scorn is heroically accomplished by male ardor symbolically discharged in delectable volleys of candied fruit, with the liberation of femininity celebrated in joyous dancing. The luxury and frolic, however, also serve to situate the celebration in the world outside the hall. Historically, the pageant is located in the early modern era by the mingling of medieval and courtly traditions, with moral personifications reenacting the scenario of salvation as a Petrarchan courtship. Materially, it is calibrated by its weapons of war: the battle is fought with rosewater, comfits, dates, oranges "and other fruits made for pleasure," weapons that proclaim the participants exempt from the prudent hoarding of comestibles.

Visually, the masque articulates the structures of Tudor society with a multiplicity of fixed and mobile icons. In Hall's description, the festive space of the banqueting hall (Fig. 13) is carefully segmented and coded in terms of hierarchical oppositions.[2] The horizontal area of the great chamber is cleaved into near and "nether end," interior and exterior to the castle battlements. Replicating the social division between "gentle" and "base,"[3] the vertical space is divided into turrets, "base fortress," "nether chamber," and *platea,* all under the domination of a "principal tower" emphatically illuminated by "a cresset burning." Within this partitioned space circulate the masquers in uniform dress, lords in blue satin and ladies in white, attire that both recapitulates the principle of segmentation and defines the participants as elements of an emblematic composition. Hierarchy is gesturally established as well as mapped and pigmented, most vividly in the relations between men and women. After their victory over malevolent femininity, the lords take the ladies they have liberated "as prisoner" and bring them "down," the interlude of after-dinner dancing introduced and justified by a scenario of forcible abduction. The jolly rescue is close to a mock rape, tolled in the rhythmic boom of a cannon that thunders the connection of dancing with masculine power.

13. Great Hall. Hampton Court Palace, sixteenth century. Crown Copyright. Historic Royal Palaces.

The masquing scenario of assault and rescue was something of a commonplace, and, containing masculine violence in a narrative of courtliness, rehearsed the civilizing of the warrior. An earlier Epiphany pageant (1512),

was made in the hall a castle, gates, towers, and dungeons, garnished with artillery and weapons of the most warlike fashion, and on the front of the castle was written *"le Fortresse dangereuse,"* and within the castle were six ladies, clothed in russet satin. . . . After this castle had been carried about the hall, and the Queen had beheld it, came the King with five other. . . . These six assaulted the castle, the ladies seeing them so lusty and courageous were content to solace with them, and upon further communication, to yield the castle, and so they came down and danced a long space. And after the ladies led the knights into the castle, and then the castle suddenly vanished, out of their sights.[4]

Here, the ladies embody both "dangerous" and consenting femininity, and the gentlemen vanish into their domain at the end, but in both pageants it is the performance of masculine martial boldness that lures the ladies out of their fortress and provides the pretext for dancing.

As pure spectacle, the Henrician pageant has been critically neglected in comparison with the poetic splendors of the Jacobean masque. Indeed, preserved in descriptions like those of Hall that admiringly detail the opulence of the setting and the lavish dress of the masquers, and lacking the glorious poetry supplied by Jonson and his contemporaries, Henrician festivity may seem inconsequential. However, read through Sir Thomas Elyot's defense of dancing in *The Boke named the Governour* (1531), which celebrates a choreography of hierarchy, it becomes apparent that the Henrician masque—to which dancing was central[5]—was more complex and formative than has been recognized, and that it anticipated the later masque in important ways.[6] The alliance of dancing and power in the Jonsonian masque has long been established, with the masque proper seen to affirm the cosmic concord centered in the king, and the revels between masquer and spectator to extend this harmony outward and downward into the court, uniting them and transforming each in turn.[7] But the Henrician masque emerged at the beginning of an absolutist trajectory that culminated in the Stuart era,[8] and nearly a century before Jonson praised dancing as "an exercise / not only shows the movers wit, / but maketh the beholder wise, / as he hath power to rise to it,"[9] Elyot defended dancing precisely for its capacity to educate the new governor. In the Henrician masque, the dancing that organized the spectacle reinforced the structures of rank and gender that consolidated political power in the monarch, performing at least some of the political work usually credited to the Jonsonian masque.

ELYOT'S DEFENSE OF DANCING

For Thomas Elyot, dancing was more than an amorous pastime or an invigorating sport; in the *Governour,* he asserts that "nobility," both moral and social, is created and confirmed in the actions of courtly dancing. The earliest English work on the education of the governing class, the book was written when Elyot was, in fact, a court outsider who had lost his minor position with the fall of his patron Wolsey and retreated to his undistinguished estate; dedicated to Henry

VIII, the volume pleased the monarch sufficiently that Elyot soon secured an appointment to the court of Charles V.[10] Elyot's *Governour* was the first of many English works on gentlemanly education, a new necessity in early modern England. In feudal society, courtly education was experiential, with young gentlemen sent as pages into household service to perfect by example their deportment and learning, a custom that persisted into the early modern era. However, the increasing importance of humanist studies among the Continental aristocracy, the Tudor willingness to elevate the sons of the lesser nobility and lower gentry into the new governing class, and the bureaucratic demand for pens instead of swords mandated the development of a more methodical system.[11] In his educational program, Elyot, following, as he asserts, the example of the ancients (and certainly the model of the Italian courtier), elevates dancing into the curriculum of English classical education: "if men would now apply the first part of their youth, that is to say from seven years to twenty, effectually in the sciences liberal and knowledge of histories, they should revive the ancient form as well of dancing, whereof they might take not only pleasure, but also profit and commodity" (fol. 82r).

Dancing was one of the physical practices that proved so useful in transforming the feudal warrior to an early modern gentleman, and the dancing imported from the Continent adapted well to the needs and preoccupations of a reforming English governing class.[12] Social mobility increased during the reign of Henry VII as a new landed nobility sprang up from the gentry and merchants. The rapid population growth and economic fluctuations of the beginning of the sixteenth century affected the different strata of society, improving the fortunes of some, diminishing those of others. Henry VII sought to restore the authority of the crown over powerful feudal families, and Henry VIII, to strengthen it further: country knights were imported to court as a power base, and ambitious younger sons supplied the growing bureaucracy. The newly elevated had to be transformed rather quickly into disciplined and useful courtiers, and physical forms of obedience were practiced with the same diligence as martial skills had been in former times.[13] The feudal warrior ethic based on honor in battle was replaced by an hierarchal "network of patronage";[14] honor was no longer won by brave deeds, but by adroit manners and tractable bodies that promoted princely trust and social acclaim. In the absence of martial rigor, the aestheticized physical disciplines of dancing and civility, less overtly aggressive but equally competitive, were prized.

Courtly dancing, like civility, instructed the ambitious if unrefined courtier to prepare and present his credentials by means of an "outward bodily propriety"[15] that affirmed the power of those he sought to represent. In a period of social transition, behavior became a new heraldry by which the courtier created his nobility and signaled his allegiance, for in the "upward training of the body," achieved by tedious and painful means, a postural metonym of hierarchy was blazoned on the upright figure of the dancing courtier. Moreover, in a time of uncertainty, when fortunes were being made and lost, when heirs were failing or were produced in superfluity, dancing was a kinetic talisman, a physical training that materialized the illusion of social control—whatever his place in the hierarchy, the dancer might reassure himself that his exertions would improve his social position as certainly as his posture.

In the *Governour,* Elyot represents dancing as an ideal of physical training that simultaneously trained the spirit. Many "wise men and valiant captains [of antiquity] embraced dancing for a sovereign and profitable exercise" (fol. 78v), he explains, and he invokes Greek pedagogy, which conveniently coincided with Tudor exigency, to prescribe dancing as a means by which "children of gentle nature or disposition may be trained into the way of virtue with a pleasant facility" (fol. 83v). Dancing invested the dancer with the honor and nobility of the courtly ideal, a kind of text written on the body that mnemonically preserved discursive values within the dancer as subject, and transmitted these by means of the dancer as object:[16] "all they that have their courage stirred toward very honor or perfect nobility, let them approach to this pastime, and either themselves prepare them to dance, or else at the least way behold with watching eyes other that can dance truly" (fols. 84v–85r). Elyot is careful, however, to identify dancing with heaven, not earth, an imitation of "the wonderful and incomprehensible order of the celestial bodies . . . and their motions harmonical" (fol. 77v).

Anticipating by centuries phenomenological theorists of the constitution of social reality through language and gesture, Elyot anatomizes the ways in which nobility was performative in courtly dancing.[17] The "right courtier," Elyot explains, is constituted through his performance of the measures, a Platonic-way-through-the-Beautiful-to-the-Good.[18] The five steps of the dance guide the moral elevation of the dancer from the "first moral virtue called prudence" (fol. 83v) to the quality of "maturity" (fol. 84v). The "singles"—a step forward, a pause, then another step—are "two unities separate in pacing forward, by whom may be signified providence and industry" (fol. 86v). The "brawle" (*branle*), an "altercation" that sways from side to side, ensures a "celerity and slowness" from which "springs an excellent virtue" (fol. 85r). The "double," three slow steps and a pause, instructs in the three branches of prudence: election, experience, and modesty (fol. 92r). The *reprise,* a step diagonally backward, teaches circumspection (fol. 86v). Practicing these movements, the dancer learns social as well as moral lessons. He learns to move in concert with others engaged in identical motions, and to relinquish improvisation. He learns to pace forward slowly, reflectively, and deliberately, covering his tracks. And he learns to advance steadily while not straying from the designated path. Dancing the measures assures the courtier of achieving "nobility" by the mastery of a formalized mobility.

Clearly, Elyot recommends dancing not because it is "timeless," but because it is timely, a discipline to be undertaken not only for pleasure, but for "profit and commodity" (fol. 82r). Elyot's description of the "honor" or *révérence* (Fig. 14)[19] that peppered dances, processions, and social interactions defines dancing as both moral and tactical:

The first [movement] of every dance is called honor, which is a reverent inclination or courtesy with a long deliberation or pause, and is but one motion comprehending the time of three other motions, or setting forth of the foot. By that may be signified that at the beginning of all our acts, we should do due honor to God, which is the root of prudence, which honor is compact of these three things, fear, love, and reverence. And that in the beginning of all things we should advisedly, with some tract of time, behold and foresee the success of our enterprise. (Fol. 85r)

In moral terms, the honor imbues the dancer with the spirit of reverence, the foundation of all the virtues. In social terms, the honor, governing relations between superiors and inferiors, is the spine of hierarchy. Therefore, the performance of respect to those above and the extraction of homage from those below not only conferred advan-

Capriol.

14. *Révérence* and *Capriole. Orchèsographie,* 1588. Fols. 26 and 28. By permission of the Bibliothèque Nationale, Paris.

tage upon the courtier himself in several ways, his actions reinforced the hierarchical social order from which the notion of "honor" emerged.[20] The display of reverence enacted in the honor was additionally prudent, for while it created and proclaimed the spiritual goodness of the courtier, it pragmatically afforded him "some tract of time" to pause, collect his thoughts, and concentrate on worldly matters of success and enterprise. The moral ascent that commenced with a gesture of reverence is thus linked with a kind of early modern career-building, with the honor transforming the dancer into both a "wise man" and a "valiant captain" to assure both worldly and otherworldly success.

The hierarchy legitimized by courtly dancing was also a patriarchy, in which the interests of male supremacy were served by constructions of feminine enclosure and dependence that preserved the sanctity of family and property.[21] Elyot explicitly defines the dancing couple as an emblem of gender relations,[22] the "associating of man and woman in dancing, they both observing one number and time in their movings . . . signifies matrimony" (fols. 82r–82v). Officially charged with political significance under the Tudors by the diplomacy of marriage employed by Henry VII,[23] the subject of marriage and its fruits was understandably a matter of concern for Henry VIII, since the Tudor claim to the throne was somewhat tenuous, and his contributions to the succession for a time seemingly less than decisive. The decline or extinction of a line was of general concern as well, as some lesser families were in a similar, if not so conspicuous, danger of dying out. Strengthening the patriarchal family through a cultural privileging of marital relations also served to strengthen the power of the state by correspondingly weakening feudal ties of extended kinship that might prove a threat to monarchical authority.[24]

If the incessant performance of the "honor" consolidated structures of rank, it also served (as the spatial inequity of the honor in the drawing in *Orchesography* suggests) to ratify female containment and subordination. In the honor, the lady dipped slightly as the gentleman "made a leg" (Fig. 14). However, as the gentleman stepped back and acknowledged his superior or dancing partner by inclining his body forward, he actually filled more space than he did when erect. In contrast, the lady's bow, with upright but lowered body and downcast eyes, confined and diminished her. Paired in heterosexual couples that visually articulated the preoccupation with patriarchal marriage, Elyot's dancers display an array of gendered virtues that support the principle of male dominance.

In every dance of a most ancient custom there dances together a man and woman holding each other by the hand or arm, which betokeneth concord. Now it behoove the dancers and also the beholders of them to know all the qualities incident to a man, and also to a woman likewise appertaining. A man in his natural perfection is fierce, hardy, strong in opinion, covetous of glory, desirous of knowledge, appetiting by generation to bring forth his semblable. The good nature of a woman is to be mild, timorous, tractable, benign, of sure remembrance, and shamefast. Diverse other qualities of each of them might be found out, but these be the most apparent, and for this time sufficient. (Fols. 82v–83r)

Drawing on classical, biblical, and humoral economies, Elyot endows the gentleman with the characteristics of "natural perfection"—strength, reason, and generative heat—that his negative image, woman, in her "good nature" lacks. Reciprocally, he ascribes to her the qualities of emotional and physical enclosure that culminate in the "shamefastness" and "soberness" that were linked inseparably with chastity.[25] These traits are learned through and expressed in the classically authorized "dance of a most ancient custom": "when we behold a man and a woman dancing together, let us suppose there be a concord of all the said qualities being joined together as I have set them in order. And the moving of the man would be more vehement, of the woman more delicate and with less advancing of the body, signifying the courage and strength that ought to be in a man, and the pleasant soberness that should be in a woman."[26] The conventions of courtly dancing anticipated the sexual division of labor in the modern family, establishing then reinforcing parameters of difference. In encoding these parameters as sacramental, Elyot obscures their human fabrication and utility.

THE HENRICIAN MASQUE

In two important ways, the Henrician masque expedited the process of social stratification,[27] through the formalization of structures of rank and gender in dancing and gesture (as Elyot so carefully explained) and in the incorporation of the monarch as exemplum into the spectacle. The function of dancing in Henrician masque may best be understood in comparison with an earlier English disguising that took place in 1377 on the eve of the accession of Richard II.

On the Sunday before Candlemas in the night, one hundred and thirty citizens disguised and well horsed, in a mummery with sound of trumpets . . . rode from Newgate [some] in the likeness and habit of esquires . . . with comely visors on their faces [and some with] black visors not amiable, as if they had been legates from some foreign princes. These maskers, after they had entered the Manor of Kennington, alighted from their horses, and entered the hall on foot; which done, the prince, his mother, and the lords came out of the chamber into the hall, whom said mummers did salute, showing by a pair of dice upon the table their desire to play with the Prince, which they so handled that the Prince did always win when he cast them. . . . After which they were feasted, and the music sounded, the prince and the lords danced on the one part with the mummers, which did also dance; which jollity being ended, they were again made to drink, and then departed in order as they came.[28]

This description presents a vivid picture of the medieval mumming on a grand scale, but it leaves one important question unanswered.

One hundred and thirty citizens confirm Fortune's favor with weighted dice; Richard entertains his welcome guests, and all dance—but with whom did princes, lords, and mummers dance? Were there women in the court that night aside from the prince's mother? Did the mummers dance with them? Traditionally, this account has been cited as evidence of a "division" between masquers and spectators, one that was "healed" when the two groups began to commingle in the masques of Henry's reign.[29] However, it can also be offered as evidence of *dancing* between masquers and spectators—unless the one hundred and thirty men danced by themselves perhaps in a sword dance or a Morris.[30] Significantly, neither the presence nor the absence of women was recorded, and women were simply absorbed into the "ungendered" masculine body.[31]

The Epiphany masque of 1512 early in Henry's reign is usually designated as the occasion when the supposed separation of masquer and spectator was "repaired" by the introduction of the Italian masquing customs.[32]

On the day of the Epiphany at night, the king with . . . [eleven others] were disguised after the manner of Italy, called a masque, a thing not seen afore in England. [T]hey were appareled in garments long and broad, wrought all with gold, with visors and caps of gold. [A]fter the banquet [was] done, these masquers came in, with six gentlemen, disguised in silk, bearing staff torches, and desired the ladies to dance. [S]ome were content, and some that knew the fashion of it refused, because it was not a thing commonly seen. And after they danced and commoned together, as the fashion of the masque is, they took their leave and departed, and so did the Queen, and all the ladies.[33]

This masque retained many of the features of earlier disguisings: vizards, torches, the element of surprise.[34] But the identity of the "thing not seen afore" has long been a matter of speculation. Was it the "garments long and broad . . . with visors and caps of gold," or the commoning between masquers and spectators? Or perhaps "a new element of gallantry and intrigue"[35] consistent with an increasing emphasis on gender roles. Whichever it may have been, if this dance between masquer and spectator repaired one division, another was created in a newly formalized division between men and women.

Hall's description of the Epiphany masque, furthermore, links two related characteristics of the Henrician masque, the formalization of gender roles in dancing and gesture, and the staging of the monarch into the court spectacle. In the earlier pageant, Richard was a participant in the sense that the casting of dice was a ritual confirmation of the prince's fortune. However, it was his visitors who were the performers, covered with vizards and casting the subtly made dice; Richard merely played himself, fortunate prince and gracious host. Henry, however, is embedded within the spectacle[36] as one of twelve masquers, his preeminence disguised by the same visors and caps of gold as worn by the others, and, "desir[ing] the ladies to dance," the same behavior. Nevertheless, his true identity, though hidden, is not long unknown, and as the king his behavior is exemplary: while seeming to be part of a community of masquers engaged in spontaneous revels, in fact, he leads them in a ritual that confirms his power much as the weighted dice confirmed Richard's good fortune.

This ritual defines the new gentleman with Henry as royal paradigm. Unlike the description of Richard's mumming from which women were erased, this passage is remarkable for its emphasis on feminine difference. In the mumming of 1377, women were, if present, subsumed into universal man; if absent, unremarked. However, in Henry's court, men and women are precisely distinguished, often, as in the Shrovetide masque, by dress of contrasting color, always by the contrasting roles they play. If in other pageants, men play the warrior who abducts the ladies by force, here, men play the courtier who charms them. The ritual of gaining feminine consent is central: the gentlemen masquers invite the ladies to dance; some ladies accept the invitation and some "that knew the fashion of it" refuse, whether out of modesty, lack of expertise, or, conversely, proficiency in playing a scenario of feminine coyness.

Gender is the fundamental category in this ritual, distinguishing masquers from ladies and regulating their interactions by prescribed gesture and precedence: gentlemen "desire" the ladies to dance, ladies do not "desire" the gentlemen. Although, in theory, ladies may accept or refuse the masquer's invitation, few apparently exercise the latter option; most dance and common together in the fashion of the masque. Behavior is consistent throughout: the ladies follow the gentlemen's lead from beginning to end, responding to the gentlemen's desire, and departing after the gentlemen have finished. Far from hiding women among the brambles of universal man, or failing to note their absence, as did the chronicler of Richard's mumming, Hall cultivates men and women in separate rows, trimming them into monitory forms according to patterns implicitly fitted to the designs of the monarch.

Disguised as entertainment and perhaps entertaining in itself, an important project of the Henrician masque was that of social segmentation, a kind of division of the kingdom into discrete units that once established were sanctioned to interact in a strictly regulated way. Both the pageants and masques shared a common structure:

they began with the entrance, often in a pageant-wagon, of the disguisers, usually divided into groups of men and women. The disguisers danced alone and then together, descended into the hall to dance, and returned to the pageant-wagon, which conveyed them out.[37] The proceedings were ordered and unambiguous, with roles clearly defined, groups of masquers segregated in space and time, and interactions between them carefully governed. Participants in English court festivities were assigned to oppositional categories: "masquer" and "spectator," "lord" and "lady." Boundaries were marked by habiliment, behavior, and location: symmetrical numbers of masquers were dressed identically in conspicuous opulence; enacted an emblematic relationship for an assortment of spectators; and were restricted to a particular space within the hall. Once established, the integrity of these groups was rigorously maintained—persons did not move into or out of the company at their own discretion. Furthermore, the time, place, and form of any interaction between them was conventionally predetermined.

A taxonomic preoccupation did not, of course, descend upon the court at the instant of Henry's coronation; the same tendencies were evident toward the end of the reign of Henry VII at the marriage of Henry's older brother Prince Arthur to Catherine of Aragon. Several elaborate entertainments were presented "to amplify and increase the royalty of this noble and solemn feast with many and diverse acts of pleasure." In one, "the likeness of a great hill or mountain" was introduced,

in whom there were enclosed eight goodly knights with their banners spread and displayed naming themselves the knights of the Mount of Love. . . . [They] hastily sped them to the . . . castle which they forthwith assaulted so and in such wise that the ladies yielding themselves descended from the castle and submitted themselves to the power, grace, and will of these noble knights, being right freshly disguised, and the ladies also, four of them after the English fashion and the other four after the manner of Spain, danced together diverse and many goodly dances. . . . And then came down the Lord Prince and the Lady Cecil, and danced two [basse] dances and departed up again, the Lord Prince to the King and the Lady Cecil to the Queen.[38]

On another evening, twelve knights descended from an arbor "of goodly manner and proportion," and "by themselves danced a long space diverse and sundry dances and stood aside. And then blew up the trumpets and therewith came a goodly pageant made round after the fashion of a lantern . . . in which were twelve goodly ladies disguised . . . [who] came out and danced by themselves in right goodly manner diverse and many dances," then "coupled" with the knights and "danced altogether a great space." On yet another, after the lords danced "deliberate and pleasantly," the ladies descended and together they "danced there a long season many and diverse rounds and new dances full curiously and with most wonderful countenance."

These celebrations anticipate the festive reproduction of hierarchical opposition in Henrician pageant: men and women, liberators and prisoners, masquers and spectators, those in Spanish costume and those in English dress. The artificiality of these categories is aestheticized by the symmetry of the subdivisions: sixteen dancers in the castle masque are divided into four groups uniform in gender and nationality. Discrete groups are isolated in space and time: twelve lantern ladies dance alone and establish their affinity before coupling with twelve knights from the arbor, and masquers and masquing ladies likewise dance separately before they combine with the lords and ladies of the court. The division of a commonwealth of revelers into symmetrical groups in distinctive dress seems an unremarkable and innocent form of amusement, and (inured as we are to the convention from balletic and operatic stagings) one not apparently saturated with social import. However, the uniform dress of English masquers was apparently unique to sixteenth-century England, not a characteristic adopted from the Continental courts, since Hall remarks on the variety of French masquing dress on the Field of the Cloth of Gold: "The French Maskers' apparel was not all of one suite, but of several fashions, of diverse silks, some cut, some broached, some had plumes that were very fair, but very beautiful was the sight."[39] The emphasis on fixed and arbitrary groups indicates a singular preoccupation with, and anxiety concerning, social fluidity, and an attempt to control it by festive means.

Court celebrations, then, rehearsed many of the ways by which the equilibrium of an unstable society might be secured: affiliation, glamorized by costly costumes, was promoted; unison movement and a suggestibility to direction were honored; and a tendency toward unsanctioned personal forays was eliminated. Masquer and spectator, lord and lady, remained for the entirety of the entertainment in predetermined roles, acting only in concert, and in the manner prescribed in the scenario. They neither wore inappropriate clothes nor changed them: identical apparel was an emblem of cohesion that reflected in miniature the sumptuary laws that increasingly striated the society.[40] And as the pageants rehearsed the larger social structures of the ranks of men, dancing rehearsed the presumably more intimate relations of heterosexual couples relentlessly signifying matrimony. The dances within the masques like the masques as a whole served to regulate the opportunity and the terms of the interactions between men and women: the gentleman was required to "desire" a lady to dance, and the lady, to respond correctly at the proper time, in harmony with her immediate community, and with the partner selected for her—she was not permitted to emerge at her pleasure from a giant lantern and couple posthaste with any knight or guest she fancied.

The pageant of the "Garden of Pleasure" (1511) visually articulated the hierarchy of gentle and base that structured relations inside and outside the court. At the celebration of the queen's churching at Richmond, a staged uprising against the courtiers of the Garden followed the pageant and dancing. After supper, the lords and ladies retired to the hall, "which was richly hanged . . . [and] scaffolded and railed on all parts" to view an interlude by the Gentlemen of the Chapel. When that entertainment was finished, "the minstrels began to play, and the Lords and ladies began to dance." The king departed unnoticed and returned with the richly dressed disguising. "When the time was come, [the] pageant was brought forth into presence, and then descended a lord and lady by couples. [A]nd then the minstrels which were also disguised also danced, and the lords and ladies danced, that it was a pleasure to behold." As the lords and ladies made ready to retire, "rude people ran to the pageant, and rent, tore, and spoiled the pageant." The king, "in token of liberality . . . appointed the ladies, gentlewomen, and the ambassadors to take the [gold] letters of their garments." As they did so, "the common people perceiving ran to the king, and stripped him into his hose and doublet, and all his companions in likewise . . . wherefore the King's guard came suddenly and put the people back. . . . and all these hurts were turned to laughing and game."[41] This pageant opposes the unlettered masses—rude people who run, rend, tear, and spoil—with lords and ladies who are orderly enough to descend by couples, civil enough to dance sufficiently well to be a pleasure to behold, liberal enough to give away their golden letters in the interests of civic peace, powerful enough to withstand an uprising, and good-natured enough to laugh it off. The lords and ladies, then, give a performance that justifies a society of entitlement.

The hierarchical model of social relations circulated by the dancing and gesture of Henrician masque was reinforced by visual emblems of social ordering that replicated the structuring principle. In an Epiphany masque in 1513, the disguisers emerged from a

Rich Mount . . . set full of rich flowers of silk. . . . On the top stood a goodly beacon giving light, [and] round about the beacon sat the King and five others, all in coats and caps of . . . crimson velvet. . . . [T]he Mount . . . came before the Queen, and the King and his company descended and danced, then suddenly the Mount opened, and out came six ladies . . . and they danced alone. Then the lords of the Mount took the ladies and danced together, and the ladies reentered, and the Mount closed.[42]

This pageant erects familiar boundaries between the men around about the beacon on the top and the ladies emerging from the base, and imposes behavioral sanctions in the form of precedence, as the king and his company descend and dance, then the Mount opens, then out come the ladies.

Furthermore, the setting is itself an icon of social structure, with actual height denoting status; the king and the male masquers, already atop the Rich Mount as it appears in the hall, are confirmed in eternal supremacy. That the monarch is the chief luminary is somewhat ponderously allegorized by the location of scenic illumination. While in earlier pageants, the light originated outside the hierarchical peak produced by common torchbearers who irradiated the masquers in a circle of light, here, the company of highlighted masquers towers over the spectators with solar radiance. Ladies, in contrast, are entrapped within the murky base of a pyramidal Mount that opens to liberate them only after the king and his company have descended and danced. That the ladies' dance follows the lords' emphasizes their separate and secondary status, one further underlined when the lords "take" them. Never on equal footing, the ladies are soon hustled back into the base and "conveyed out" in the tightly closed Mount.

The visual trope of the Rich Mount, a familiar sight in Henrician masque, repeatedly confirmed a gendered hierarchy, displaying the monarch and his courtiers upon a lofty promontory and disgorging ladies from its base. If ladies were occasionally elevated above the men, as when they inundated the lords with rose water, they were usually imprisoned and isolated, helpless in the nether end of a castle tower.[43] Lady Scorn and her company of cross-dressed choirboys fought from underneath the base fortress; even after they were "driven out of the place" and the ladies were "brought down" out of their isolation, the ladies were still prisoners. In most pageants, though, ladies were situated firmly beneath the lords throughout, as in the entertainment for the French ambassadors in 1527. Following a debate on the relative importance of riches and love, a mount appeared, covered with rich stones, roses, pomegranates, and eight lords, who "descended from the mount and took ladies and danced diverse dances." Then, eight other ladies, including the future Queen Mary, emerged from a cave to dance with the lords, but their dances were suddenly interrupted when six other lords with masks and long garments, masquers who were "not known," entered and "took ladies and danced lustily about the place."[44]

Related to the images of lusty masculine dominance circulated in courtly dances and replicated in iconic settings, the form of the monarch's appearance in pageants and masques enforced the notion of male privilege. Typically, Henry, in the company of a number of other lords, disguised himself in spectacular apparel, surprised the spectators with an intrusion into the hall, danced with the ladies, and disvisored as dramatically as possible. In the Epiphany masque, Henry deftly inserted himself into the spectacle, his primacy concealed by the identical dress worn by the other knights. Appareled in garments long and broad, wrought all with gold, the masquers were clearly aristocrats, but social distinctions among them were effaced by impenetrable costumes and masks. Yet the preeminence of the king, though concealed, was not unknown, so that Henry enacted not a "spectacle of rule," but a spectacle of role, the paradigm of the new gentleman.[45]

After the banquet was done, Henry led the masquers, sharply delineated by their glittering dress and the light from the staff torches that surrounded them, in a bold intrusion into a passive company. "[F]ierce, hardy, strong in opinion, covetous of glory, desirous of knowledge" expressed in "advancing of the body," the masquers desired the ladies to dance; some of the ladies, those "tractable [and] benign" were content, but the "timorous, of sure remembrance, and shamefaced" declined "because it was not a thing commonly seen." After the masquers and ladies "danced and commoned together . . . they took their leave and departed." Henry's was an example that the court was obliged to follow.[46] But concealing his identity, and therefore not acknowledging the court's duty to imitate him, Henry rehearsed his courtiers in social difference by disguising power as pleasure.

In one respect, though, Henry's performance was inimitable. Unlike the rest of the court, the king frequently changed roles during the masque, and this source of dramatic excitement was an important emblem of his power. Often, he began the festivities as a spectator, but when the attention of the court was occupied with the performance, he surreptitiously "shifted himself" and returned as a masquer. After one Shrove supper "began the dancing, and every man took much heed to them that danced. The king perceiving that, withdrew himself suddenly out of the place, with certain other appointed for that purpose [and returned with the lords in opulent masking dress] of blue velvet and crimson, with long sleeves all cut and lined with cloth of gold."[47] Unlike other courtly participants, the identity of the king was not fixed: he had the license to change his apparel as well as his rank during the masque.[48]

On some occasions, the king abruptly withdrew when the attention of the court was occupied with the dancing, and returned visibly more impressive, adorned with the regulated perquisites of gentility. On others, as after the pageant of the Rich Mount, he shed masquing dress to return in royal guise, the most impressive role of all: "Then the King shifted himself and came to the Queen, and sat at the banquet which was very sumptuous."[49] In sum, Henry was repeatedly seen to descend into the anonymity of masquing lords, to startle the spectators with an unexpected entrance, and—recalling Henry Richmond—to rise like a Rich Mount above the other lords as he disvisored. Henry's assertion of the right to the ultimate mobility, that of remaking himself king, coincided with a strategic concentration of the court on his performance as a man: when Henry performed in a masque, dancing was an exercise that indeed showed the mover's power to rise and enlightened the beholder to it, strengthening the social hierarchy from the courtly base of commoning dancers right up to the top of the mount.

A century later in *Henry VIII,* Shakespeare conflated the celebration at Wolsey's with another chronicled banquet at York Place,[50] to dramatize the "first dance" of Henry and Anne Boleyn that led to the English Reformation.[51] As a Lord flirts heatedly with Anne, one of the Cardinal's guests, the banquet is interrupted by the entrance of a "noble troupe of strangers, / For so they seem. Th'have left their barge and landed, / And hither make, as great embassadors / From foreign princes" (1.4.53–56). The intrusion, however, is not an embassy but a masque: "Enter King and others as Maskers, habited like shepherds. . . . They pass directly before the Cardinal, and gracefully salute him." Out of "great respect they bear to beauty," the shepherds have left their flocks and "[c]rave leave to view these ladies, and entreat / An hour of revels with 'em" (1.4.63–72). The Cardinal bids the masquers "take their pleasures," the Masquers choose ladies, and the King chooses Anne, to whom he extends the courtesy of a kiss. The Cardinal offers the now-overheated King some "fresher air . . . [i]n the next Chamber," and the scene ends as King and company withdraw to continue the festivities:

> Lead in your Ladies ev'ry one. Sweet partner,
> I must not yet forsake you. Let's be merry,
> Good my Lord Cardinal: I have half a dozen healths
> To drink to these fair ladies, and a measure
> To lead 'em once again; and then let's dream
> Who's best in favor. Let the music knock it.
>
> (103–8)

In this short scene, Shakespeare borrows the devices of the Henrician masque: the sudden intrusion of the masquers, the disguised king, the commoning of masquer and spectator. But the sensual scene—with dances that are merry, not moral, characterized by consuming heat, not by stately restraint, instruments of male appetite, not of masculine control—owes as much to the antidance writing of later Puritan critics, who sought to unravel the spectacle of royal power that Hall and Elyot so painstakingly wove. However, that Shakespeare dramatizes as a dance an encounter that was both conclusive and generative recognizes the dancing of the Henrician masque as a practice that transformed English society and empowered the monarch—if perhaps not in the ways that Elyot imagined.

Through dancing and spectacle, then, the Henrician masque reproduced the concentration of authority at the patriarchal pinnacle,

and circulated rituals of power that informed later ages and generated resistances at multiple sites. Although the Henrician masque
has not been commended for the perfection of Jacobean masque that
resides in a unity of decor, poetry, music, and dance, these pageants
were amply unified—and not by a verbal text. Had the pageant and
dancing by themselves proved inadequate to realize the courtly design, certainly a spoken text would have been required and preserved.[52] It appears, however, that in the Henrician era, the discursive
work of the masque was sufficiently accomplished by the rehearsal in
miniature of the principles of social ordering, and the terpsichorean
elevation of the sovereign. If ideology is "the obviousness of culture,
what goes without saying, what is lived as true,"[53] then the political
project of the dancing in Henrician masque involved rendering natural, even enjoyable, a stratified society under an absolutist ruler.

TWO

Imitating the Stars Celestial:

Rival Discourses of Dancing
in Early Modern England

Early in his defense of dancing in *The Boke named the Governour,*
Elyot recalls the legend of Proteus, supposedly the first dancer,
who "turned himself into sundry figures, as some time to show himself like a serpent, sometime like a lion, other whiles like water, another time like a flame of fire, [signifying] to be none other but a . . .
crafty dancer, which in his dance could imagine the inflections of the
serpent, the soft and delectable flowing of the water, the swiftness
and mounting of the fire" (fol. 77r). Although Elyot rejects the Protean myth of origin, the image conveys the shape-changing, bodily
modulation, and self-mastery that rendered dancing an indispensable element of courtly self-fashioning. Moreover, it recalls the met-
aphorical transformations that dancing underwent in sixteenth-
century England—now a quenching stream, now a consuming
flame—as it was discursively appropriated and debated by competing social interests.

The controversy over dancing, smoldering since antiquity, flared
brightly in early modern England; like plays and poetry, dancing
became a battle-line in various social struggles, and generated a related body of adversarial writings.[1] Dancing itself took many
forms—the popular dances of English festivity, the courtly dances
imported from the Continent, and the permutations that evolved as
elite practices were disseminated into the city and among the country gentry. Potentially, then, dancing signified in many ways, and
therefore might be mobilized to promise control or threaten license,
to confirm agency or enforce dependence, to consolidate or contest
power. The imaginative authority that dancing exerted as a forma-

tive social practice is witnessed by the energetic attempts to gain control *of* it, with arguments for and against citing the same fables and features, but turning them one way or another to exalt dancing or condemn it.

Courtly dancing was a kinetic discourse, and as Continental dances were embraced or resisted by the middling sort, distinct linguistic discourses of dancing evolved to manage it. Elyot's patriarchal discourse was modified by the mercantile and medical discourses of the city, contradicted by the moralistic discourse of Puritan adversaries, and amplified by the sovereign discourse of John Davies' *"Orchestra"*—which in turn generated succeeding discourses *on* Renaissance dancing. The essential joy of dancing did not figure prominently in early modern debates, and the dancer's physical pleasure was secondary to defenders and critics alike. Apologists justified dancing as morally uplifting, socially prudent, physically salubrious, and mentally refreshing. Adversaries expressed less concern that dancing was pleasurable in itself than that it encouraged the pursuit of pleasure and provided the occasion for sin: "an introduction to whoredom, a preparative to wantonness, a provocative to uncleanness, an [entry into] all kind of lewdness."[2]

PATRIARCHAL DISCOURSE

In the *Governour,* Thomas Elyot argues at some length that dancing, embraced by "wise men and valiant captains . . . for a sovereign and profitable exercise" (fol. 78v) is "not to be reproved" (fol. 74r). On the contrary, he explains, it is "of an excellent utility, comprehending in it wonderful figures, or as the Greeks do call them, Ideas, of virtues and noble qualities" (fol. 84r). Because the movements of the measures simultaneously imitate the perfection of the cosmos (fols. 77v–78r) and represent the ideal of marriage (fol. 82v), dancing offers "both recreation and meditation of virtue" (fol. 84r), and "very honor or perfect nobility" may be achieved by performing, or even beholding, its actions (84v). Many of the elements of Elyot's defense, including the reference to Proteus, were borrowed from Lucian's dialogue *The Dance,* which enumerated dancing venerables, praised its moral and instructional value for both dancers and beholders, and linked dancing with an eternal cosmic "concord."[3]

Elyot, however, modifies Lucian's defense in significantly patriarchal ways.[4] Lucian's dialogue focused primarily on the narrative dancing of the male mime, but Elyot's defense on the festive dancing of the heterosexual couple that signified matrimony (fols. 82r–82v). Lucian does allude briefly to a dance that portrays manliness and femininity, in which "boys and girls together . . . move in a row and truly resemble a string of beads. The boy precedes, doing the steps and postures of young manhood and those which later he will use in war, while the maiden follows, showing how to do the woman's dance with propriety; hence the string is beaded with modesty and with manliness."[5]

Both Lucian and Elyot describe dances in which the man is dominant—preceding the girl, more vehement than the woman, but Elyot's portrait is much more detailed, contrasting specific traits of masculinity and femininity and the ways in which these qualities are expressed in movement (fol. 83r). In Elyot's measures, the "string of beads" is broken into couples, each a private and self-contained emblem of gendered virtues whose actions are not only enlivening but transformative, teaching abstract moral qualities and tangible social behavior with equal verve. Since masculine precedence was performative in courtly dancing—the gentlemen began and ended the dance, led the lady through it, and later had the most splendid variations—one of the moral lessons the measures taught was that of feminine subordination.

Where in Lucian's dialogue, dancing was a timeless way of expressing the parts of the dancer's soul and teaching the beholder "much that happened of old,"[6] for Elyot, dancing is a way to master the present and secure the future. Elyot's arguments in favor of dancing are ostensibly moral appeals,[7] but these are politically coded throughout, dressed in a pervasive administrative imagery of "powers and offices" (fol. 84r). Merging reverence with expedience, Elyot links ethical concerns with worldly matters of "success" and "enterprise" (fol. 85r), and in the dedication to Henry VIII, consecrates his moral arguments to earthly power with a book that "treats of the education of them that hereafter may be deemed worthy to be governors of the public weal under your highness" (Sig. a2v). Elyot emphasizes social hierarchies in relation to dancing where Lucian did not: his "public weal" is hierarchical, "a body living compact or made of sundry estates and degrees of men" (Sig. A1r), and so are the dances that affirm it. Ranked as defensible or indefensible, the former are the dances of the elite, "basse dances, bargenettes, pauvions, turgions, and rounds" (fol. 81v), comparable to those of the classical Golden Age. The latter dances, however, with "a spice of idolatry," or "unclean motions [that] irritate the minds of the dancers to venereal lusts" (fol. 75v), are akin to

> that kind of dancing which was used in the time . . . when everything with the empire of Rome declined from their perfection, and the old manner of dancing was forgotten, and none remained but that which was lascivious and corrupted the minds of them that danced, and provoked sin as semblably some do to this day. (Fol. 74v)

Elyot defends the courtly dancing presumably descended from antiquity at its height, and not the "corrupted" practices, implicitly popular, that preserved the lascivious customs of imperial decline.

If Elyot early modernizes classical arguments in favor of dancing, he also mobilizes classical cosmology to respond to contemporary warnings that dancing was provocative of lust and license. On the contrary, Elyot insists that courtly dancing is "among the serious disciplines for the commendable beauty, for the apt and proportionate moving, and for the crafty disposition and fashioning of the body" (fol. 81r), because it replicates heavenly forms.

> The interpreters of Plato do think that the wonderful and incomprehensible order of the celestial bodies, I mean stars and planets, and their motions harmonical, gave to them that intensely and by the deep search of reason behold their courses in the sundry diversities of number and time, a form of imitation of a semblable motion which they called dancing or saltation. Wherefore the more near they approached to that temperance and subtle modulation of the said superior bodies, the more perfect and commendable is their dancing.[8]

The beautiful and apt body crafted by dancing was, in more than one sense, a "classical" body: finished, symmetrical, closed, its actions controlled and its dangerous passions contained.[9] Courtly dancing, for Elyot, was not a servant of the senses but the handmaid of wit; it did not incite to bodily vice but assisted the reason, "as much as it is very expedient that there be mixed with study some honest and moderate . . . recreation to . . . quicken the vital spirits lest . . . being much occupied in contemplation or remembrance of things grave and serious might happen to be fatigate, or perchance oppressed" (fol. 83v). For those who contemplated the heavens with a "deep search of reason," dancing was the idiom of intellect, the movements of the foot and body "expressing some pleasant or profitable affects or motions of the mind" (fol. 81v–82r).

MERCANTILE DISCOURSE

As courtly dancing spread into the city and countryside, and with the agent of its transmission an itinerant peddler who taught his skills for a fee, a mercantile discourse evolved that resonated with transactions, vocations, and deals. Not, alas, recorded firsthand in English texts, it was, however, preserved in two colorful and important French treatises that were both widely known: Antonius de Arena's *Ad suos compagnones studiantes . . .* [10] and Arbeau's *Orchesography*. While French social formations clearly differed from those of sixteenth-century London, evidence of this discourse in England may be found in the unmistakable responsiveness of succeeding moralistic attacks and medical defenses. Arena, for example, recommends that the dancer make the most of his amorous opportunities: "I exhort you to learn the dances in which you may bestow prolonged kisses. . . . Whoever dances these may call himself happy since he quaffs the beautiful lips of the damsels."[11] That the antidancing tracts dwell on what Stubbes sees as "smooching and slobbering one of another"[12] strongly suggests this aspect of mercantile discourse circulated in England. Moreover, the private papers of men associated with the Inns of Court show evidence of a set curriculum of dancing and, as Arbeau referred back to Arena, it is likely that the French dancing masters in England referred to both or to the same spoken maxims.[13]

In England, the great merchants eschewed dancing from their masques, and the city fathers attempted to regulate the proliferation of dancing schools. But for up-and-coming lawyers and merchants' wives, dancing was an indispensable skill,[14] and the ambitious sought to master the intricacies of the cosmic dance with the expectation that their personal fortunes would rise and sparkle like a star in the heavens. To this end, they had to invest in themselves. "You have to spend money if you want to learn dancing," the barrister Antonius de Arena reminded his students peevishly, "for no man teaches without money. Everyone wants to learn, but no one wants to pay. That's why almost no one can dance perfectly."[15]

In order to dance perfectly, the aspirant needed to transform his body from grotesque matter to classical instrument. Elyot's defense purports to describe the dancer's Platonic metamorphosis, but his images from beginning to end are those of completion and control: his governor is always already there, dancing perfectly. Arena, however, contrasts a dreaded carnival bulk that gapes inopportunely with the trim form of gentility through which prosperity will be gained. His foremost concern is the securing of bodily apertures. The dancer must wipe his mouth before kissing the ladies and keep it closed when dancing: "since the flies have a habit of flying about they could easily fly into your gaping mouth and choke you." The dancer must refrain from spitting, blowing his nose with his fingers, or drooling ("do not dribble at the mouth. No woman desires a man with rabies"), eating onions, belching, and breaking wind ("never fart when you are dancing; grit your teeth and . . . hold [it] back." The gallant should "maintain a smiling aspect when dancing. . . . Some people look as if they want to shit hard turds," and must tie up his codpiece securely lest it fall to the ground and trip him.[16] But when he falls, he must "get up quickly and go back to finishing the dance bravely—pa-trim pe-tro-lo—without complaining at all."[17]

Once transformed, this sleek, dapper figure is ready for polite society, and the marriage market. A common mercantile defense of dancing argued its usefulness in the making of a worthwhile marriage: "Dancing is practiced to reveal whether lovers are in good health and sound of limb, after which they are permitted to kiss their mistresses in order that they may touch and savor one another, thus to ascertain of they are shapely or emit an unpleasant odor, as of bad meat. Therefore, from this standpoint, quite apart from the many advantages to be derived from dancing, it becomes essential in a well ordered society."[18] Mercantile defenses supported some of the assumptions of the elite: the desirability of a dignified self-presentation and the capacity of dancing to expedite it. Nevertheless, patriarchal and mercantile discourses were also at odds, since the sensual tests of touching and savoring essential to the evaluation of perishable matrimonial fodder were those that the transformation to an impermeable, courtly body were ideally designed to impede.

MORALISTIC DISCOURSE

The association of dancing and marriage, whether related to Elyot's image of dancing *as* marriage or the assertion that dancing facilitates a salubrious match, was one of the most roundly refuted in moralistic discourse. Northbrooke, for example, explains that marriages made by dancing are inherently defective, "contracted by these arts and acts wherein a regard is had only to the agility and beauty of the body," and concludes that "although honest matrimonies are sometime brought to pass by dancing, yet much more often are adulteries and fornications wont to follow."[19] Another detractor is even more to the point: God alone can make a marriage, and without the assistance of dancing.[20] With their lengthy enumerations of Biblical interdictions, antidancing tracts were negative replications of humanist defenses. They were also characterized by ingenious explanations as to why "a time to dance" in practical terms meant a time *never* to dance,[21] catalogues of dancing's inflammatory properties, and examples of the myriad ways in which dancing "blow[s] up Venus' coal."[22]

Where mercantile discourse confirmed dominant assumptions, morally based attacks by Northbrooke and others disputed the profitable spirituality of the measures that Elyot promoted, and inverted humanist tropes of defense in a kind of adversarial self-fashioning.[23] Although these attacks have been characterized as "Puritan opposition to dancing," Puritanism was a broad-based movement that included gentry, merchants, craftsmen, apprentices, and the laboring poor, so a "typical Puritan attitude" was difficult to define.[24] The attempts to regulate dancing schools and the absence of dancing in civic festivity testify to an official urban antipathy, but the affiliations, objectives, and arguments of adversaries and defenders alike were often less than clear and consistent. Apologists for dancing were, like Elyot, apologists for courtly dancing, but detractors attacked both courtly dancing as a Papist export, and popular practices as part of the Catholic and pagan past. Prosecutions involving popular customs accelerated in London and the provinces over the century preceding the English revolution,[25] but in Milton's *A Masque Presented at Ludlow Castle,* courtly dances were banished to the antimasque, and "country dances," well on their way to becoming the signature of the Puritan elite, were performed in the masque.[26]

If in patriarchal discourse dancing shaped a virtuous body and in mercantile discourse marketed an appealing one, in moralistic discourse, dancing fashioned a monster. For Elyot, dancing was beautiful and good, a fortification that enclosed, controlled, and protected both the dancer and society, but for Northbrooke, dancing was ugly and bad, a yawning portal to license and defeat. Courtly humanists praised dancing as an inspiring spectacle of conduct that reflected heavenly forms and promoted moral and physical splendor, but moralistic writers inverted patriarchal tropes, castigating dancing as a corruptive display that reflected hellish designs and engendered moral and physical decay. Where Elyot praised the dancer's prudent gentility, Northbrooke derides a "scabbed and scurvy company."[27] Curiously, Northbrooke, who excoriated courtly practices as Papist,[28] appropriates the portrait of the dancer abloom with scabs and lesions from Vives' *Instruction of a Christian Woman,* in which lascivious dancing is said to be the cause "that so many young women lie pocky and scabbed, in [hospitals], and lazer houses, and go a begging."[29]

Point by point, Northbrooke refutes Elyot's defense. Where Elyot pronounces that "all dancing is not to be reproved," Northbrooke's spokesman primly counters: "I find that [in the Scriptures] dancings were oftentimes reproved."[30] As for the cosmic origins of dancing, Northbrooke scoffs: "Some other suppose that men, when they beheld the sundry motions of the wandering stars, found out dancing. Others affirm that it came from the old Ethnics, etc. But whatsoever these say, St. Chrysostom, an ancient father, sayeth it came first from the devil."[31] But while Northbrooke repeatedly rejects the divinity of the cosmic dance[32] he does not discard the image, but feminizes it: the motions of dancing stars are not orderly and fixed but "wandering." Once domesticated, the image is inverted and reappropriated—dancing originated not from above, but from below, to subvert masculine virtue.[33]

For the governor, dancing was an important means of social and individual control, but for the moralist, dancing was the practice that drove society *out* of control, and that needed *to be controlled.* To Elyot, dancing was a means of moral elevation for dancer and beholder; Northbrooke, however, replies that dancing does not restrain the passions but inflames them, and therefore does not teach good behavior or improve bad, but unleashes man's inherent evil:

[Dances] are . . . snares and offenses, not only to the dancers but also to the beholders; for they stir up and inflame the hearts of men, which are otherwise evil enough, even from their beginning, and that thing which is to be suppressed and kept under with great study and industry (as the lust of the flesh, the lust of the eye, and the pride of life) the same is stirred up by the wanton enticement of dances. . . . O deceitful dance! It is the mother of all evil, the sister of all carnal pleasures, the father of all pride.[34]

Dancing does not *signify* "providence and industry" to Northbrooke as to Elyot (fol. 86v); instead, "great study and industry" are required to *resist* it.

While Elyot asserts that "in the good order of dancing a man and a woman dance together" (fol. 82r), Northbrooke insists that in the best dancing, men and women dance "apart by themselves." The couple dance that Elyot praises as an image of holy matrimony Northbrooke regards with particular alarm as a pernicious decline from biblical times when

[the] women of Israel, for joy of their delivery . . . danced not with young men but apart by themselves among women and maidens. . . . Also their dances were spiritual, religious and godly, not after our hoppings, and leapings, and interminglings men with women, etc. (dancing every one for his part), but soberly, gravely, and, matronlike, moving scarce little or nothing in their gestures at all, either in countenance or body. They had no minstrels or pipers to play unto them, but they took the timbrels in their own hands . . . not as our foolish and fond women used to mix themselves with men in their dance.[35]

Where Elyot moralized the new Continental dances as classical models of propriety and rectitude, and implicitly deplored popular practices as carnal and degrading, Northbrooke condemns the recent developments in courtly dancing, dismissing capers as common "hoppings and leapings," and ridiculing flamboyant *galliard* variations ("dancing every one for his part"). Ironically, though, he seems to imagine the biblical probity to which the Puritan should aspire as a combination of early Renaissance caroler, "moving scarce little or nothing in their gestures at all, either in countenance or body," and medieval folk dancer, with "no minstrels or pipers to play unto them."

If in the *Governour*, dancing was praised as an ennobling exercise for both dancer and beholder, for Northbrooke,

there is no sight more ridiculous, nor more out of order than dancing. This is a liberty to wantonness, a friend to wickedness, a provocation to fleshly lust, enemy to chastity. . . . Dancing is the vilest vice of all, and truly it cannot be said what mischiefs the sight and hearing do receive thereby, which afterward be the causes of communication and embracing. They dance with discordant gestures . . . monstrous thumping of the feet . . . maidens and matrons are groped and handled with unchaste hands, and kissed, and dishonestly embraced, and the things which nature hath hidden and modesty covered, are then often, by means of lasciviousness, made naked. . . . [It is] an exercise, doubtless, not descended from heaven, but by the devils of hell devised, to the injury of the Divinity, when the people of Israel erected a calf in the desert [and] after they had done sacrifice . . . rose up to sport themselves, and singing, danced in a round.[36]

The dances that "betokeneth concord" to Elyot are "discordant" to Northbrooke, and the troublesome calf that Elyot sacrificed with "[o]ther fables there be which I omit for this present time" (fol. 78r) becomes Northbrooke's coup de grâce (Fig. 15).[37]

The only ground on which Elyot and Northbrooke meet is an admiration for feminine restraint in dancing "soberly, gravely, and, matronlike." For Northbrooke, though, this restraint was conspicuously absent from the dancing of his contemporaries, from whose company he pointedly does not exclude

CXXII

Concurrunt illic pompofa fuperbia:luxus:
Et petulans faltus:& furiofa venus:
Nam venus imprimis/choreis folatur in illis:
Hanc fequitur pedibus turba petulca citis.
Ludus in orbe quidem eft nullus damnofior ifto:
Contaminat ftimulis pectora cafta fuis:
Ludus & ifte quidem:non pax/fed pugna videtur
Clamando currunt/vociferantcp nimis.
Quis locus immunis:quem non vefania talis
Contaminat/templi vix loca tuta manent.
Clerus:& in cappa monachus:puer atcp puellæ
Et iuuenes blandi:decrepiticp fenes:
In girum faltant pedibus:ductantcp choreas:
Atcp incompofitis motibus vfcp ruunt.
Rufticus in circo teneram cum flectit amicam:
Non fitis hunc tota nocte/die ve premit.

¶ Of leppynges and dauncis and folys that pas theyr tyme in fuche banpte.

incle. attendæ
tes de fta. rel.
de vi. & ho. cl.'
cũ decorem.

Prouer.ij.

Virg.ij.geor.
Iudith.ij.

Choree fatuitas

Nil placet i to
ta fapiétibus
vfcp chorea.
Quod iuuet/
aut profit:cõ=
deceat ve bo=
nos.In circu=
tu impii am=
bulant.

y.f.

15. Dance around the golden calf. Albrecht Dürer, *Ship of Fools*, 1494, 1509. STC 3545. By permission of The Folger Shakespeare Library.

the queen herself, known to dance with enthusiasm.[38] Somewhat impudently does Northbrooke liken English dancing schools to "houses of bawdry" that teach young women to hold onto men's arms "that they may hop the higher."[39] What woman nowadays, asks Northbrooke blandly,

> will be known to have skill of dancing, etc.? For what chastity of body and mind can be there, where they shall see so many men's bodies, and have their minds enticed by the windows of their eyes, and by the means of the most subtle artificer, the devil. . . . [W]hatsoever they are that have any care of gravity and honesty have utterly condemned this filthy dancing, especially in maidens.[40]

So much for the Virgin Queen, who learned "in the Italian manner to dance high,"[41] and has been—wrongly, it turns out—associated with the celebrated painting of a "high" dance that hangs at Penshurst Place.[42]

MEDICAL DISCOURSE

The 1570s and early 1580s saw the flood of antidance treatises that offered vivid warnings against the ignescent properties of dancing, and macabre descriptions of the physical and moral lesions sure to result. One of the most interesting responses to their arresting images of lust in action is Richard Mulcaster's defense in *Positions Concerning the Training up of Children.*[43] London teacher and high master of Saint Paul's, writer on the teaching of Latin and English, contributor to city pageants honoring Elizabeth and James, and deviser of masques that his pupils performed at court, Mulcaster was truly a cultural liaison between court and city. His alliance with city interests and his function as guild spokesman were substantial,[44] and with his defense of dancing, he functioned as an apologist for a controversial aspect of court culture at a time when the controversy was at its height. As headmaster of the Merchant Taylor's School, Mulcaster might be expected to condemn dancing rather than defend it; his defense thus witnesses the complex and shifting attitudes toward elite culture. He negotiates through roiling social currents by assuming a protoscientific, class-neutral stance, grounding his defense of dancing in the humoral body rather than the figure of nobility.

Unlike most defenders or critics of dancing, who affected a lofty objectivity, Mulcaster personalizes his defense, emphasizing his own vulnerability as an egalitarian appeal.

Dancing of it self declareth mine allowance, in that I name it among the good and healthful exercises which I must needs clear from some offensive notes, wherewith it is charged by some stern people, lest if I do not so, it both continue itself in blame still, and draw me thither also with it, for allowing of a thing that is disliked, and by me not delivered from just cause of misliking, which by my choice do seem to defend it.[45]

Surprisingly for a teacher and scholar, he rejects the models of humanist defense and scriptural attack; in contrast to Elyot and Northbrooke, who copiously cited ancient authorities, Mulcaster generalizes perfunctorily: "[dancing] seems to have served for great uses in old time, both athletical for spectacle and show, military for armor and enemy, and physical for health and welfare; so many and so notable writers make so much and so oftentimes mention thereof in these three kinds."[46] More enthusiastically, he responds to the discourse of disease used by the antidance critics and their metaphors of inflammation and infection, rehabilitating the moral heat and sores of antidance argument as natural properties within the humoral system, and tempering the inflammatory disposition of dancing to purge it of impurity.

If lately dancing has been condemned, Mulcaster continues, it is because the hygienic element has been lost, and "it is used for pleasure and delight only, and beareth no pretense of style of exercise directly tending to health."[47] He proceeds to counter the salacious image of dancing as the ruin of the dissolute by reaffirming the salubrious properties that can ensure glowing health. Up to a point, he is on sound Galenist ground, for exercise was believed to be productive of natural heat, purgative of excrements, and encourager of sound sleep.[48] John Jones, Mulcaster's contemporary, praises exercise as "the stirrer-up of natural heat, quickener of sleepy nature, consumer of superfluities, strengther of the parts, death of diseases," and notes that "comely dancing is most commended . . . for preserving the healthy spirits as also for strengthening the sound body."[49]

Mulcaster begins his defense by transforming the malevolent heat against which the moralists raved to a comforting warmth:

The sad and sober commodities which be reaped by dancing in respect of the motion applied to health be these: by heating and warming, it driveth away stiffness from the joints, and some palsylike trembling from the legs and thighs . . . is a present remedy to succor the stomach against the weakness of digestion, and rawness of humors. . . . [I]t so strengtheneth and confirmeth aching hips, thin shanks, feeble feet as nothing more; in delivering kidneys and bladders from the stone, it is beyond comparison good.[50]

Emphasizing the salutary nature of the heat generated in dancing, and its wholesome effect on both extremities and organ systems, he counters the incendiary vision of an activity that "stirs up and inflames the hearts of men."[51] Furthermore, he recommends dancing as a kind of master purge: where for Northbrooke, dancing fractures the fragile carapace of goodness and releases the evil within ("that thing which is to be suppressed and kept under . . . is stirred up by the wanton enticement of dances"),[52] for Mulcaster, "delivering kidneys and bladders from the stone, [dancing] is beyond comparison good." Here, however, Mulcaster's medical discourse begins to diverge from medical practice. For "stone in the reins," treatments included purgations and plasters of herbs, copious drinking of liquids, reclining with hips raised, catheterization, and the immersion of the yard in hot oil. For "stone in the bladder," possible remedies might involve potions of fennel, lovage, chamomile, or goat's blood, the consumption of a raw salted sparrow, or the elevation of the patient's hips to expedite the stone's discharge.[53] None of these seems compatible with dancing.

Mulcaster neatly deploys medical discourse to confute the Puritan assertion that there is *no* time to dance. Dancing, he emphasizes, while an incomparable purge, must be undertaken with reason, not "mistimed . . . used after meat, when rest is most wholesome . . . when digestion should have all the help of natural heat," but rather should "by rule of physic go before meat, and not be used but long after, as a preparative against a new meal, and a disburdener of superfluities against the surcharge of a new diet."[54] Dancing must not only be used in the proper interval, but by a judicious community, and those who have

weak brains, swimming heads, weeping eyes, simple and sorry sight must take heed of it, and take an eye to their health, for fear they be dizzy when they dance, and trip in their turning, or rather shrink down right when they should cinquopace. Such as have weak kidneys and overheated, may displease themselves, and increase their diseases, by increasing their heat.[55]

Mulcaster's warning seems consonant with medical cautions concerning the provocation of dizziness by exercise: "when the head is [heated] so the humors being dissolved do turn about in the brain"; therefore, if one is prone to dizziness, "let his exercise be moderate." [56]

But this caution also reveals the real nature of Mulcaster's concern, which is not medical but social, not with injury but with embarrassment—shrinking right down when one should cinquopace, or "displeasing." [57] The image of the shrinking dancer subtly engages a common trope of the controversy over dancing, the trope of fallen man. In the ideal, courtly dancing articulated a variety of assumptions concerning man's upright posture: defenders insisted that the dancer's erect carriage and exquisite high capers demonstrated his natural, moral, and social privilege. Conversely, antidance writers warned incessantly against the bone-breaking threat of actual tumbles as well as the dancer's inevitable moral decline. "I have known diverse [dancers]," cautions Stubbes, "have in short time become decrepit and lame, so remaining to their dying day. Some have broke their legs with skipping, leaping, turning, and vaulting, and some have come by one hurt, some by another, but never any came from thence without some part of his mind broken and lame." [58] Mulcaster, however, counters the fear of falling with the promise of mastery. If the choice of dance, from the staid and *almain*-like to the springing *galliard,* is made "upon [one's] knowledge of his own body, and his emptiness or [satiety]," [59] no one need worry about "displeasing" himself in the course of his exertions.

Quite late in his defense, Mulcaster finally specifies just what kind of dancing he recommends: courtly Continental "galliards." Immediately, a crowd of discrete yet related discourses invades his medical argument. First enters classical aesthetics: dancing should not be the servant of the passions, but must dominate them with "*order* in time, with *reason* in gesture, with *proportion* in number, with *harmony* in music, to appoint it . . . both seemly and sober . . . as it may prove an exercise of health." [60] Next comes a patriarchal-moralist hybrid: children should learn dancing because it teaches them while young "to resemble the manners, affections, and doings of men and women," which serves both as a beneficial social training and as an inoculation against license, since regular early exercise will "stay [children's] overmuch delighting therein in further years."

Mulcaster concludes his defense with a discourse of civility, praising the suppression of gesture that distinguished courtly dancing from popular forms. Ideally, he writes, the dancer presents "nothing . . . but the bare motion, without that kind of hand-cunning [in which] the skill seemed then to rest most in the use of the upper parts, and gesturing by the hand. The credit of our dancing now is to represent the music right . . . and with such a grace to use the legs and feet as the old dancers used their arms and hands."[61] In the new dances of the elite, the hands were immobilized as a way of disconnecting the new courtier—perhaps an erstwhile tailor—from a context of manual labor or martial rigor. The idle hand of "our dancing now" performed and signified its distance from the worlds of work and war, while pedimentary anapests embedded the dancer in a context of humanist learning. Therefore, Mulcaster, like Elyot before him, specifically excludes traditional dances while recommending courtly ones as a medical regimen. In so doing, he promotes the cultural separation of the urban gentry from the common sort, and the alliance of this estate with an international elite.[62] To close, he reverses Elyot's moral argument: "as the motion is for health, the meaning [is] for good."

SOVEREIGN DISCOURSE

The many descriptive stanzas of John Davies' "Orchestra, Or a Poeme of Dauncing"[63] have long served in the absence of English dancing treatises as the authority on English dancing practices. The poem responds to earlier discourses and, as a font of epigrams for literary commentators and dance historians, has generated succeeding ones. Originally, it may have been intended satirically, for dancing's advocate is the slimy Antinous of the *Odyssey,* here a "fresh and jolly Knight" (stanza 5); but it evolved into a diligent courtier's ingratiating defense of dancing against moralist objections, undertaken by means of a sovereign discourse purified of dissonant elements. In "Orchestra," dancing—an exercise favored by Queen Elizabeth and a spectacle admired by King James—becomes a metaphor for social order,[64] and the supremacy of dancing a metonym of court authority. Davies neither defends dancing as moral nor acclaims it as wholesome, but acknowledges the efficacy of dancing as an instrument of power—"Thus they who first did found a commonweal. . . . By dancing first the peoples hearts did steal" (stanza 86)—even as he mythologizes it as the transcendent organizing practice of civic life.

If courtly dancing was a privileged practice of self-fashioning, Davies, a member of the educated governing class typically addressed by civility books and dancing treatises, was a paradigm of upward mobility. His father was a provincial tanner who died young, leaving Davies' Oxford education to his wealthier, landed mother. Admitted to the Middle Temple, Davies was temporarily banished for an assault upon the friend to whom he had dedicated his poem of dancing; not much of a dancer himself, he nevertheless admired the skill in others, and praised it with much invention. Davies managed to effect his restoration a few years later, and may have presented his poem as an entertainment for the queen.[65] Upon the instant of her demise, however, he methodically departed for Scotland, eventually finding favor with the new king for his "*Nosce Teipsum.*" James appointed Davies attorney general for Ireland; regrettably, however, the culmination of Davies' career was not to be enjoyed: the self-fashioned courtier-servant elevated by a lifetime of deference died on the eve of his installation as Lord Chief Justice.

Although a full account of the poem is not possible here, the features of its discourse of dancing are worth noting. Like Elyot, Davies borrows liberally from Lucian: the image of the cosmic dance, the figure of Proteus, the identification of dancing with gender relations. And like Elyot, when Davies praises dancing, he praises courtly dancing. However, Davies' defense, in contrast to the apologies of Elyot and Mulcaster and the attacks of Northbrooke and others, aspires to epic proportions. Elyot sanctifies the movements of the dancing couple and extols the moral effect on the self-fashioner, Mulcaster praises the physical and social benefits for the mature gentleman, and Northbrooke laments the lascivious ruin of man and woman alike. Davies' vision, however, embraces an entire commonwealth, a dancing body politic.

> Concord's true picture shineth in this Art,
> Where diverse men and women ranked be,
> And every one doth dance a several part,
> Yet all as one, in measure do agree.
> Observing perfect uniformity.
>   All turn together, all together trace,
>   And all together honor and embrace.
>   (Stanza 110)

And his defense takes the form of a poetic narrative of its development from primordial chaos to the celestial figures of Elizabethan court masque.

The splendid pageant of civic order is shown to be achieved by the regulation of individual and group movement, the engenderment of the dance, and the deletion of popular and foreign matter. At the center is the image of the cosmic dance.

> Learn then to dance you that are Princes born
> And lawful lords of earthly creatures all,
> Imitate them, and thereof take no scorn,
> For this new art to them is natural.
> And imitate the stars celestial.
>
> (Stanza 60)

Here, Davies identifies celestial order with an earthly hierarchy of princes born who imitate the stars and lord it over all other creatures, an order that began in the original moment of elemental harmony (stanza 17), and will endure from the creation "[u]ntil that fatal instant should revolve, / When all to nothing should again resolve" (stanza 28). And this order is universal, for "perfect forms of dancing" adorn "every province of the imperial sky" (stanza 48). Furthermore, Davies slyly elevates the dance-loving monarch above controversy by transforming a personal enjoyment of the morally vexed pastime of dancing into a duty that Princes born must undertake.[66]

Three times, Davies recounts the extrapolation of dancing from the cosmos in the form of the round, perhaps seeking with a numerical charm to cancel the image of sinners jumping up and down around a calf. Significantly, he represents the choral dance—traditional, and the figure of community—as imposed from above, effectively erasing the popular origin of courtly forms. First, he offers a genetic myth in which dancing begins as an elemental truce negotiated under Love's auspices:[67]

> Dancing (bright Lady) then began to be,
> When the first seeds whereof the world did spring,
> The Fire, Air, Earth, and Water did agree
> By Love's persuasion, Nature's mighty King,
> To leave their first disordered combating,

> And in a dance such measure to observe
> As all the world their motion should preserve.
>
> (Stanza 17)

The emergence of the world from chaos occurs when Love, the dancing-master, persuades the warring elements to dance with "measure," comporting themselves like courtly dancers who "neither mingle or confound, / But every one doth keep the bounded space / Wherein the dance doth bid it turn or trace" (stanza 18).

Having ordered the "natural" world, Love turns to human society.

> The comely order and proportion fair
> On every side did please his wandering eye,
> Till glancing through the thin, transparent air
> A rude disordered rout did he espy,
> Of men and women that most spitefully
>   Did one another throng and crowd so sore,
>   That his kind eye in pity wept therefore.
>
> (Stanza 29)

Transformed from a divine creator to a secular administrator, Love possesses the absolute power to realize an advantageous social design.

> And swifter than the Lightening down he came
> Another shapeless Chaos to digest
> He will begin another world to frame
> (For Love till all be well will never rest)
> Then with such words as cannot be expressed
>   He cuts the troups that all asunder fling
>   And ere they wist, he casts them in a ring.
>
> (Stanza 30)

Where natural order was established by a mighty king endowed with superior reason and diplomacy, the institution of a better world demands household skills on a colossal scale to sweep away Chaos and arrange the scrambled "troups" into a tidy ring. In this narrative, social hierarchies are amply justified, for Love at the apex is endowed with superior strength, sagacity, diligence, and compassion, while the invidious throng who "spitefully . . . crowd so sore" is a teeming repository of disagreeable qualities.

By the third repetition of the creation-story, the throng is mollified, and Love no longer needs to "fling" dancers into a circle; instead, he patiently teaches a compliant flock the "rounds and winding hays to tread" (stanza 64). Strategically, Davies conflates the round with the *farandole,* the paradigm of popular festivity in which a chain of dancers curved through open spaces in a spontaneous procession. Merging this dance with a protocourtly one, and representing both not as traditional and improvised but as devised and taught, Davies again erases the thronging populace from the history of English dancing. And since "wild whirling" might well challenge "civil order and conveniency" (stanza 74), Davies contains popular unruliness within courtly forms:

> where keep the Winds their revelry,
> Their violent turnings and wild whirling hays?
> But in the Air's tralucent gallery,
> Where she herself is turned a hundred ways,
> While with those Masquers wantonly she plays;
> Yet in this misrule, they such rule embrace
> As two at one encumber not the place.
>
> (Stanza 47)

What commences as transgressive revelry of violent turnings and wild whirlings that might play wantonly with courtly merrymakers is soon revealed to be nothing more than an antimasque, in which, as in other courtly diversions, misrule never gets out of hand since antimasquers courtly "rule embrace," and graciously cede their places to the masquers.

Controlled by Love, Davies' dancers are emptied of agency: repeatedly, Davies' credits the master choreographer, and carefully expunges the populace. Motions are not improvised by the dancers, but are demonstrated, combined, and choreographed by the dancing master:

> Then first of all, [Love] doth demonstrate plain
> The motions seven that are in nature found;
> *Upward,* and *downward, forth* and *back again,*
> *To this side,* and *to that,* and *turning round:*
> Whereof a thousand brawls he doth compound,
> Which he doth teach unto the multitude.
>
> (Stanza 62)

Once again, Davies performs an erasure of popular festivity, refusing to allow the possibility of a dance that is not imposed by an authority: although he calls the foregoing dance a "brawl," the "motions seven" he enumerates are those of the courtly measures.[68]

Like Elyot, Davies affirms differences of gender as well as status through the medium of dancing. The fashionable dances of the late sixteenth century that Davies goes on to celebrate—the *pavane,* the *galliard,* the *coranto,* and the *volta* (all imported from the Continent, which Davies neglects to mention)—emphasized gender difference with their distinct variations for gentlemen and ladies. Davies embodies this property by representing the *pavane* as a decorous moon and the *galliard* as a bold sun, drawing on at least two ideologies of gender difference: humoral economies in which the woman was cold and moist, and religious analogies in which Eve was inferior to Adam as the moon to the sun.[69] His stanzas reproduce Arbeau's economic and sexual coding while slightly revising his images of masculine wealth and feminine modesty. The *pavane* that served to establish the gentleman's wealth and social standing with vestimentary display is transformed into an image of the gentleman's pampered, virginal dependant:

> Who doth not see the measures of the Moon
> Which thirteen times she dances every year?
> And ends her pavine thirteen times as soon
> As doth her brother, of whose golden hair
> She borroweth part, and proudly it doth wear.
> > Then doth she coyly turn her face aside,
> > That half her cheek is scarce sometimes discride.
> > > (Stanza 41)

Indeed, this lady displays masculine riches while performing both virtuous "shamefastness" and courtly coyness as she turns her face aside and receives the spectators' admiration of her borrowed finery with the prescribed glance of virginal modesty.

If the *pavane* is a modest maid who shines with borrowed light, Davies' *galliard* is a lustrous rover, ardently leaping, furiously rotating:

> A gallant dance that lively doth bewray
> A spirit and a virtue Masculine
> Impatient that her house on earth should stay
> (Since her self is fiery and divine)
> Oft doth she make her body upward flyne,

With lofty turns and capriols in the air
Which with the lusty tunes accordeth fair.
(Stanza 68)

Both dances confound the execration of the moralists: Davies' *pavane* douses Venus's coal, and his fiery *galliard* recasts the impostumed heat of the moralists as the defining humor of sublimity. Moreover, the "lofty turns and capriols in the air" (Fig. 14), clearly a "more diverse and pleasing show" (stanza 67) than the lady's placid modesty, patently validate masculine ascendancy.

However, at the same time Davies emphasizes gender differences with these dances, he introduces dancers who transcend gender categories: the mythical figures of Proteus and Teiresias (stanzas 81–83), and most important, the queen herself. Both Davies' *pavane* and his *galliard* resonate with tropes of the cult of Elizabeth. The *pavane* invokes the legendary chastity of the moon goddess (helpfully, the moon's half-descried cheek averts her eyes from the enticing sight of "so many men's bodies" on the dancing place). The fervent *galliard* is, unexpectedly, also a woman, who "[i]mpatient that her house on earth should stay . . . doth she make her body upward fly," much like the queen who danced high, elevated by a "fiery and divine" spirit and "virtue Masculine" of a King, and a King of England, too.[70] In double-gendering the queen, Davies elevates her well above Northbrooke's house of bawdry, and signifies marriage, between the monarch's two bodies.

The last dance that Davies celebrates, the *volta,* might have been considered a powerful argument on Northbrooke's side. Full of hoppings and leapings (and probably gropings, since the gentleman lifted the lady high by grasping her under the busk and boosting her behind with his knee), the dance elevated the lady and "made naked" those "things which nature hath hidden, modesty covered."[71] Davies, however, urbanely rehabilitates the dance, dignifying both dancers and beholders.

> Yet there is one [dance], the most delightful kind,
> A lofty jumping or a leaping round,
> Where arm in arm, two Dancers are entwined,
> And whirl themselves with strict embracements bound,
> And still their feet an Anapest do sound:

An Anapest is all their music's song,
Whose first two feet are short, the third is long.
(Stanza 70)

His strategy is twofold. He lowers the lady, so that she does not dance above, to tantalize or threaten, but "arm in arm" with the gentleman. And he reforms the dance itself: its embraces are not groping but "strict," and dancers are entwined arm in arm, not hand in busk, so the dance is no longer immodest but "delightful." Furthermore, he deflects attention from human to humanist anatomy, from handling by unchaste hands to feet that measure anapests.

Davies' "sovereign" discourse, then, both affirms structures of rank and gender and disarms dangerous urban tropes. The queen, identified with undefiled princess *and* divine prince, is both partners of a sanctified couple: a queen chastely married to sovereignty. The monarch is therefore not contaminated but purified by dancing. Furthermore, where Elyot represented dancing as the consolidating practice of the select, Davies praises courtly dancing as a universal practice that incorporates and erases everything but itself. In the "perfect, fortunate, triangled isle" of England, everything dances courtly dances: the sea dances about the land with "measure" (stanza 49), the vine entwines the elm in "just order" (stanza 56), the birds fly in "perfect form triangular" (stanza 57), and even the streams want to study dancing with Love (stanzas 52–54), who, like an Italian dancing master, has invented "a hundred million" variations (stanza 73).

The ultimate vision of the poem is of a brilliant masque that celebrates with cosmic dances "the only wonder of posterity, / The richest work in Nature's treasure"—the "fortunate, triangled Isle" of England (stanza 121). In an emblem of eternal glory, "things to come, present and past . . . represent in lively show / Our glorious English Court's divine Image, / As it should be in this our golden age" (stanza 126). Embracing all of space and time, the divine image of the English court unfolds over the prospect of the *orchestra* in the forms and "changes" of courtly dancing, simultaneously fixed and ever-renewing. The spectacle is the culmination of history in a new Golden Age, and at the same time, is only an instant in a rush toward enduring glory. Where Elyot defended dancing for the improvement of the elite, the anonymous dancing masters sold the techniques of upward mobility, Northbrooke rejected the festive authority of both pagan past and monarchical present, and Mulcaster withdrew into a private realm of personal hygiene, Davies choreographs a nation. Furthermore, transforming the ancillary and precipitate into the transcendent and timeless, he anticipates the imperial age by praising the "true nobility" of an exclusionary practice that figures "the world's consent" to a world "where all agree and all in order move" (stanza 96). And it is this sovereign discourse that has until recently shaped our vision of English dancing.

THREE

Hands, Feet, and Bottoms:

Decentering the Cosmic Dance
in Shakespeare's Comedies

Shakespeare's comedies often end with a dance, we have been assured, because they move from confusion to order, from misfortune to prosperity, and dancing is an image of concord that celebrates this festive resolution.[1] Certainly, in the comedies, the patriarchal social order is disrupted and apparently restored, and in two, *Much Ado About Nothing* and *As You Like It,* the restoration is celebrated with dancing. The vision of dancing as ineffable harmony, however, imposes an identity upon the variety of dancing practices on the public stage, even as it discounts the social uses of courtly ones. As Shakespeare's theater was an eclectic enterprise, incorporating elements of the elite culture of the learned minority and the popular, oral culture of the majority,[2] so dancing in the public theatre was multifarious—the common player might be called upon to perform an expert *galliard,* a dignified measure, or a vigorous Morris with equal aplomb.[3] Encompassing a wide range of practices, the dancing of Shakespeare's theater was a metonym of the interactions and circulations in the society it reflected and generated, with courtly dancing reinscribing hierarchy through codified movement, and popular dancing celebrating affinity with traditional motions. Mingling with popular practices on a public stage, courtly dancing betokened more than concord, and even served to articulate competing assumptions.

On the public stage, courtly dancing was seen from, and presented, various social perspectives. The dances that visually articulated an elite ideal were executed not by aestheticized ladies and gentlemen for the purpose of attaining a position within the courtly sphere, but were imitated by male artisans, apprentices, and wage earners in order to gain a livelihood from a paying audience; the discontinuity between the representations and the representers themselves abraded the courtly veneer.[4] The performance of a dance signifying matrimony by a man and a cross-dressed boy, and the assumption by player-artisans of the gestures of aristocratic self-fashioning as easily as they donned the cast-off clothes of the nobility unsettled structures of rank and gender alike, undermining the inevitability that the image of the cosmic dance was recruited to assert. Therefore, while the dances with which some of the comedies conclude may resemble the revels dancing of court masque, they do not effect the resolute closure of elite dances as performed within the court. Dancing on the public stage was not a monolithic activity, but a kinetic economy: competing cultural assertions were visually articulated in the diverse traditions of dancing, and were certainly understood as such by their audiences.

A MIDSUMMER NIGHT'S DREAM

In *A Midsummer Night's Dream,* elite and popular traditions of dancing are unusually coextensive, oscillating with and debating one another throughout the play, yet in critical representation, the dancing has been imagined as a festival of reconciliation, and a "universal symbol" to "comment on and affect the major pattern of order and disorder in the action." The rustic Bergomask performed by the mechanicals serves "as an anti-masque to the singing and dancing of the fairies which ends both the first night of the wedding festivities and the play itself." The "glimmering light" that the fairies bring invokes the order of the firmament, and the fairies' carole "bind[s] together religion and fairy lore," bringing the play to a harmonious close.[5] The conflicts of the play are resolved in a dance that "expresses and confirms [the] recovered amity" of Oberon and Titania, a symbolic dance of concord that serves to transport us "beyond the realm of actuality."[6] But the dances of *A Midsummer Night's Dream* are more than a cosmic fantasy, or even a festive reconstitution of the patriarchal power.[7] Recent commentary on *A Midsummer Night's Dream* has focused on the intricate interactions among society, stage, and culture,[8] and it is these relations that are so clearly articulated on the public stage in the diverse and semiotically complex practices of dancing.

Certainly, the ending of A *Midsummer Night's Dream* engenders a sense of reconciliation, for the warring lovers are reconciled, the night is reclaimed for the sprites, and the fairies are joined in a round: "Hand in hand, with fairy grace, / Will we sing, and bless this place" (5.1.399–400).[9] But the fairies' dance is specifically defined within the play itself not as a courtly cosmic dance of the sort believed to signal a return to the natural order of the heavens, but as something quite different. The dances that dominate A *Midsummer Night's Dream* are the rounds and hays associated with popular festivity, traditional dances of the May Game and Midsummer Eve that cosmic refinements supposedly replaced. Although Titania and Oberon on one occasion dance a courtly dance (4.1.84–90), this is not the last dance of the play; instead, it is the linked dance of the fairies, not a "cosmic" dance, that brings the play full circle. And if the ending of this play "reaffirms essential elements of a patriarchal ideology [as it] calls that reaffirmation into question,"[10] at the end of the play as throughout, dancing is an important means by which this is achieved.

In A *Midsummer Night's Dream,* dancing quickly establishes an opposition between the popular tradition—oral, medieval, native, and communal—associated with Titania,[11] and elite culture—literate, modern, foreign, and solitary—associated with Oberon. The round danced by Titania and the fairies is an emblem of connection, each dancer facing toward the others, hands linked in a collective embrace. This is the dance of an oral tradition: "First, rehearse your song by rote, / To each word a warbling note" (5.1.397–98), instructs Titania, recommending the mnemonics of group repetition as the mechanism of cultural transmission rather than the formal study of a written score.[12] This tradition is immediately defined as feminine: "our round" (2.1.140), "our ringlets" (86), and the first dancing of the play involves Titania and her fairies when she invites them to "a roundel and a fairy song" (2.2.1) before sending them winding through the forest on errands of vernal housekeeping.

Oberon, however, has withdrawn from popular culture, and not only refuses to dance, he impedes the dancers. "Never," Titania reproaches,

> since the middle summer's spring,
> Met we on hill, in dale, forest, or mead,
>
> . . . .
>
> To dance our ringlets to the whistling wind,
> But with thy brawls thou hast disturbed our sport.
> (2.1.82–83, 86–87)

A "brawl" was, of course, a "noisy, turbulent quarrel." But it was also a dance, and a different kind of dance—boisterous where the round was serene, transitional where the round was traditional. From the French *branler,* "to sway from side to side," the *branle,* or brawl, was a French dance of popular origin that in France was danced in both court and countryside. There were many versions of this dance, distinguished from one another by gestural pattern;[13] that manual labor was central to this dance, in more ways than one, perhaps gave it the thrill of the forbidden that it sometimes enjoyed in England.[14] In *Love's Labor's Lost,* Moth evokes both the sexual and the popular associations of the dance when he suggests that his master win his love with a French brawl:

jig off the tune at the tongue's end, canary to it with your feet, humor it with turning up your eyelids, sigh a note and sing a note, sometime through the throat, [as] if you swallowed love with singing love, sometime through [the] nose, as if you snuffed up love by smelling love. (3.1.11–17)

Provocatively, Moth associates the dance, not with the chaste figure of gentility, but with the grotesque, open body—tongues, eyelids, throats, and noses—representing the brawl as a sexually charged blazon of the senses. Furthermore, since courtly dancing had by this time lost its "natural accompaniment of song,"[15] Moth's description defines the brawl as a transitional form, one that dances out conflicting cultural pressures in the linkage of old, new, popular, and courtly elements.

In England, the "brawl" was often ornamented with the kind of choreographic complexity that removed it from the improvisational province of popular culture, and advanced it into the realm of elite exercise. In *The Malcontent,* the dapper courtiers seek to outdo one another with their refinements:

—We will dance; music! We will dance.
—"*Les quanto*," lady, "*Pensez bien*," "*Passa regis*," or Bianca's brawl?
—We have forgot the brawl.
—So soon? 'Tis wonder.
—Why, 'tis but two singles on the left, two on the right, three doubles forward, a traverse of six round; do this twice, three singles side, galliard trick-of-twenty, corantopace; a figure of eight, three singles broken down, come up, meet, two doubles, fall back, then honor.[16]

To dance this, a dancing master's notation and instruction are surely required. Furthermore, this choreographed morsel is not a traditional pleasure but a virtuoso performance, a hybrid display piece set to dazzle with its complexity and the pyrotechnics of the "lofty turns and caprioles in the air" of the *galliard*. This is the sort of vehicle that an upwardly mobile courtly aspirant might purchase from an itinerant dancing master to display the dexterous, agile feet that set him apart from the crowd, and with the "galliard-trick," well above it.

Most likely, Oberon's noisy brawl was this kind of dance, and therefore represents a covert cultural assault on Titania. He imports tricky French customs designed for the privacy of a smoky hall that cloak sexuality and self-promotion in the guise of civility; he replaces shared popular festivity with an aggressive performance, and transforms dancing from a communal ritual into a conquest. His rejection of shared tradition results in the abandonment of the site where gentle and common interact. Festivity disappears from the neighborhood—"The human mortals want their winter cheer; / No night is now with hymn or carol bless'd" (2.1.101–2)—and the deterioration of common space is emblematic of the cultural break:

> The nine-men's-morris is fill'd up with mud;
> And the quaint mazes in the wanton green,
> For lack of tread, are undistinguishable.
> (98–100)

As the play continues, Oberon withdraws even further into elite isolation. Titania invites him once again to "patiently dance in our round, / And see our moonlight revels" (140–41), attempting one more time to draw him back: "If not, shun me, and I will spare your haunts" (143). Oberon, however, imposes unacceptable conditions, and Titania departs, leaving Oberon outside the circle, where he confides to Puck a curious reverie:

> once I sat upon a promontory,
> And heard a mermaid, on a dolphin's back,
> Uttering such dulcet and harmonious breath,
> That the rude sea grew civil at her song,
> And certain stars shot madly from their spheres,
> To hear the sea-maid's music.
>
> (149–54)

Oberon refuses Titania's invitation to dance, preferring a solitary fantasy that with impressive specificity reinscribes the male performative, envisioning himself, not with a partner or within a community, but alone upon a promontory, while a mermaid, entwined around a leaping mammal of considerable proportions, caresses the waters with her dulcet song and precipitates an eruption of "stars [shooting] madly from their spheres" that pleasurably shatters an implacable cosmic dance.

In the form of high *caprioles,* cosmic eruptions were the centerpiece of the masculine pyrotechnics that exploded over the dancing place; height was the patrimony of the gentleman, and soaring capers, exclusively male, an analogue of masculine prowess. As the breathless boasts of the two seedy courtiers in *Twelfth Night* suggest, the measure of a man was the height and amplitude of his "kickshawses": "I can cut a caper," crows Sir Andrew, "[and] I think I have the back-trick simply as strong as any man in Illyria." "Wherefore are these things hid? wherefore have these gifts a curtain before 'em?" gasps Sir Toby admiringly, before neatly topping his fellow dancer. "My very walk," he exults, "should be a jig; I would not so much as make water but in a sink-a-pace"—proposing to relieve himself, presumably, in the pause following the five steps of the six-count *galliard.*[17] As Sir Toby intimates, courtly dancing articulated and defined as exclusively masculine a virtuosic control far beyond the powers of the leaky feminine body.[18]

As might be expected in the light of his fantasies, Oberon waits to dance with Titania until she has been subdued by his enchantment. Then he proposes a different kind of dance, one in which the man leads and the woman follows: "Sound, music! Come, my queen, take hands with me, / And rock the ground whereon these sleepers be" (4.1.75–76). Titania, we recall, has urged Oberon to "patiently dance in our round, / And see our moonlight revels" (2.1.140–41); she does not claim him (*"my* King"), or seek to draw him away from the community ("take hands with *me"*). He, however, has declined to "patiently" dance in a round, but instead, offers his hand, a gesture that immediately defines the kind of dance he has in mind: the couple dance that served as an icon of gendered comportment. "Come, *my* Queen," he orders, "take hands with *me"* (emphases added). Oberon may use a more tactful expression than a blunt command to "take my hand," but he clearly is not inviting her to dance *with* him. Instead, Oberon takes charge of the lady like a well-schooled gentleman; he does not join a dance already in progress, but initiates one, establishing his dominance in a gesture that designates its inevitable response.[19] Oberon commands, and Titania, having by now been well brought up, accedes.

Oberon proposes to celebrate his restored amity with Titania not by joining her dance, but by inviting her to follow him in a courtly dance in which "whether forth or back or round he go, / As the man doth, so must the woman do."[20] His invitation to "rock the ground" practically specifies a courtly dance, one that rejects the linked hands of the group and privileges the dexterous feet of the individual that tap out intricate metrics with energetic footwork. It might have been a *tourdion,* a proto-*galliard* danced "with the feet kept close to the ground," or perhaps it was an *almain,* with percussive "jumps and springs."[21] The courtly dancing that constructed gender difference was a writing in which the practiced movements of the feet traced geometric patterns on the floor as they imitated poetic meters; transcribed in the treatises of the dancing masters, it was written to "foot the bill," not "handed down" as a community tradition. Titania's dance with Oberon is often seen as the evidence of a natural reconciliation: "The dance of Oberon and Titania is the ritual which ratifies the reconciliation of the fairy rulers, and symbolizes the renewed dance in the realm of nature which depends upon them. It corresponds inversely to the dance of Titania's fairies from which Oberon was absent, and to his earlier refusal to dance with her on her terms."[22] However, this is not only a dance that "betokeneth concord" between man and woman, it is a dance that explicates the conditions upon which concord is achieved; in the terms of the cultural opposition associated with dancing in the play, the dance of Titania

and Oberon articulates the subordination of popular culture to a patriarchal elite.

This is not the last dance of the play, though, nor the dance that,
as Oberon expects, spreads through "Duke Theseus' house trium-
phantly, / And bless[es] it to all fair prosperity" (4.1.89–90). It is
not, in fact, a gendered couple dance, rehearsing precedence from the
first proffered hand, that ultimately celebrates the play's marriages,
but the rustic Bergomask, that honors something quite different.
Theseus impatiently calls his "manager of mirth" for a bouquet of
elite festive practices: masks, dances, revels, play, music, delight
(5.1.32–41). However, Theseus and his court are not finally entertained by a courtly diversion, but a "palpable-gross" one. Bottom's
play, which precedes the dance, is frequently received as a burlesque
on popular attempts to master the refinements of elite culture,[23] and
the awkwardness of the "[h]ard-handed men . . . Which never labour'd in their minds till now," considered the source of the play's
humor, always at the expense of the uneducated. But the play-
within-the-play does not patronize the players, it rather "internalizes
and distances" the relationship between aristocratic patron and artisan player, effectively repudiating Theseus's condescension.[24] And if
the mechanicals' play is "carefully articulated as a rejection of
learned, humanist entertainments,"[25] the mechanicals' dance that
follows may be an equally explicit rejection of the structures of gender and hierarchy reproduced by courtly dancing.

Traditionally, the Bergomask has been viewed from the perspective of the courtly humanist as a continuation of the joke on the
naïveté of the awkward "mechanicals," an antimasque to be subsumed into a courtly finale: "There is a double strain of humor here.
A bergomask was originally a clumsy dance in ridiculous imitation
of the peasants of Bergamo. Shakespeare has his clowns, already inept, performing a dance imitating the inept."[26] However, the Bergomask in *A Midsummer Night's Dream* may have been much more than
humor at the expense of the lower classes, or simple opposition of
the "grotesque" and the "graceful."[27] Disclaimed by Theseus as "*your*
Bergomask," the dance perhaps offered an alternative model of gender relations, one patently in opposition to Oberon's dance of
"amity": where the courtly couple was isolated, enclosed, regulated,
and heterosexual, the popular couple was gregarious, intimate, improvisational, and often ungendered. Furthermore, it may have dis-

76

played not the ineptitude but the skill of the "rude mechanicals," and in so doing decentered the "cosmic" dance of Oberon and Titania. If, as has been suggested, the roles of the fairies and the mechanicals were doubled,[28] the round and the Bergomask were bodily identified, and popular dances outnumbered, surrounded, and overwhelmed Oberon's courtly imports.

Bergamasca was a term that embraced peasant dances and related musical forms from the Lombard region of Bergamo and involved a circular procession followed by a dance of two or more couples.[29] The *bergamasca* had a traditional form that was transmitted in the dancing, unlike courtly dances whose cachet derived from a unique and choreographed version, available only to those who could pay for the distinction. The relationship, if any, of the mechanicals' Bergomask to the *bergamasca* is unknowable, but Bottom's invitation to "*hear* a Bergomask dance between two of our company" (5.4.353–54), locates it within a popular, oral tradition. With the sequence of two couple dances, *A Midsummer Night's Dream* visually articulates gender first in one way, then in quite another, as Oberon and Titania dance a courtly dance, and then Pyramus and Thisby, perhaps, dance a popular one. Much as De Bry's "Court and Country Dancers" revealed the constructedness of gender identity and relations in courtly dancing, the contrast of Bottom's dance with Oberon's may have revealed the finesse of the courtly dancer as etiolation, and presented an alternative to it.

In *A Midsummer Night's Dream,* the Bergomask, like the dance between Oberon and Titania that signified matrimony was, of course, not performed by a man and a woman, but by a couple of men, a substitution that in both cases functioned to deconstruct elite practice.[30] In the Bergomask, though, the homology of the dancers operated somewhat differently. Where the masculinity of the player of Titania is suppressed, that of the Thisby player is foregrounded when the mechanicals decide which of them will play "the woman's part" (1.2). In this scene, femininity is established as only one of many characteristics to be assumed as easily as a disguise of dress or voice: Bottom, for example, boasts of a repertoire of gendered voices ranging from "monstrous little" (1.2.52) to heartwarming roar (70). Gender identity is not innate or absolute, but is defined as a role to be played, donned, or discarded with the same ease as an orange-tawny beard—to assume a female identity, Flute need only conceal his darkening upper lip, speak in a "small" voice (50–51), and dance with small steps. The dramatically established certainty concerning the actual gender of the Bergomask dancers, as well as its irrelevance to a successful performance of gender, unmasks as artifice the "naturalness" of the courtly couple.

Extradramatic knowledge concerning the Bergomask dancers that Shakespeare's audience no doubt possessed also reinforced the artificiality of the courtly dancers. And it is likely that the Bergomask, far from being merely an antimasque, was, instead, a star attraction; the role of Bottom, it is believed, was one of the vehicles created for Will Kempe, a series that came to an end in 1599 when he left the company for his "nine days wonder," an extended Morris dance across the English countryside.[31] A certified popular dancer among the play's imitation courtly couples, Will Kempe, celebrated for his mastery of the jig and other popular forms,[32] personified popular traditions and relations. Furthermore, Kempe may not only have danced in the Bergomask, he may have added his own virtuosic specialties.

Long ago it was suggested that the Bergomask may originally have combined comedy with exciting acrobatics,[33] but the Bergomask has traditionally been considered a clown dance, performed by Bottoms "in a grotesque and clumsy way." However, when performed as a male solo dance, the Morris for which Kempe was known featured high leaps and elaborate capers much like those of the *galliard*. When the Morris was performed as a pantomime, the hobbyhorse, close kindred of the ass, did most of this jumping.[34] Since Kempe's skill was so extraordinary that a jig was composed to honor it, and since he clearly did not hang a curtain before his wonders, it does not seem improbable that he added a showpiece of the kind of improvisational performance to which Hamlet objected. If so, this Bergomask was not a further display of artisan clumsiness, but a superior display of their adroitness.[35] The image of Bottom elevated in Kempe's high capers—capers only dreamed about by Oberon—may have presented a formidable visual challenge to the myth of elite supremacy and popular inadequacy.

The Bergomask of A *Midsummer Night's Dream* may both sequentially replace and theatrically surpass the courtly couple dance, but it is still not the last dance of the play. Yet another epilogue follows, in which Oberon seems to have discarded the courtly practices that he attempted to import, and to have commandeered the popular dances that he formerly disrupted. As Titania did earlier, Oberon sends the fairies off on a procession through the house past the sleeping lovers.

> Through the house give glimmering light
> By the dead and drowsy fire,
> Every elf and fairy sprite
> Hop as light as bird from brier,
> And this ditty, after me,
> Sing, and dance it trippingly.
>
> (5.1.391–96)

And Titania immediately responds:

> Hand in hand, with fairy grace,
> Will we sing, and bless this place.
>
> (399–400)

Her couplets, "carole measure," suggest that she dances a round with the fairies before they depart on Oberon's orders, whereas he directs and oversees their actions.[36] Titania's habit of mind is still equitable—each word gets its warbling note, and the entire place is blessed—but Oberon makes distinctions: he will go himself to the "*best* bride-bed," and though "each several chamber" will be blessed with "sweet peace," only "the *owner* of it . . . Ever shall in safety rest" (420) (emphases added). Seemingly, masculine surveillance and control have replaced Titania's communal round, and the hierarchy and authority of the cosmic dance have been restored.

The play does not end with this dance either, but with Puck's keen "slight"-of-hand. Left alone with the audience for the third and final epilogue, Puck addresses his audience in the player's conventional plea.

> If we shadows have offended,
> Think but this, and all is mended,
> That you have but slumber'd here,
> While these visions did appear.
> And this weak and idle theme,
> No more yielding but a dream,
> Gentles, do not reprehend:
> If you pardon, we will mend.
>
> (423–30)

Puck, echoing Titania's carole measure, evokes the oral contracts of the old marketplace[37]—"If you pardon, we will mend"—while seeming to distance the conflicts of culture and gender that have occupied the play, and which have not fully been resolved, by defining them as illusory, "visions" and "a dream." He returns once more to old assurances, concluding by seeming to reach out to his audience as Titania had reached out to the fairies, and to Oberon:[38]

> as I am an honest Puck,
>
> . . . .
>
> We will make amends ere long;
> Else the Puck a liar call:
> So, good night unto you all.
> Give me your hands, if we be friends,
> And Robin shall restore amends.
>
> (431, 434–38)

"Robin Goodfellow," though, was an urban trickster, not a woodland sprite.[39] While Puck first seems to be proposing that the spectators join hands in the fellowship of the fairies' round, in fact, he is demanding that they use their hands to applaud the performance of *A Midsummer Night's Dream* that they have just attended. In doing so, he defines the player as the purveyor of a commodity, and evokes the bargain between player and audience that will momentarily expire.

Puck does not propose a communion of audience and players, but a division into separate functions; not a fusion of the worlds of stage and audience, but a transaction between them; not a flight into the supernatural, but a return to the material. His trick frames the dance of the fairies and distances it, so that the *Dream* does not evaporate into a harmonious dance of blessing that transports its audience into a magical dream-world, but pointedly returns the spectator to his "local habitation" and its practices. Puck's gesture neither repairs the patriarchy with the fable of the cosmic dance nor makes the "social body whole again"[40] by reinstating the old festivity that embraced all classes of society. Puck's guileless invitation turns out to be a trick: he is not asking for social inclusion, but, in a social inversion, for his audience of gentles to use their hands. And his audience is left with empty hands. Why?

Perhaps to reject the timeless image of community, an imaginary unity based on the cosmic dance and the medieval round—"antick fables" and "fairy toys" (5.1.2–3) of cosmic harmony and pastoral simplicity—and to evoke a more timely one. The dancing in *A Midsummer Night's Dream* is not an "airy nothing" that evokes cosmic concord to restore "order," but, identified within the play itself as an interested social practice, serves to give this fantasy a "local habitation and a name." The juxtaposition of popular with courtly dancing has both reproduced the conditions of public performance and permitted the beholder to "apprehend / [m]ore than cool reason ever comprehends" about the social construction of rank and gender. In *A Midsummer Night's Dream,* dancing has not naturalized an order, but has revealed it to be provisional and man-made. Puck therefore closes the play not with an image of the universal cosmic dance but with the impact of a terrestrial one, ending this eclectic epithalamion on a reassertion of the urban contracts of the middling sort—in much the same way as the stage jig served to reestablish the popular equilibrium of a stage top-heavy with historical monarchs.[41] The new dance for gentles and mechanicals is a commercial contract between the artisan of images and those who construct their lives with dreams.

MUCH ADO ABOUT NOTHING

From the courtly forests of *A Midsummer Night's Dream,* Shakespeare moved, a few years later, to the urban setting of *Much Ado About Nothing.* In both comedies, dancing plays a crucial role, is associated with linguistic forms, and seems to effect a restoration of patriarchal order.[42] At the same time, however, dancing additionally complicates this resolution, the variety of practices in *A Midsummer Night's Dream* and discourses of dancing in *Much Ado* resisting the order that it ostensibly reinstates. But there are important differences between the two plays. In *A Midsummer Night's Dream,* popular dances visually dominate the action while courtly dances for the most part occur offstage, and the play ends not with a real dance but with an evocative gesture. In *Much Ado About Nothing,* courtly dancing is central to and may conclude the play, providing a real test of interpretive tropes of concord. Moreover, dancing and language are both separately interrogated and explicitly linked as patriarchal practices, and

since the linguistic paradigm of "wit" has been incontestably rejected when the final dance begins, the triumph of patriarchy is qualified at best.

Messina is depicted at the outset as a wonderland for those of rank:
as the play opens, Don Pedro returns from a glorious campaign having lost "few of any sort, and none of name" (1.1.7). Yet this is no
idyll: it soon becomes evident that Messina is a material world, not
unlike the English city, in which questions of inheritance govern
both affection and action. Claudio, having established his martial
prowess, decides that the time is auspicious to be smitten with Hero,
and prudently inquires if she is her father's heir (1.1.294); Don John,
excluded from a patrimony by his illegitimate birth, consequently
prides himself on being a "plain-dealing villain" (1.3.32). Given the
importance of economic stability, life in Messina understandably
centers on the pursuit of an advantageous marriage of the kind expedited by dancing in mercantile discourse, in which the bride is
an enriching and unblemished repast: Leonato expects Hero to accept the proposal of the Prince (2.1.66–67), but is equally agreeable
to a marriage with Claudio (2.1.302–4); Don Pedro, elder exemplary, benevolently undertakes to engineer the matches of Hero with
Claudio and Benedick with Beatrice, but promptly turns on Hero
(4.1) when it appears that she is damaged goods.

Despite temporary reversals, the play ends comedically with the
firm betrothal of two young couples, an event celebrated in merry
dancing that begins as dialogue concludes. Adversaries to marriage
and to dancing—Don John, Borachio, and Conrade[43]—have been
eliminated; Hero's value has been restored in the eyes of those who
will marry her and marry her off; Benedick's reluctance to marry has
been overturned; and the unacceptable challenges of the "Lady['s]
Tongue" have been silenced, presumably forever. "Let's have a dance
ere we are married, that we may lighten our own hearts and our
wives' heels," trumpets Benedick (5.4.117–20)—his levity on the
subject of female chastity in questionable taste in the light of Hero's
recent experience—and the lovers join in the sort of dance that
might be expected to lighten men's hearts by giving them the upper
hand. But does the play end "happily" with a dance that shows that
"harmony is restored"?[44]

In *Much Ado About Nothing*, dancing has an authoritative speaker,
and it is Beatrice, who explains her "wit" as an auspicious cosmic

influence: "there was a star danced, and under that I was born" (2.1.335). Early in the play, she invokes the association of marriage and dancing as a warning to Hero of the dangers of matrimony. The two scenes of dancing that follow reflect and confirm aspects of her warning: in the first, four ladies are courted in a dance by their disguised partners; in the second, Margaret offers a dance to cheer a nervous Hero on the morning of her wedding day. At the play's end, a newly silent Beatrice seems to agree to follow Benedick in a dance of his selection, at a time of his choosing, to the accompaniment of his bad jokes on chastity; it is difficult to believe that her dancing star has served her very well. But her observations on marriage and dancing expressed early in the play definitively dismantle the mythology of the dance of marriage, so that at the end of the play the couples do not simply submerge beneath it.

If the dancing couple "signifies matrimony," what kind of a dance is marriage?

For hear me, Hero: wooing, wedding, and repenting, is as a Scotch jig, a measure, and a cinquepace; the first suit is hot and hasty, like a Scotch jig, and full as fantastical; the wedding, mannerly-modest, as a measure, full of state and ancientry, and then comes repentance, and with his bad legs, falls into the cinquepace faster and faster, till he sink into his grave. (2.1.72–80)[45]

Certainly, this is not Elyot's cautious progress from prudence to maturity. Beatrice suggests the opposite: that neither dancing nor marriage elevates the participant through an ennobling imitation of the motions of the cosmos, but rather fatally exhausts him. Neither is this a dance of companionate marriage, for it is increasingly isolating, with the lady moving out of the picture as the dancer struggles alone in center stage. Wooing, wedding, repenting, and dancing are presented from the distance of a spectator, but this dancer does not "all amaze [who] at his beauty gaze"; instead, he appears to be awkwardly propelled through disparate and discontinuous dances "hot and hasty" and "mannerly-modest," with the coda an uncontrollable dance-of-death.

Marriage and courtly dancing privileged masculine dominance, and Beatrice's warning to Hero quietly calls attention to the progressive disappearance of the female partner. The Scotch jig was a popular form that charmed Londoners with its "rustic or provincial" qualities, and consisted of a song-and-dance that recounted a courtship in repeating refrains, spiced with vigorous danced enactments. In the song, male and female voices alternated, and the woman, who took the refrain, had the last word.[46] In the measures, the smooth walk of the governor, each torpid step was a complex system of material and social demands; the lady and gentleman did the same dance together, though the gentleman led. But in the cinquepace, the gentleman was displayed alone in variations of exhausting complexity, with jumps ever higher, turns ever longer, feet crossed with increasing rapidity, while the lady "easily [did] slide / And smoothly swim with cunning hidden art."[47] The girl of the Scotch jig is the song—without her power of refusal, there would be no song to sing—but marriage is a compact that if she should ever "get the upper hand," she will obey the "Measure's law" and "[wheel] about, and ere the dance should end, / Into her former place . . . transcend."[48] The disappearance of the woman in Beatrice's dance, then, parallels her loss of agency in the dance of marriage.

But Beatrice renders the husband's marital doom even more appallingly, with satiric images that undermine masculine privilege and suggest that perhaps the putative beneficiary has the most to lose. For the gentleman, she suggests, patriarchal marriage is a complex and painful endeavor, necessitating confusing adjustments and awkward tacks: wooing is so pleasurable that neither song nor dance alone can contain it, but wedding restrains the dancer into an ineffable immobility, and married life is a male solo performance the demands of which increase as the means decrease. The pleasures of courtship are chilled by a wedding of economic and political duty, and the infelicitous outcome of such a marriage, not between man and woman but to a system of social relations, is the compulsive and pointless upward mobility vainly sought by an exhausted self-fashioner.

This dance of marriage is a futile social climb, the popular jig replaced by a humanist cadence, in turn superseded by the solipsism of the Continental courtier; through it, Beatrice deconstructs the assumptions of upward mobility central to patriarchal and mercantile discourses of dancing. "Repentance" has a million different variations to make him sorry, dancing on painful limbs that can no longer perform their saltations but which, despite a depleting expenditure of effort, hasten their owner's mortifying fall. The envied model of social advancement, who leaps high, turns dexterously, and twinkles his inexorably progressing toes to classical metrics, whose burgeoning power is confirmed by the admiring glances of his lady, is here inverted as his loss of power, gazed upon, grows infinitely vast.

With this baleful introduction, the masquers enter for a postprandial dance with the ladies. "The revellers are ent'ring, brother: make good room," calls Leonato (2.1.84), recalling the Vice from an old morality play—and indeed, this dance marks the activation of deception, as the Prince, disguised, undertakes to woo Hero in Claudio's stead, with Don John and Claudio prophetically observing the courtship as they will later watch the staged scene that compromises Hero.[49] This dance of misunderstanding and disguise is an active metonym of the play's larger actions, as the dancers advance toward and retreat from one another, misrepresent themselves and mistake the designs of others.[50] If the dance, as the pattern of the dialogue indicates, is the measures, it is performed out of sequence, for the measures articulated the sanctity of marriage. The masquers' dance, though, slow and deliberate, evokes both the calculations of parental contracts and the premeditation and duplicity involved in their negotiation. Furthermore, contrary to Elyot's assertions, these measures do not provide a moral foundation, but prove to be, as threatened in moralistic discourse, a staging area for dishonor.

This masquers dance does, however, fix the association of language and dancing as patriarchal practices by measuring out the interactions between men and women, and circumscribing the number and length of their exchanges.[51] The dialogue seems to reflect the dance in a way that suggests that dancing structures language: "Lady, will you walk about with your friend?" asks Don Pedro (2.1.87), presumably offering his hand, which Hero accepts, "So you walk softly, and look sweetly, and say nothing, I am yours for the walk."[52] But fissures open between word and gesture: "I am yours for the walk; and especially when I walk away," teases Hero (90). In the measures, however, the lady does not "walk away" from the gentleman—any more than her partner, like a damsel, walks softly, looks sweetly, and says nothing.[53] The disjunction between word and dance subjects them both to scrutiny, and engenders the suspicion that both may diverge from the ideal much as the sink-a-pacer declined from his aspirations.

If the dance enacts the courtship of Hero and Claudio in miniature as their falling and rising fortunes sweep past in the dancing couples who part and meet,[54] it also foreshadows its grave end. Antonio is a particularly inappropriate dancing partner for Ursula, ill-matched both in age and status; an "oddity as a dancer" with his "dry hand" and his "waggling" head,[55] he recalls old Repentance with the bad legs ready to sink into his grave. Ursula recognizes him: "I know you well enough; you are Signior Antonio . . . I know you by the waggling of your head . . . Here's his dry hand up and down: you are he, you are he" (2.1.113–19). Antonio, however, rejects her identification, claiming, in a twist on self-fashioning, self-counterfeit (116). Significantly, the men in this dance, which reveals their imperfect self-fashioning—and their imperfect self-knowledge—are masked, while the women are probably not.[56] Ursula, though, kindly follows Antonio's lead, attributing to him the quality which he patently desires, but which he conspicuously does not possess: "Come, come, do you think I do not know you by your excellent wit?" (122).

Male identity is again at issue, though probably once again, not in doubt, when Beatrice and Benedick dance. Like the other couples, Beatrice and Benedick accompany their dance of marital harmony with a genial set of verbal sorties. "Will you not tell me who told you so?" "No, you shall pardon me." "Nor will you not tell me who you are?" "Not now" (2.1.125–28). However, Beatrice and Benedick break the pattern of four-transaction segments that replicate the measures of music established by the other couples, when Beatrice stops the dance.[57]

BEATRICE.	Did he never make you laugh?
BENEDICK.	I pray you, what is he?
BEATRICE.	Why, he is the prince's jester; a very dull fool; only his gift is in devising impossible slanders. None but libertines delight in him, and the commendation is not in his wit, but in his villainy, for he both pleases men and angers them, and then they laugh at him and beat him. I am sure he is in the fleet; I would he had boarded me.
BENEDICK.	When I know the gentleman, I'll tell him what you say.
BEATRICE.	Do, do, he'll but break a comparison or two on

> me, which peradventure, not marked, or not
> laughed at, strikes him into melancholy, and
> then there's a partridge wing saved, for the fool
> will eat no supper that night. . . . We must fol-
> low the leaders.

BENEDICK.   In every good thing.

BEATRICE.   Nay, if they lead to any ill, I will leave them at
the next turning.

(133–54)

Here, Beatrice egregiously flouts courtly custom, for in courtly dancing, the gentleman is privileged to begin the dance, and to end it by
returning the lady to her original place.[58] But Beatrice breaches the
established pattern of short sallys with two passages completely un-
suited by their length and syntactical complexity to the accompaniment of a stately dance, passages the sense and humor of which would
be extremely difficult for an audience to grasp were the speaker in motion. When she begins to move again—"We must follow the leaders"—she once more takes the lead away from Benedick. And she
concludes this skirmish in their war of wits as the victor, by asserting
a dominance that terpsichorean usage did not customarily allow: "if
[the leaders] lead to any ill, I will leave them at the next turning."

The next turn after these destabilized measures of courtship is the
"Light a love" with which Margaret offers to entertain a miserable
Hero on the day of her wedding (3.4.44): "Do you sing it, and I'll
dance it" (46). Again, propriety is disrupted, for the "Light a love"
promises to be a lively and amorous song-and-dance, perhaps a jig.[59]
This dance, though, will not lead to a wedding full of state and ancientry, but to one that will deprive Hero of her "mannerly-modesty"
so that she sinks into her grave.[60] Ironically, Margaret, who proposes
this entertainment, has the previous evening unwittingly ensured
Hero's misfortune. But even though Hero, Beatrice, and Margaret
know nothing of the bride's impending calamity, they are worried
by the changes that even a mannerly-modest marriage brings. Hero's
heart is "exceeding heavy" (25); and surfacing from beneath her
torrent of quips emerges Beatrice's sudden realization, "'Tis almost
five a' clock, cousin, 'tis time you were ready. By my troth, I am
exceeding ill" (52–53), her anxiety instantly denied by a jolly
"Heigh-ho."

Quite frequently, Beatrice repudiates a serious intent in the impudent verbal sallys that uniformly mark her interactions. She skirmishes not only with Benedick (1.1.118–45), she thrusts and parries with equal relish with Hero, Margaret, Leonato, the Prince, often softening her edge with the equivalent of a "Heigh-ho," or the demurral that she speaks "all mirth and no matter" (2.1.330). But a war of wits is still a war, serious business and man's work, and predicated upon a victory: the necessity of having the best or last word is commensurate with the necessity of having the best or last blow. Exceptionally endowed with the verbal adroitness that she credited to her dancing star, Beatrice wins most of her contests. But at the moment when Hero is slandered, she abandons the witty conceits that have served her so well, and simply cries: "O, on my soul, my cousin is belied!" (4.1.146). She is even more direct when Benedick seeks to console her: "Kill Claudio" (289), she demands, and efficiently extracts his promise.

As she began to do in their dance, Beatrice continues to lead Benedick in important ways. In response to her example of candor, Benedick again follows her lead. He seeks out Claudio and the Prince, and finds them laughing at Leonato and Antonio, who are distraught about the treatment of Hero. They attempt to include Benedick in their levity, realizing only with difficulty that he really is angry, and no longer interested in recreational defamation.

DON PEDRO.	Welcome, signior, you are almost come to part almost a fray.
CLAUDIO.	We had like to have had our two noses snapped off with two old men without teeth.
DON PEDRO.	Leonato and his brother. What think'st thou? Had we fought, I doubt we should have been too young for them.
BENEDICK.	In a false quarrel there is no true valor. I came to seek you both.
CLAUDIO.	We have been up and down to seek thee; for we are high-proof melancholy, and would fain have it beaten away. Wilt thou use thy wit?
BENEDICK.	It is in my scabbard: shall I draw it?
DON PEDRO.	Dost thou wear thy wit by thy side?

CLAUDIO.	Never any did so, though very many have been beside their wit. I will bid thee draw, as we do the minstrels, draw, to pleasure us.
DON PEDRO.	As I am an honest man, he looks pale. Art thou sick, or angry?
CLAUDIO.	What, courage, man! What though care killed a cat, thou hast mettle enough in thee to kill care.
BENEDICK.	Sir, I shall meet your wit in the career, and you charge it against me. I pray you choose another subject.
CLAUDIO.	Nay, then, give him another staff: this last was broke cross.
DON PEDRO.	By this light, he changes more and more: I think he be angry indeed. (5.1.114–42)

Benedick, though, refuses to be drawn back into the game. Appalled by the callousness of his erstwhile friend, he challenges him:

You are a villain. I jest not; I will make it good how you dare, with what you dare, and when you dare. Do me right, or I will protest your cowardice. You have killed a sweet lady, and her death shall fall heavy on you. Let me hear from you. (144–50)

However, Benedick is not finished yet. Claudio is abashed by his challenge, but the Prince babbles on, nervously attempting to recall Benedick to his former self, even invoking Beatrice as ultimate authority:

I'll tell thee how Beatrice praised thy wit the other day. I said, thou hadst a fine wit: "True," says she, "a fine little one." "No," said I, "a great wit:" "Right," says she, "a great gross one." "Nay," said I, "a good wit." "Just," said she, "it hurts nobody." (158–63)

Don Pedro, though, succeeds in recalling Benedick not to witty games but to real hurts, with the result that Benedick not only rejects his friend, he curtly breaks with his patron as well, breaching male cohesion on two fronts.

BENEDICK.	Fare you well, boy, you know my mind. I will leave you now to your gossip-like humour. You break jests as braggarts do their blades, which,

> God be thank'd, hurt not. My lord, for your
> many courtesies I thank you. I must discontinue
> your company. . . . You have among you kill'd a
> sweet and innocent lady. [*Exit.*]

DON PEDRO.   He is in earnest.

(185–94)

Not only does Benedick break fraternal ties, he rejects the gentle-manly paradigm of sport, the war of wits that both wounds and serves as an evasion of the importance of things, a game that he now understands not as a noble contest, but as petty and "gossip-like hu-mour." He views verbal duels not as being won, but as being lost ("You break jests as braggarts do their blades") and not a sign of power, but of impotence ("which, God be thanked, hurt not").

The use and misuse of language is the pivot on which the play turns, and when language is misused to slander Hero, Beatrice re-jects the forms that have facilitated this injustice: the leaders have led to ill, she has left them at the turning, and she has taken Bene-dick with her. Confirming the choices of Beatrice and Benedick is the example of Dogberry, who stumbles into the linguistic briars of malaprop with an alacrity that models itself after the wittiness of his betters. But unlike those with rhetorical skills who deliberately misuse language, Dogberry can see and listen to others, talents that enable him to penetrate Don John's plot and bring the perpetrators to justice (4.3). Interestingly, Dogberry, was, like Bottom, believed to be one of Kempe's parts, and they have striking similarities—both are "asses," both aim at erudition but miss the mark. And one popular dancer played them both, which serves to link Dogberry's honesty with the young woman born under a dancing star, and to undermine further the integrity of the dances of the elite.

The ending of the play, with Beatrice submissively joining Bene-dick in his dance, might be one more victory for the patriarchal es-tablishment, that is, if Hero and Claudio are the "leaders" whom Beatrice follows "both . . . at the ball and subsequently to the altar."[61] Beatrice appears to follow Hero's example in another way, too, falling silent as Hero does on her first wedding day; in sharp contrast to her eloquence during her earlier dance with Benedick, Beatrice becomes conspicuously quiet when interrupted, perhaps with a kiss from Benedick to "stop [her] mouth" (5.4.97), and remains uncharacteristically silent thereafter. Is Beatrice, with Hero, successfully reincorporated into the woman's place of walking softly, looking sweetly, and saying nothing in a masculine courtly dance? Even worse, is she the object of a renewal of masculine slander in the form of Benedick's sophomoric remark about light-heeled wives?

Curiously, it is Beatrice who has anticipated much that seems objectionable in the final episode. Early in the play, when Claudio jabbers excitedly on his first acquisition of Hero, Beatrice, in Benedick's presence, prompts her friend: "Speak, cousin, or (if you cannot) stop his mouth with a kiss, and then let him speak neither" (2.1.310–11). And Beatrice herself initiated the "light heels" joke on the first wedding day.

> MARGARET.   Clap's into "Light 'a love"; that goes without a burden. Do you sing it, and I'll dance.
>
> BEATRICE.   Ye light 'a love with your heels! then if your husband have stables enough, you'll see he shall lack no barns.
>
> (3.4.44–48)

Although Benedick may not be aware of the source of his witticisms, the audience of the play surely is, and although she is silent, it is Beatrice who has the last word. Mouths are stopped with kisses and the tournament of wit has ended in a draw. When the pipers play the final dance, they certainly do not accompany a constipated matrimonial processional, nor a fancy *galliard,* but most likely a "rustic and provincial" jig in which both man and woman are heard. Moreover, the light-heeled dance is less a commemoration of patriarchal victory than a celebration of female generation, for it is Beatrice's association of dancing with "barns," at least as much as discourses of rank and wealth, that resonates in the closing dance.

To the champions of male bonding, the marriage of Beatrice and Benedick is a sad occasion that formalizes the disruption of masculine society and the "ending of happiness"[62]; and yet, those relations and practices have been shown to make deadly demands and have debilitating consequences. Benedick's hectic insistence on a dance (reminiscent of Theseus's call for "mirth" and "revels") before the measured nuptials that dancing should follow, seems hasty, impulsive: for a moment, he suggests the desperate, sinking husband of Beatrice's image just enough to imply that he has managed only narrowly to avoid the same fate. To supporters of female agency, the marriage might also seem a sad occasion, with Beatrice submitting passively to her husband. It is she, however, who has led him every step of the way with cunning hidden art, beyond the solitary sink-a-pace of witty display.[63] The multiple couplings of the final dance may erect a facade of patriarchal triumph, but its foundations are shaky, undermined by Benedick's demonstrated willingness to follow his wife, and by Beatrice's lingering image of the floundering sink-a-pacer. In *Much Ado About Nothing,* Shakespeare represents marriage, dancing, and "wit" in all their deficiencies, so that at the play's end, patriarchal order is reinstated, not restored.

FOUR

The Nervy Limbs of Elizabeth Cary:
Resisting Containment

E lizabeth Cary's *The Tragedy of Mariam*,[1] as the first original play
written by a woman to be published in English, promises distinctive access to a feminine perspective on the cultural practices that
shaped gender relations. While there is no dancing in *The Tragedy of
Mariam*, there are multiple associations to it. References to dancing
made both by her admirers and the author herself frame the play,
discursive tropes of dancing are pivotal to it, and formally, it documents the enclosure and rigor of the classical body. Dancing was an
accepted discourse of social relations, and paradigms of difference
were circulated through images of dancing in Cary's chamber play
even as they were in Shakespeare's comedies. Furthermore, in Cary's
play, as in those of Shakespeare, patriarchal norms were not only circulated, they were resisted. But they were resisted somewhat differently: where Shakespeare presents alternatives to dominant practices,
Cary seems to accept that there are no alternatives, shaping her text
and assumptions to conform with elite customs. However, as a
woman and therefore subordinate, she challenges them in the very
act of mastering them. In *The Tragedy of Mariam*, images of dancing
vividly articulate the inner division and overt confinement that patriarchal strictures generated for the educated woman, while Cary's
energetic compliance with the dramaturgy of enclosure foregrounds
its rigidity, and in so doing transforms oppression into the potential
for affirmation.[2]

While Cary, reportedly an isolated and self-educated child and a
diligently pregnant wife[3] probably did not dance with the frequency,
skill, or enthusiasm of more frivolous ladies, as a woman of high
status, her familiarity with the practice might be expected, since
dancing was an important feature of the education of upper-class

women.[4] Cary reportedly wrenched her classical education, and even her skills with the needle, alone and by guile from unsympathetic parents, who rationed her candles in an attempt to limit her reading and writing, and she may not have benefited from much instruction in dancing either. However, as Elyot observed, dancing exerted a profound influence on beholders as well as dancers, and Cary's credentials as a spectator are verified by a report of her pleasure in Sir Henry Cary's appearance in a court masque, and her connection with the Villiers, to whom de Lauze dedicated the *Apologie de la Danse*.[5] Therefore, it is safe to assume Cary's familiarity with the discourse of dancing, whether or not she was accomplished in practice.

Courtly dancing was potentially a source of conflict for the educated woman. For all women, it was a practice that performed masculine agency and feminine dependence, learned under the guidance of a "male cultural authority" in the person of a dancing master who was of a lower social status than the woman he instructed, but, paradoxically, as a man, superior.[6] The measures of the cosmic dances subordinated women and appended them to men, yet courtly dancing was also associated with socially privileged status. For the woman who was classically educated, the image of the cosmic dance was potentially even more unsettling, associated as it was with both feminine submission and the masculine learning to which she aspired. Dancing and classical studies were equally a means of women's "immasculation"[7] which imbued in them a set of propositions to which their insufficiency was central. Alone, each promised a qualified transcendence, but taken together, evoked contradictory assumptions.

The dominant discourses of dancing have been preserved in men's writing; but was there a "woman's discourse of dancing" in the Renaissance? Unfortunately, it seems that women rarely wrote about dancing directly. In one of the few instances, Margaret Clifford, Lady Cumberland, uses a metaphor of dancing in an autobiographical letter to represent the advances and reversals of her life.[8] Margaret Cavendish, in *The World's OLIO*, has provided one of the few examples of any length.

Kissing dances are commonly dances which were invented by the meaner and ruder sort of people, at wakes, at fairs; which kind of people knows not the ceremonies of modest civilities, for country dancing is a kind of rude pastime, and cannot be called truly a dance, but a running in [figures]. For the true art of dancing is measured figures, by the feet in divided times, for the feet keep as just distance of times as notes of music. Dancing is compounded of measures, figures, and motion. Measure is geometry, figure is symmetry, and motion is division.[9]

Here, Cavendish identifies with elite categories of gentle and base, privileging modest civilities over rude fairs, regulated dancing in "measured figures" over immoderate "running." Measured feet, the anatomical means of propulsion in dancing and the structural unit in the classical metrics that dancing often replicated, were associated in both systems with masculine dominance. However, in the traditional ideology of the body politic, the foot, the lowest extremity, corresponded more aptly with the (often unlettered) woman and servant. For the learned woman, therefore, discourses of dancing evoked contradictory positions and, while fixing her in a social system, emphasized her conflicting identifications.

DANCING AS AUTHORIZING TROPE

The poem often cited as evidence of Cary's authorship of *The Tragedy of Mariam,* the "Muses Sacrifice" of John Davies of Hereford,[10] offers Cary an apposite tribute that rests heavily on the cosmic dance.

> Cary (of whom Minerva stands in fear
>   lest she, from her, should get Arts Regency)
> Of Art so moves the great-all-moving Sphere,
>   that ev'ry Orb of Science moves thereby.
>
> Thou Makest Melpomen proud, and my Heart great
>   of such a Pupil, who, in buskin fine,
> With feet of State, doth make thy Muse to mete
>   The Scenes of Syracuse and Palestine.
>
> Art, Language; yea; abstruse and holy Tongues,
>   thy Wit and Grace acquir'd thy Fame to raise;
> And still to fill thine own, and others Songs;
>   thine, with thy Parts, and others, with thy praise.
>
> Such nervy Limbs of Art, and Strains of Wit
>   Times past ne'er knew the weaker Sex to have;
> And Times to come will hardly credit it,
>   if thus thou give thy Works both Birth and Grave.

. . . .

> But your Three Graces, (whom our Muse would grace,
>   had she that Glory that our Philip had,
> That was the Beauty of Art's Soul and Face)
>   you press the Press with little you have made.
>
> No; you well know the Press so much is wronged
>   by abject Rhymers that great Hearts do scorn
> To have their Measures with such Numbers thronged
>   as are basely got, conceived, and borne.

In this poem, Davies links with Cary the celestial images from "*Orchestra*," representing Cary as the aspiring sun of a cosmic dance wherein "Art so moves the great-all-moving Sphere, / that ev'ry Orb of Science moves thereby." As in the earlier poem, the hierarchical principal written in the skies is realized in the form of a dance, and the play itself is honored as an exemplary dance of the "nervy Limbs of Art" to the "Strains of Wit." The dexterity of Cary's "feet of State," in which anatomy and poetry intersect, is so extraordinary, Davies suggests, that even goddesses are apprehensive.

Paradoxically, however, Davies not only praises Cary's poetic accomplishments as accomplished dancing; he praises her for not performing in public, denigrating "abject Rhymers" who seek to "press the Press" as unskilled dancers whose "Measures" are with "Numbers thronged," recalling the other John Davies who scorned the "disordered rout" that "most spitefully / Did one another throng and crowd so sore" (stanza 29). Davies' compliment to Cary's accomplishment is double-edged, for in dancing the part of the sun, with feet of State and dressed "in buskin fine," she dances the gentleman's part, trespassing gender boundaries as she has in the act of writing. However, the same dance that Cary has mastered also promises to bring her down: when performed correctly, the measures maintained "the bounded space" between ranks and genders; by invoking this dance, Davies sounds a tacit warning to an exceptional woman.[11]

THE TRAGEDY

The Tragedy of Mariam has been recognized as an effort by Cary to resolve some of the difficulties and conflicts of her private life, particularly a "mind-body rift" resulting from "her attempt to live the 'masculine' life of the mind while devotedly carrying out the role and duties of a woman." [12] The issue of power relations on which the play turns centers on the linguistic problematic of a woman's public voice: [13] what can a woman say, to whom, and with what consequences? As in *Much Ado About Nothing,* speech is inextricably associated with dancing. Mariam's conflict between "social and ideological pressures to conform and submit and an inner imperative to resist and challenge authority," [14] between her need to be "chaste" and her desire to be free, is articulated by two related and opposing images that link dancing and language: the contained woman is represented by the regulated foot, and the free woman by a gaping mouth.

Adapted from Lodge's translation of Josephus's *Jewish Antiquities,* the tragedy recounts the last day of the life of the virtuous and beautiful Queen Mariam. During the single day of the action, her husband, the ruthless Herod, who has been reported dead, returns; Mariam, unable to flatter him, is put to death as a result of the intrigue of his unscrupulous sister Salome, who can. Mariam is torn between conflicting claims, between her wifely duty to keep silent at her husband's strategic murder of her kin, to greet him as he wishes in spite of her feelings, to comply with his retribution for her failings, and her personal desire to speak what she feels, to grieve for her family, and to escape her death sentence. Finally rejecting the polarities of patriarchal speech embodied in Salome, the model of opportunist speech, and Graphina, the model of opportune silence, [15] Mariam accepts her death with "a dutiful, though scornful, smile" (5.1.52).

Certainly, *The Tragedy of Mariam* is the tragedy of the silenced woman, both as dramatized in the Hebrew Queen Mariam and as lived by her creator Elizabeth Cary—the right to a voice was crucial to the life of the poet as well. Cary's parents kept private their daughter's learned voice, sending her husband Sir Henry letters in Elizabeth's name ghost-written by a less-accomplished girl, and Cary dutifully withheld her full name from her tragedy and circulated it privately. Cary endeavored not only to play but to live her wifely role of deference, and encouraged her own daughter to both "Be and Seem"; however, when she decided to seem the Catholic that she was, she was deprived of the roles of wife and mother in whose performance she had invested so much, unable, like Mariam, to reconcile two sets of opposing demands.

Cary's play opens with Mariam's privately voiced concern about the statements made in her public voice, and with their immediate recantation, in an anguished soliloquy of guilt and anxiety over her crimes of speech.[16]

> How oft have I with public voice run on?
> To censure Rome's last hero for deceit:
> Because he wept when Pompey's life was gone,
> Yet when he lived, he thought his name too great.
> But now I do recant, and Roman lord
> Excuse too rash a judgment in a woman:
> My sex pleads pardon, pardon then afford,
> Mistaking is with us but too too common.
> Now do I find by self-experience taught,
> One object yields both grief and joy:
> You wept indeed when on his worth you thought,
> But joy'd that slaughter did your foe destroy.
> So at his death your eyes true drops did rain,
> Whom dead you did not wish alive again.
>
> (1.1–14)

The first line articulates the association of speech and ambulation that informs the play. Her censuring voice, she recognizes, is censurable whether or not the object of censure is culpable, simply because it runs on. Terrified at the danger in which her unregulated voice has placed her, Mariam attempts to trap it in a double net of feminine submission: she recants, judges her judgment "too rash," pleads "pardon, pardon," laments that "[m]istaking is with us but too too common." She finally succeeds in halting her censuring voice by turning it back on herself, internalizing the fault about which her public voice ran on. Invoking the principle of measure—"One object yields both grief and joy"—she reciprocally exonerates her husband as she censures herself, and, in a solitary *volta,* argues that what seems censurable as hypocrisy is not, in which case, she as the censurer is in the wrong. Mariam's first linguistic dance constitutes an attempt to fortify herself in a secure silence, and to rationalize its necessity.

MORAL MEASURES

The conflict between Mariam's impulse to run on and the need to stop herself is finally resolved when she justifies her own death, her final arrest, in a moral judgment that is paradoxically ambulatory:

> Had I but with humility been graced,
> As well as fair I might have proved me wise:
> But did I think because I knew me chaste,
> One virtue for a woman might suffice.
> That mind of glory of our sex might stand,
> Wherein humility and chastity
> Doth march with equal paces hand in hand,
> But if one single seen, who setteth by?
> (4.559–66)

Unexpectedly, Cary represents humility and chastity as a dancing couple in a sedate procession. They march "with equal paces hand in hand," emphasizing the insufficiency of the single virtue: she "did . . . think because [she] knew [her] chaste, / One virtue for a woman might suffice"—but it does not, at least not in the public eye ("But if one single seen, who setteth by?"). The humility with which Mariam has not been graced is the correct kind of "public voice," that is, the absence of a private one. This image of virtues pacing together, which accents Mariam's unescorted chastity, is central to her self-condemnation, and to the play: voice and dancing body are paired at a pivotal dramatic juncture when Mariam's actions are measured by "the measure's law" of feminine incompletion.

Cary's use of the dancing metaphor to deliver a moral judgment is crucial; it identifies courtly dancing as patriarchal disciplinarian. The moralization of physical deportment was customary in the Renaissance: allegorical dancing couples and couple dances were no doubt familiar to Cary,[17] but the dance to which Mariam refers is recognizably Elyot's moralized measures, in which "the first moving in every dance is called honor," the next signifies the "celerity and slowness" of maturity (fol. 85r), and the

third motion called singles, is of two unities separate in pacing forward, by whom may be signified providence and industry, which after every thing maturely achieved . . . maketh the first pace forward in dancing. (fol. 86v)

These pacing virtues, "separate" but inseparable, articulate the ideal of gender relations, the association of man and woman that signifies matrimony in "vehement" and "delicate" movements. In Mariam's image, the cultural injunctions that she has violated by standing alone and acting vehemently coalesce to define her fault, and justify her solitary destiny.

GENDERED MOVEMENTS

In some of the extant copies, Cary's play is prefaced with a dedicatory sonnet[18] structured by familiar gendered images of the cosmic dance.

> When cheerful Phoebus his full course hath run,
> His sister's fainter beams our hearts doth cheer:
> So your faire brother is to me the sun,
> And you his sister as my moon appear.
>
> You are my next beloved, my second friend,
> And when my Phoebus' absence makes it night,
> Whilst to the Antipodes his beams do bend,
> From you my Phoebe, shines my second light.
>
> He like to Sol, clear-sighted, constant, free,
> You Luna-like, unspotted, chaste, divine:
> He shone on Sicily, you destined be,
> T'allumine the now obscurèd Palestine.
> My first was consecrated to Apollo,
> My second to Diana now shall follow.

Cary's sonnet is strikingly reminiscent of Davies' cosmic dance of *pavane* and *galliard* in "*Orchestra.*" In the latter, the Moon dances a shorter dance, "end[ing] her pavine thirteen times as soon / As doth her brother," she shines with his borrowed light, she displays the delicacy of chastity, "coyly turn[ing] her face aside, / That half her cheek is scarce sometimes discride." In contrast, the *galliard* is "fiery and divine," with a "spirit and a virtue Masculine." Cary's Phoebus is likewise sanguine and free, where his sister, like Davies' Moon, is "fainter" and chaste. By introducing her tragedy with a coupled cosmic dance, Cary activates the cultural assumptions that structured relations between men and women—relations that were distilled in the practice of courtly dancing. As the unequal distribution of "radiance" in the astral imagery of both Davies and Cary suggests, the dancing couple rehearsed gender roles that were progressively disparate.

In the *galliard*, the gentleman was the "dancer" (Fig. 16) and the "damsel" was scenery and audience; the dancer selected a partner, the damsel waited patiently to be chosen. In a drawing of Negri's "Rules for Ladies" (Fig. 17), *Regola IV*, "On Asking a Lady to Dance," the lady sits impassively, her "half-discride" cheek and phlegmatic countenance displaying lunar coolness and courtly containment, her hands arranged into a tranquil pose of detachment.[19] The gentleman, in contrast, appears eager to perform a few passages with his well-muscled legs while the damsel, who keeps to her house, remained fixed on the "same spot."[20] The bodies of both ladies and gentlemen were rigorously enclosed by the erect posture of aristocracy, but while dancing masters instructed the gentlemen in what to do, usually, as in *Regola V*, "Warning a Lady Not to Touch Her Skirt While Dancing," they admonished ladies to be still.[21]

Other conventions associated with dancing likewise fixed the courtly woman in a spot, and isolated her there, as Negri's drawings so felicitously suggest. The movement of her eyes was strictly disciplined. The lady was not to meet the gentleman's gaze, but simply to absorb it: she should "set her head, and . . . regulate her eyes, which should always be level with one's height when dancing," and when bowing, should lower and raise her eyes with her body, "without stopping to regard any person fixedly, for that savors of effrontery."[22] She was estranged from her body by the gown that concealed her while it displayed the wealth and rank of her husband, for the stiffened bodices that encased women's torsos replaced their own con-

16. The gentleman dances. *Le Gratie d'Amore*, 1602. Dance Collection, The New York Public Library for the Performing Arts, Astor, Lenox, and Tilden Foundations.

17. Rules for ladies. Illustrations, *Le Gratie d'Amore,* 1602. Dance Collection, The New York Public Library for the Performing Arts, Astor, Lenox, and Tilden Foundations.

tours with the geometrical shapes of their padded costumes.[23] Even the woman's relation to the spot upon which she stood was disrupted by the high chopines often worn when dancing; deprived of direct contact with the ground, with a center of balance set precariously high, she was forced to rely on the proffered support of the gentleman in order to totter, hand in hand, with equal, careful, and diminutive paces.[24]

Dancing was an occasion of feminine physicality otherwise considerably restricted, recommended as an exercise particularly suitable for sedentary young girls, who "are not free to take walks, or go here, there, and everywhere about the town as we may without reprehension."[25] However, both the movements of the dances and their ideological overlay codified masculine disapproval of feminine mobility, and served not as liberation but as additional constraint. Even the simple act of "pacing" was, in an intimidating application of the principle of "hierarchical dualism,"[26] deliberately gendered: dances invariably started not with the right foot, as might be expected, but with the left, since the right is the "fortress . . . [and] provides strength and stability," while the left is "weaker."[27] Paces, while inseparable and equivalent, are not really "equal." It is Mariam's knowledge of this fact that reverberates in her seeming resignation to a condition that is naturalized as walking in a stately dance, but which is anything but natural.

THE ABSENT BODY AND THE UNCHASTE VOICE

The courtly body danced according to "the laws of symmetry and perfect theory,"[28] with geometry realized on the body by costume and choreographic design, and with uniformity ensuring that the dancer would be "gallant and worthy to be acclaimed, admired, and loved."[29] This constructedness was emphasized by the absence of the body from Renaissance treatises,[30] an absence also notable in *The Tragedy of Mariam.* While saying much, often about saying less, the characters of this chamber play are twice disembodied: the body parts acknowledged by the play are those of blazon, not anatomy, vestiges of a legible surface that belongs to the reader.[31] Cary's bodies are tropological: time comes on winged feet, bosoms ope to a new friend, foreheads are blotted with dishonors, eyes gaze on the beloved, ears are enchanted, hearts and minds waver, and some cheeks are purer than others. Like the body of courtly dancing, the body of poetic trope was a construct that sustained female subordination, and these body parts enforce patriarchal hierarchies: to recall Mariam to the realities of her wifely role, her mother reminds her that "it is no boot, / To let the head contend against the foot" (1.4.259–60).

On the infrequent occasions when a woman is supplied with an anatomical body part in *The Tragedy of Mariam,* it is usually a foot, the lowest extremity, as well as an instrument of measure; not surprisingly, the movement of this foot is shown to be restricted. The Chorus takes care to explain quite clearly Mariam's duties as a wife in vivid and kinetic terms that recall the engenderment of dancing.

> It is not enough for one that is a wife
> To keep her spotless from an act of ill:
> But from suspicion she should free her life,
> And bare herself of power as well as will.
> > Tis not so glorious for her to be free,
> > As by her proper self restrained to be.
>
> When she hath spacious ground to walk upon
> Why on the ridge should she desire to go?

> It is no glory to forbear alone,
> Those things that may her honor overthrow
>> But tis thankworthy if she will not take
>> All lawful liberties for honor's sake.
>
> (3.215–26)

Feminine restraint in movement is equated with feminine spot-lessness and subordination; not only should Mariam remain in her authorized spot—mythologized as "spacious ground"—she should not even aspire to leave it. Furthermore, it is preferable for her willingly to enclose herself even further within her allotted spot: "tis thankworthy if she will not take / All lawful liberties," since feminine "glory" resides in immobility. Unlike Mariam, Salome needs no lectures from the Chorus, but discursively tailors her movement to conform with patriarchal expectations: "Tell Silleus," she says, that "my brother's sudden coming now: / Will give my foot no room to walk at large."

As the constrained body recedes, the vocal apparatus is fore-grounded, and where the body is regulated, closed, and chaste, the mouth is open, erotic, and destructive.[32] Herod's ambition is an insatiable "cruel mouth that gaping stood" (1.98), Salome's mouth poisons where it kisses (2.334), Herod recognizes that "[his] word though not [his] sword made Mariam bleed" (5.189), and his abandoned wife Doris longs for a murderous tongue to avenge her (4.609). Women's tongues, if mobile, are sexualized, Mariam's being both "alluring" (4.430–31) and too quickly moved (1.234), and Salome's loading Mariam's name with scandal (3.96); if quiescent, they are chaste—Graphina's infant tongue bespeaks her innocence (2.17), or is tied up in amazement (53). The speech act is a sexual act, and liberal speech a form of inchastity. Whatever Mariam's virtues, the Chorus observes, her unchaste speech is a perverse penetration that condemns her:

> And every mind though free from thought of ill,
> That out of glory seeks a worth to show:
> When any ears but one therewith they fill,
> Doth in a sort her pureness overthrow.
>> Now Mariam had (but that to this she bent)
>> Been free from fear as well as innocent.
>
> (3.245–50)

Herod, too, concludes, in a similarly improbable image of speech as a sexual act, that she is unchaste because of the fact, not the quality, of her speech: "It may be so: nay, tis so: she's unchaste, / Her mouth will ope to every stranger's ear" (4.433–34).[33] The open, spewing mouth of the transgressive woman was a commonplace of misogynist discourse, and it is disconcerting to find it reproduced by a woman writer as the self-condemnation of a woman's need to "forbear alone."

FORMAL PERFECTION

The rigidity of the poetic and dramatic forms of the play that articulate this image is also curious, for it suggests an unsettling allegiance on Cary's part to patriarchal paradigms. Cary is insistent on the correctness of her dramaturgy, repeatedly asserting her compliance with classical dramatic standards as a kind of mute rhetoric by which the writer can make herself understood and persuade her readers that she is worthy to be acclaimed, admired, and loved. The final Chorus is an example of this methodical perfection, and is wholly lacking in the ingratiating tone characteristic of many a stage epilogue, as, for example, George Chapman's Epilogue to *Bussy D'Ambois:*

> With many hands you have seen D'Ambois slain,
> Yet by your grace he may revive again,
> And every day grow stronger in his skill,
> To please as we presume he is in will.
> The best deserving actors of the time
> Had their ascents; and by degrees did climb
> To their full height, a place to study due.
> To make him tread in their path lies in you;
> He'll not forget his makers, but still prove
> His thankfulness, as you increase your love.[34]

Where Chapman acknowledges the continuing dependence of his play on the grace and love of its audience, Cary does not cajole, but firmly presents the reasons for which approbation is deserved.

Cary's Epilogue, as well, provides a formal statement of the play as a whole.

> Whoever hath beheld with steadfast eye,
> The strange events of this one only day;

How many were deceived? How many die
That once to day did grounds of safety lay?
　　　It will from them all certainty bereave,
　　　Since twice six hours so many can deceive.

This morning Herod held for surely dead,
And all the Jews on Mariam did attend:
And Constabarus rose from Salom's bed,
And neither dreamed of a divorce or end,
　　　Pheroras joyed that he might have his wife,
　　　And Baba's sons for safety of their life.

To night our Herod doth alive remain,
The guiltless Mariam is deprived of breath:
Stout Constabarus both divorced and slain,
The valiant sons of Baba have their death.
　　　Pheroras sure his love to be bereft,
　　　If Salome her suit unmade had left.

Herod this morning did expect with joy,
To see his Mariam's much beloved face;
And yet ere night he did her life destroy,
And surely thought she did her name disgrace.
　　　Yet now again so short do humors last,
　　　He both repents her death and knows her chaste.

Had he with wisdom now her death delayed,
He at his pleasure might command her death:
But now he hath his power so much betrayed,
As all his woes cannot restore her breath.
　　　Now doth he strangely lunaticly rave,
　　　Because his Mariam's life he cannot save.

This day's events were certainly ordained,
To be the warning to posterity;
So many changes are therein contained,
So admirable strange variety.
　　　This day alone, our sagest Hebrews shall
　　　In after times the school of wisdom call.

　　　　　　　　　　　　　　　　　　(5.259–94)

Four times in six stanzas Lady Cary directs the attention of her readers to her adherence to the unity of time, and to her pedagogic rigor:
she has presented "[t]he strange events of this one only day" not for
entertainment but as a "school of wisdom," since "[t]his day's events

were certainly ordained, / To be a warning to posterity." Clearly, however, if an unseen hand ordered the events of "twice six hours," it was the hand of Lady Cary herself, since in the *Jewish Antiquities* the events of "this day alone" spanned considerably more than a year, and the characters were not, as in the play, personified virtue and vice in didactic opposition.[35]

The concerns of the closing Chorus are formal, and as a result of the regularity of the verse, the symmetrical form of a padded courtly dancer materializes on the page. Like the preceding four, this Chorus is constructed of six six-line stanzas, composed of a quatrain and couplet. A stanza of introduction and one of conclusion enclose the center section of four stanzas: in the first is recalled the happy expectations of the morning, in the second, the unhappy outcome of the night; the third repeats the juxtaposition of expectations and outcome; and the fourth concludes the section, as the play itself concludes, with a postdramatic chorus-in-miniature. This Chorus applauds, not the audience, but the shaping hands of Lady Cary, who, guided by classical norms, has represented Mariam's story in a way that vigorously exceeds them. Of course, Cary, writing a chamber play, did not have to concern herself with pleasing a paying audience. But neither did Fulke Greville, who, like Cary, wrote closet drama at the encouragement of the duchess of Pembroke;[36] nonetheless, the closing choruses of *Mustapha,* notably less rigid, suggest that Cary's formal perfection is personal, not conventional.

The preoccupation in the final Chorus with the realization of venerable models is characteristic of the play as a whole, giving the play, shaped to conform with Horatian precept and Senecan example, a poetic and dramaturgical surface that is "unspotted." The formal features of the play are a blazon of dramaturgical perfections: it is written in five acts marked off by an interstitial Chorus; the acts themselves are segmented into scenes according to Elizabethan custom by the introduction or exit of a character; the speaking actors in each scene number no more than three; there is no resort to divine intervention; scenes of violence such as the death of Mariam are not enacted but are narrated by the *nuntius;* the Chorus moralizes with a most conservative bias the events of the preceding act, and prepares an interpretation of those to come. The regularity of the verse enhances the effect of flawless construction, and contributes to the sturdiness of the text as a dramatic object with well-defined outlines and elaborate reinforcements, designed to entice the eye with symmetrical pleasures. Lengthy speeches are carefully divided into precise and equivalent quatrains; for variety, a sonnet may be embedded within a speech, or a couplet may be used to bring a scene to a close.[37] To complete the post-and-beam construction, lines and quatrains are bound together internally and to one another by prolific use of chiastic schemes.[38]

Mariam's opening soliloquy, as a structured object with precise outlines internally reinforced, provides the model for the play, and codes the chiasmic support structure. The soliloquy is cross-hatched, like the Epilogue and the play as a whole, by figures that solidify the form, and that are immediately associated with Mariam's constriction. Her inner division is expressed in a series of chiastic schemes and paradoxes that serve, at the same time, to bind "her" up again: she "wept indeed when on his worth [she] thought, / but joyed that slaughter did [her] foe destroy" (13–14); "he wept when Pompey's life was gone, / Yet when he liv'd, he thought his name too great" (3–4); and later: "I now mine eyes you do begin to right / The wrongs of your admirer. And my Lord" (69–70). If Shakespeare used crossover schemes at times of "self-satisfying self-reflection" or on occasions where a "crucial . . . choice has to be made between antithetical possibilities,"[39] Cary seems to be using these figures to point to the impossibility of either alternative. Lacing up the lines, these figures suggest both Mariam's imprisonment within a patriarchal tradition and the antithetical internal tensions for which the binding is intended to compensate. Mariam's lament is contained in a series of formal paradoxes: the object yielding grief and joy, tears for the worthy husband and joy at the slaughtered foe, sorrow for the one wished dead, the one who "saves for hate, and kills for love" (1.64), the one who "to shun [her] ranging, taught [her] first to range" (28). Early in the speech she cries out for freedom—"Oft have I wished that I from him were free" (18)—but this cry is silenced in a poetic figure.

Cary's prodigious poetic and dramatic regularity cumulatively textualizes the enclosed classical body.[40] As a dramatic object, *The Tragedy of Mariam* is very like a courtly dancer, skillfully shaped to please in compliance with classical models. Not only does Cary accede to these norms, though: her mastery both surpasses that of male playwrights, and immodestly calls attention to itself. The very rigidity of her formal chastity, to which she so carefully points, engenders a potential opposition within the text. Cary appears to surrender with vigor and pleasure to formal restrictions, but in the Epilogue, she boasts rather too boldly of having done so. Within the play itself, the unruly feminine voice is silenced. However, through the metaphor of the dancing body it continues to speak of subordination, and, by doing so, protests it. The allusion to gendered dances in the prefatory sonnet evokes the constraints upon the woman to which the events of the play will bear witness; but the image of the dancer of only one pace foregrounds the feminine lack of agency that the act of writing the play rejects. While seeming to disappear into formalism, Cary simultaneously remains visible above the "spacious ground" of patriarchal restriction. The rigidity of Cary's "nervy limbs," therefore, not only functions collusively to reproduce the systems of her oppression, it becomes a language of protest against them, a way to be free by being chaste.

Rehearsing for Empire:

Dancing in the Early Jonsonian Masque

In Jonson's *Masque of Queens,* presented at Court on 2 February 1609, a riotous dance of Witches is dispersed by a transformation wrought by Heroic Virtue, and replaced with a "bright bevy" of legendary Queens. The antimasque is set in a smoky inferno, whose denizens raise charms to "blast the light" and dance to "strange and sudden music." As their dance reaches its height, a blast of "loud Music" heralds the appearance of "a glorious and magnificent Building . . . [with a] Throne triumphal . . . circled with all store of light." The dark, disorderly matriarchy vanishes instantly when the glittering symmetry of the masque appears, its glories "scarce suffering the memory" of the Witches' presence. The courtly triumph is celebrated in verses and songs, and in dances that "graphically disposed" the masquers "into letters" to fill the newly emptied space.[1]

With *The Masque of Queens,* the court masque settled for a time into a structure of grotesque antimasque, transformation scene, and elegant court celebration.[2] The contrast between antimasque and masque worlds was visually realized not only scenically, but in contrasting dances. In the sublunary realm of the antimasque, clowns, monsters, witches, and other beasts, impersonated by professional players,[3] disported themselves in bizarre or comical popular dances; at a musical cue, this world disappeared, and was replaced by a lofty masque kingdom of courtiers dressed as classical deities, heroes, and nymphs, who imitated the harmonies of the heavens in songs and dances.

The court masque has proved a fertile field for scholarly cultivation, and several strains of inquiry have complicated traditional political readings that understood the Jacobean masque as a celebration and circulation of royal harmony.[4] The nuptial and diplomatic occasions for which the masques were produced, and the court politics that shaped them, have been investigated.[5] The role of Queen Anne in their composition has been reassessed and the masques reinterpreted as a challenge to male absolutism.[6] And recently it has been argued that the masque, shaped by tropes of racial difference, facilitated the formation of England's imperial identity.[7] Certainly, the occasions for which the masques were staged were crucial, and the queen's influence on certain English masques cannot be underestimated, for the form was by no means a unitary glorification of monarchical power but rather a complex collaboration shaped by diverse interests, and articulated a variety of meanings. However, the part played by dancing in the imaginative facilitation of the colonial enterprise has not been considered, and as a discursive exercise of aristocratic self-fashioning and spatial redefinition, courtly dancing was from its inception potentially implicated in European expansion.

As England's project of plantation accelerated in the early seventeenth century,[8] the court masque, with *The Masque of Queens* as paradigm, focused intensely upon the containment of difference, opening in a "society of strangeness" that was erased and replaced by the "lines and signs of royal education."[9] The transformation scene, in which rough environs and oafish popular dances were replaced with glorious symmetries devised by Jonson, Jones, and Giles, repeatedly enacted the triumph of European civility in theatrical figured dances that affirmed monarchical culture and social dances that mimed its universal dissemination. As the antimasque of "strangeness" was erased from the court, the dancing place was transmuted into a virgin land for courtly expansion, a "blank page" for European writing.[10]

Three oppositions common to colonialist discourse informed the court masque: darkness and light, the overflowing female and enclosed patriarchal bodies, and barbarian speech and European "letters."[11] These linguistic tropes were visually articulated in contrasting masque dances, the grotesque dances of the antimasque that mingled subordinating discourses of gender, race, and rank,[12] and the theatrical and social dances of the masque that mapped the hall in a form of patriarchal writing. While the masque dances doubtless signified in as many ways as the variety of scholarship on the masque attests, as a formal opposition of material practices they additionally functioned as a "cultural rehearsal" of the management of space and subordination of difference imperative to the possession of the "removed mysteries" of the New World.[13] Furthermore, as a complex rite of the dominance of a feminized "barbarian" by the European aristocrat, they asserted courtly control over a colonial enterprise fraught with subversive potential, since it was, in fact, accomplished not by the governors but by the sort of men who did not rule.[14]

EXTENSIVE SPACE

Dancing was one of the multiplicity of practices by which space was reconfigured in the early modern era, though perhaps the least credited. Medieval space was hierarchical, a field of "emplacement," with discrete areas designated as celestial and sublunary, sacred and profane, protected and exposed, orderly and disorderly. With Galileo, however, an "extensive" space was constituted, "infinite, and infinitely open."[15] By the beginning of the seventeenth century, the great voyages had been sailed, oceans and continents had been discovered by the Europeans, the globe had been circumnavigated. Exploration was made possible by technical advances in shipbuilding and instrument-making, and the advent of a modern geography: Ptolemy's *Geographia* mediated between the emblematic *mappamundi* and the local *portolani,* and Ortelius's *Theatrum Orbis Terrarum* made realistic representations of earthly space widely accessible.[16] The new geography contributed to a new way of imagining terrestrial space, one that, by providing "diagrams of the possible," actually invited exploration.[17] Not only were voyages made, accounts of real and imaginary adventures were widely available as the printing press brought far-off regions within the reach of the common imagination, and reading accounts of Columbus' voyages and Mandeville's travels stimulated the impulse to experience the novelties of distant lands.[18]

Optical perspective in drawing and painting helped to develop a sense of extensive space. Cartography indebted to Ptolemy's *Geographia* influenced the visual arts as well as navigation, contributing to Brunelleschi's development of artificial perspective "by which space was conquered practically and theoretically by means of the centric ray."[19] Drawing and painting, which "helped the mind to think spatially by first training the eye," were likewise influential in the development of a new sense of space: "By helping men to 'see' the countryside as a whole rather than as a mass of separate impressions, and training their imaginations by presenting them with perfectly believable landscapes, the painter was enabling them to project the imagination beyond the frame of a painting, beyond what was visible to what could be conjectured, and similarly to urge it from the known part of the map to envisage its unexplored regions as knowable."[20] The landscape backgrounds of the early Renaissance became the foreground, and by the sixteenth century, landscape painting was established as a genre. Vast and distant spaces were not only there to know, they were there to own, conveniently framed, sized, and shaped to be purchased, possessed, and displayed.[21]

But exploration of space did not only occur out-of-doors; a reconnaissance in miniature was taking place inside the banquet hall. Concurrent with the rise of modern geography, with exploration and with travel narratives, with perspective and with landscape painting, another spatial discipline took shape, the practice of courtly dancing. As the era of the great voyages commenced around the beginning of the fifteenth century, the dancing of the elite began its separate development, reshaping space by occupying it in a new way. The earliest dance theory of Domenico and his school situated man at the center of a bounded space, and commended him to fill it, in the same way that the perfection of human proportion was calculated in terms of its expansion to the limits of a geometrical form.[22] During the fifteenth and sixteenth centuries, the dancers in the processional measures, a compendium of terpsichorean "techniques for appropriating space,"[23] studiously mapped the hall in a precursor of global exploration, orbiting the perimeter of the festive space while the couples in the parade simultaneously traced the four directions.

Toward the end of the sixteenth century, while social dances like the *galliard* polished gender distinctions with variations that coded smoothness as feminine and elevation as masculine, others such as the *sarabande* and the *canary* confirmed a preoccupation with foreign exoticism and strange encounters. The *sarabande,* supposedly invented by the Saracens, was a sinuous, gliding dance accompanied by guitar and castanets, so in vogue that even little children (of gentle birth) knew it: the duchess of Buckingham proudly wrote to the duke that their infant daughter "loves dancing extremely, and when the *sarabande* is played, she will set her thumb and finger together, offering to snap."[24] The origin of the *canary* was surrounded by mystery and ambiguity: either it was "common in the Canary

Isles" *or* was derived "from a ballet composed from a masquerade in which the dancers were dressed as kings and queens of Mauretania, *or else* like savages in feathers dyed to many a hue" (emphasis added). In most social dances, the couple moved in unison around the hall or danced together in place, but in the *canary,* they repeatedly mimed the moment of encounter. The gentleman led the lady to the far end of the hall and left her there, returning to dance passages that were "gay but nevertheless strange and fantastic with a strong barbaric flavor"; he withdrew, she followed his example, and they alternately sallied and retreated until the music ended.[25] Like the finger-snapping *sarabande,* the *canary* supplied its own auditory accompaniment, with flamenco-like *tappements du pied.* These also functioned as a mimetic synechdoche of the subjection of land and woman, since in colonialist discursive formations, the imprinted land was female.[26] In at least two ways, then, the *canary* was a kinetic precursor of the early Jonsonian masque, mediating event and fantasy to reenact, and simultaneously deny, an imperial narrative.

But by far the favorite dance in the early seventeenth century was the *coranto,* one that covered more ground with increasing speed, reflecting the recognition of space as open, accessible, and ripe for the taking. As new techniques of chorography allowed Englishmen to "take visual and conceptual possession of the land on which they lived,"[27] so did new choreography. By the time of the early Jonsonian masque, the *coranto* had replaced the *galliard* in fashion, and monopolized the revels. As its name announces, the *coranto* was a running dance, performed in sets of couples who swiftly circled the hall several times, settling briefly but regularly to rehearse with mimed flirtations ("be mine!" "not yet!") the gestural tropes of gender difference. Unlike the sober procession of the measures that traversed the perimeter of the hall with dignity and moderation, or the *galliard* in which the gentleman jumped and twirled, the *coranto* circled ever more swiftly and feverishly. Moreover, during its reign of popularity, the *coranto* gathered momentum as the basic step was increasingly streamlined to expedite a more rapid passage,[28] building to a climax in which accelerating perambulations of the hall simultaneously enclosed the area within its compass and challenged its outer limits. The *coranto* enacted an aggressive consumption of space, an appetite for expansion: "everywhere it wantonly must range / And turn and wind with unexpected change."[29] As the dance of favor, it dominated the revels portion of the masque with a festive enactment of expansion and inscription.

EUROPEAN LETTERS

Toward the end of the sixteenth century, as the *galliard* and the *coranto* prevailed in the social dancing of the revels, the theatrical dances of the masque proper were influenced by the figured dancing that had originated in the French court. For the Grand Ballet at the end of *Le Balet Comique de la Royne* (1581), a court masque for Catherine de' Medici, Balthazar de Beaujoyeulx devised an entertainment with as many as forty figures that was admired and subsequently emulated all over Europe.[30] In figured dancing, eternal truths and hidden meanings were ostensibly contained in and revealed through geometric forms,[31] and its legibility depended on cultural knowledge of the meaning of certain shapes, numbers, and letters. The significance of some of these—triangles, circles, squares, diamonds—was inherited from a variety of mystical traditions from Christian exegesis to popular demonology, but other symbols were devised for the occasion and interpreted for the spectators in program notes.[32] The fashion took nearly two decades to blossom in England, and neither theoretically nor practically was it ever taken to Balthazarian lengths. However, by 1604, Samuel Daniel describes a dance from *The Vision of the Twelve Goddesses* as consisting of "diverse strains framed unto motion circular, square, triangular, with other proportions exceeding rare and full of variety,"[33] and figured dancing became a familiar feature in the theatrical portion of the early Jonsonian masque.

As a colonial discourse, figured dancing functioned in two ways: as an emblem of literacy that ratified cultural dominance, and as a performance of courtly instrumentality that consolidated the authoritarian state. Neither figures nor ideology in dances were new; both popular and courtly social dances formed traditional or choreographed patterns, and social dances as well as theatrical figures inscribed elite doctrines on and with the dancing body. Figured dancing differed, though, in that it re-presented the written symbol and the process of writing on the extensive plane of the hall *as a theatrical spectacle;* writing thus became a dramatic subject as well as an aesthetic object. Moreover, the expressive medium used to "trace out the ground in signifying patterns"[34] was the elite community itself, moving in unison into recognizable figures, then suspending motion to be read by the monarch. Under his gaze, each self-fashioned courtier was diminished to a mere point in a symbolic design that correspondingly strengthened the power of the monarch as authorial reader. As Franko explains of French masque,

geometrical dance assimilated the individual performer to the group, just as it assimilates the patterns of the group to a simulacrum of language. In geometrical dance, the body of the courtier or of the maid of honor to the queen was reduced to a signifying element or semantic particle of the sovereign's proper name or of a visual figure containing some message about the sovereign. Thus, the text exerted a power over the body's action, absorbing each individual will within the "idea of a social body constituted by the universality of wills." . . . Geometrical dance projected a physical lexicon whose signatory was the king.[35]

In English masques, as in *The Masque of Queens,* monarchical supremacy and courtly literacy were explicitly embodied in figured dances that spelled out the names of the royal family. Unlike the shared circles of traditional dances, these figures of court community were not emotional expressions but impersonal statements, and the power they celebrated was not local and bounded but national and extensive.

BLACKNESS AND BEAUTY

The masques of *Blackness* (1605) and *Beauty* (1608) established figured dancing in English court festivity as the privileged sign of European culture; significantly, these are the masques that together form a prototype for the "eradication of foreign difference" central to *Queens* and later masques. *Blackness* and *Beauty* celebrate the "lightness" and "stability" of the European male through constructions of "female darkness" that articulate the "twin concerns of patriarchy and imperialism."[36] In *The Masque of Blackness,* the Ethiopian Nymphs' dark color is irreconcilable with true beauty and must be banished. Originally, they were "as fair / As other Dames" (163–64), but then the sun "shone / On their scorched cheeks with such intemperate fires" (174–75), and they are "now black, with black despair" (164). After much grieving over their imperfection, they see a vision that promises that the remedy will be found in the land of "a greater Light / Who forms all beauty with his sight" (194–95). In "Albion the fair" (206), the sun of Britania "shine[s] day and night, and [is] of force / To blanch an Ethiope and revive a Corse" (254–55). Niger is thus urged to

> Call forth thy honored Daughters, then;
> And let them, fore the Britain men,
> Indent the land with those pure traces
> They flow with, in their native graces.
> Invite them, boldly, to the shore,
> Their beauties shall be scorched no more:
> This sun is temperate and refines
> All things, on which his radiance shines.
>   (258–65)

At this cue, the Nymphs advance in the pure traces of the measures, "severally presenting their fans, in one of which were inscribed their mixed names, in the other, a mute Hieroglyphic," authorially selected for "strangeness," "antiquity," and Ethiopian origin (266–74). They dance alone, "make a choice of their men" (291) and dance "several measures and corantos" (301–2). The courtly dances that the Nymphs perform—and, more important, the figured ones they do not—serve to celebrate the inner lightness of the darkened Nymphs, and the outer light of the Britains.

In neither *Blackness* nor *Beauty* is there an antimasque of popular dances; *The Masque of Blackness* itself functions as the antimasque of "strangeness." In the first masque, the black Nymphs perform the courtly dances that reveal their inward lightness, but while black they do not shape the refined figures of "royal education" as they might have been expected to do, since figured dancing was already a feature of the English court masque. They approach the "Britain men" with "pure traces," moving "boldly, to the shore," not pausing to form European figures, but presenting fans on which are inscribed strange, Ethiopian ones. The couple dances between the Nymphs and Britains that follow, the measures that signify matrimony and the *corantos* that mime paradigms of gender, articulate instead the colonization of the "dark" lady by the light man.[37]

The Nymphs' progression from couple dances to figures in *The Masque of Beauty* is the signal of cultural transformation. In *The Masque of Blackness,* the Nymphs' dancing is specifically *not* "hieroglyphic": the black Nymphs carry fans lettered with strange symbols, but do not trace these figures on fair Albion. However, in *The Masque of Beauty,* the daughters of Niger, bleached white, perform figures in multiples—"curious Squares and Rounds" (303) and then "a most curious Dance, full of excellent device and change, end[ing] in the figure of a Diamond" (320–21). After the *galliards* and *corantos* danced with "excellent graces" (364–65), comes a third dance "not to be described again by any art but that of their own footing," which recedes even further into elite privacy by "ending in the figure that was to produce the fourth" (376–79). Having left their blackness in the waves and received "true beauty" (58–59), the Nymphs are authorized to inscribe the metaphysical signs of European light.

Where in the masques of *Beauty* and *Blackness* difference is a smudge easily removed from the faces of the Nymphs, in *The Masque of Queens* alterity is multiply determined and subject to more drastic measures. The Witches, dark women played for comedy by low-status men, are a tangle of discourses of gender, genre, status, and race. Supernatural creatures whose dispositions and deeds most preoccupied the monarch,[38] their appearance and actions reflect patriarchal notions of unruly women in need of correction. At the same time, the Witches' female unruliness also reflects imperial stereotypes of indigenous societies used to justify their dispossession— societies in which European norms of class and gender were inverted by idle men and working women, by barbarians who hunted like gentlemen, by communities not permanent but itinerant.[39]

From their entrance, the Witches—Suspicion, Credulity, Falsehood, Malice, Rage, Mischief, and so forth—are disagreeably "fluid": they emerge severally, dress differently, their "noise" is cacophonous, their gestures bizarre. They come forth to

a kind of hollow and infernal music . . . [f]irst one, then two, then three . . . till their number increased to eleven, all differently attired, some with rats on their heads, some on their shoulders, some with ointment-pots on their girdles, all with spindels, timbrell, rattles . . . making a confused noise, with strange gestures. . . . These eleven Witches [begin] to dance, which is an usual ceremony at their convents or meetings. (30–45)[40]

The Witches commence their ritual prematurely, before their Dame has arrived, and abandon it unfinished. They are blind to their own imperfections, even prefer them: "We must not let our native manners, thus, / Corrupt with ease. Ill lives not, but in us" (143–44). Not simply ignorant of patriarchal order, they intend to eradicate it.

> I hate to see the these fruits of a soft peace,
> And curse the piety that gives it such increase.
> Let us disturb it, then, and blast the light;
> Mix Hell with Heaven, and make Nature fight
> Within her self, loose the whole henge of things,
> And cause the Ends to run back into their Springs.
>
> (144–49)

The "Scourge of Men, and Lands" (223) threaten to flood the world with chaos, snuff the heavenly light, and "untie the knots" (220) of intricate social ordering.

These Witches are indeed marvels, but they are revealed to be marvels of impotence. They begin their rites oblivious to the absence of their Dame (46–47); they charm her to "quickly aroint, and come away" (50–51) but must repeat their charms incessantly ("Comes she not yet? / Strike another heat!") before she appears (96–97). The Dame invokes "Fiends and Furies," calls on her "Three-formed Star," and leads the Witches in vile spells, but these efforts are fruitless:

> All our Charms do nothing win
> Upon the night; our Labor dies!
> Our Magic-feature will not rise,
> Nor yet the Storm! We must repeat
> More direful voices far, and beat
> The ground with vipers, till it sweat.
>
> (284–89)

Additional charms are equally powerless:

> Not yet? My rage begins to swell.
> Do not, thus, delay my spell.
> I call you once, I call you twice,
> I beat you again if you stay me thrice.
>
> (297–300)

But in spite of the fact that the Dame flaunts her challenge to masculine power by beating the ground with vipers and carrying an un-
subtly phallicized "torch made of a dead man's arm, lighted, girded
with a snake" (98–99), the Witches' threats, like their music, are
"hollow." The demonic power to bring chaos traditionally resides in
verbal spells, but the words of these Witches have no magic. They
assay a monotonous incantatory dance to conjure their destructive
powers:

> Around, àround,
> Around, àround,
> Around, àround,
> Till a Music sound,
> And the pace be found,
> To which we may dance,
> And our *charms* advance.
> (337–43)

Their odious plots are doomed to fail, though, for their powers are
defused by their barbaric mispronunciations.[41]

   Their climactic dance to "strange and sudden Music" is typical of
the dances of the antimasque, an icon of otherness that inverts every
aspect of courtly custom,[42]

full of preposterous change, [and] gesticulation . . . [the Witches] do all
things contrary to the custom of Men, dancing back to back, hip to hip,
their hands joined, and making their circles backward to the left hand,
with strange fantastic motions of their heads and bodies.[43]

The Witches do not face one another in protocourtly fashion, treading "rounds and winding hays" in well-formed rings, but revert
"back" to the "shapeless mass of things."[44] Dancing "hip to hip," they
overflow their "bounded space" onto one another, unrestrained, not
regulated. Their movements are random, not uniform, their changes
"preposterous"; like the dancers in elite representations of popular
rounds, they are visibly dismembered by the "strange fantastic motions" that jerk their heads and limbs disjointedly. At the height
of their exertions, when patriarchal structures might be expected to
topple, their own world disappears instantly and completely.[45]

In the heat of the dance, on the sudden, was heard a sound of loud music,
as if many instruments had given one blast. With which, not only the
Hags, but their Hell, into which they ran, quite vanished, and the whole

face of the scene altered, scarce suffering the memory of any such thing. (354–57)

With its evaporation, the challenge to the masque world is proved as hollow as their music and their curses.

In place of the Witches' Hell, a wondrous spectacle appears,

a glorious and magnificent Building, figuring the House of Fame, in the upper part of which [are] discovered the twelve Masquers sitting upon a Throne triumphal erected in form of a Pyramid and circled with all store of light. [Perseus descends] expressing heroical and masculine Virtue. (359–62)

The scene proclaims itself man-made, an "erected" image of European architectural and literary technology.[46] In an emblem of an orderly and predictable aristocratic culture, the complete company of twelve masquers is revealed ensemble, fixed in "the upper part," and Heroic Virtue descends from the pinnacle for a polite introduction of the twelve Queens, none of whom is late.

The company of Queens consists of eleven Amazonian warriors, impersonated by court ladies, and the Queen herself. These legendary warrior women reportedly lived apart from men except, as Elyot might put it, when "appetiting by generation to bring forth [their] semblable" (fol. 82v–83r); like the Dame, they bore arms, and like the Witches, killed male infants (176). Although their societies were long defunct in the Old World, there were reports of Amazonian communities in the New. The existence and habits of Amazons, who variously represented both female unruliness and "militant female virtue," were something of a cultural preoccupation, and an assortment of anxieties over the "other," whether of race, class, or gender, were displaced onto these warrior women who, rather like the Witches, inverted all the customs of patriarchal society.[47]

However, though the court ladies play warriors, the threat of female dominance is contained: these Queens are warriors from societies either mythical or extinguished, and the only contemporary and actual queen is Queen Anne, a queen by marriage who receives the "luster of her merit" from her husband.[48] As if to emphasize the ruliness of these Amazons, and their compliance with masculine desires, Jones dressed Penthesilia in a diaphanous parody of martial gear (Fig. 18) that exhibits the amplitude, not to say the presence, of both breasts; since Amazons were believed to burn off one or the other in

18. Penthesilia. Inigo Jones, *The Masque of Queens,*
1609. Devonshire Collection, Chatsworth. Reproduced
by permission of the Chatsworth Settlement Trustees:
photograph Courtauld Institute of Art.

the interests of more efficient archery,[49] the assumption of militant
femininity by the ladies of the court is exposed as mere role-playing,
by which the maternal function crucial to a patriarchal society was
uncompromised. And although the ladies, in a gesture that might
be considered aggressive, "take out" the men for the revels, this con-

ventional inversion was practiced at least since the Henrician masque, and was inevitably set right:

> What if by often enterchange of place
> Sometime the woman get the upper hand?
> That is but done for more delightful grace,
> For on that part she doth not ever stand,
> But as the Measures' law doth her command,
> She wheels about, and ere the dance doth end,
> Into her former place she doth transcend.[50]

Not only is female unruliness controlled by the symmetrical substitution of compliant Amazons for threatening witches; the Witches themselves, in an emblem of female containment, are bound and incorporated in groups of four into the Masquers' triumphal procession (710–720).[51] Slavery had long been justified as a necessary transition from "savagery" to "civility,"[52] and with the "Scourge of Men and Lands" replaced by "heroical and masculine Virtue," Fame orders the Hags taken captive (472). The masquers descend in the balanced formation that visually confirms the excellence of their social structure, and, to ratify their dominance, mount three chariots, rising high above the bound Hags who are driven in front (710–20). The masquers then enclose the imperfectly utilized territory that they have annexed by circling the dancing place in a symmetrical procession that both registers their claim and serves as an example of the productive exploitation of spatial resources. The celebration culminates with dances that are "right curious, and full of Changes" (732)—a repeated display of fluidity fixed—"[a]fter which [the masquers] took out the Men, and danced the Measures . . . almost to the space of an hour with singular variety" (732–38).

If the dances of the Witches threatened patriarchal order by inverting codified customs, the dances of the masquers restore this order by embodying sanctioned rules. The Hags danced to "strange and sudden Music," but the Queens' consorts are complete and harmonious. Where the Witches' changes were awkward and "preposterous," those of the Queens are "subtle, and excellent"; the Witches' dance was arbitrary and unruly, "with strange fantastic motions of their heads and bodies," but in the Queens' dance, kinetic multiplicity is unified into "singularity," and aestheticized into "variety." The Witches' dance disintegrated at its climax, but that of the Queens perpetuates "almost to the space of an hour." The Witches clung to each other and did "all things contrary to the custom of Men," but the Queens seek out the men and perform the dances that confirmed masculine control. If the feminine power of legendary warrior women is contained in the present in the person of a man-made Queen, so women's power of choice in taking out the men is contained by a performance of the social dances in which women follow.

The tenure of the Witches is brief, and they are replaced at no cost to their conquerors. The masquing world that supplants them, in contrast, makes transcendent claims for immortality and empire: the final song praises the "Royal Queen of the Ocean" (656), and the dance expands her domain outward, into the future and the distance.

After [the song], they danced their third Dance, than which a more numerous composition could not be seen: graphically disposed into letters, and honoring the name of the most sweet, and ingenious Prince, Charles, Duke of York, wherein beside that principal grace of perspicuity, the motions were so even and apt, and their expression so just as if Mathematicians had lost proportion, they might have found it. (749–56)

The tribute is an exemplary display of writing that evenly inscribes letter by letter on the courtly prospect. In symmetrical figures, the dancers colonize the captured space with the symbols of a new succession, the name of a masculine heir, extending into the future the knots that the Witches have failed to untie.[53] Having witnessed the conclusive reclamation of courtly territory in a spectacle of writing, the revelers celebrated by dancing the *galliards* and *corantos* (757) that restated patriarchal ideology, and in fluent and sweeping movements promulgated it through an ever-expanding realm. The elaborate ritual dislocation, modeled in *The Masque of Queens,* of the "accidental" world of the antimasque by the cosmic harmonies of the masque served both to rehearse and justify the replacement of threatening barbarians with orderly European monarchists.

The "masque of enlightment" continued to be staged over the next several years. In *Oberon, the Fairy Prince,* the dances of antimasque and masque again oppose and replace a dark world with a light: the "first face of the [antimasque] appeared all obscure . . . a dark Rock, with trees beyond it . . . all wildness" (1–3). Once again, discourses of difference converge in the antimasquers: in the company of Satyrs, the lability and sexual appetite attributed to women

124

in misogynous discourse are linked with popular associations and practices. An engraving of twelve dancing satyrs on the title page of Braithwait's *Natures Embassie* (1621) shows the satyrs with unexpectedly prominent, feminizing, breasts (and a corresponding absence of the expected body parts), a resistance to being in step reminiscent of the Witches, and brashly clasped hands that recall peasant dances (Fig. 19).[54] Like the Witches, the Satyrs make a disorderly entrance, "running forth severally, from divers parts of the rock," drawn from wilder places, hopping with "antique actions" while they attend the ravishment of the "princely one" who will "fill with grace, / Every season, every place" (63–64).

In their dance, the Satyrs "[t]rap [their] shaggy thighs with bells, / That as [they] do [they] strike a time, / In [their] dance shall make a chime" (121–24), "antique actions" that were probably the Morris, performed wearing bells rung by the dancers' vigorous movements, and a specialty of the professional players. As in *The Masque of Queens,* "strangeness" is articulated in a dance that conflated discourses of gender, rank, and race. The Morris was not only a popular dance that might feature a cross-dressed boy playing Maid Marian, it was believed to be of "Morrish" origin, and sometimes the dancers darkened their faces with ashes.[55] Over time, though, the "blackness" of the Morris was erased, and it ultimately became

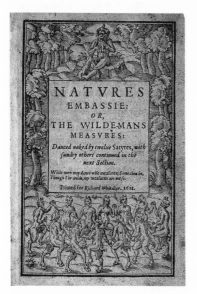

known as the English national dance that celebrated "lightness," the blackening of the face explained as a fertility trope, since the ashes were derived from the trees of bounteous England.

Within the Satyrs' antimasque, as in *The Masque of Blackness,* lingers a masque of beauty: when the rough scene of dark surfaces opens, a "bright and glorious Palace" is discovered, "like another sky of

19. Dance of satyrs. *Natures Embassie,* 1621. STC 3571. By permission of The Folger Shakespeare Library.

lights" (139, 144). A second "antique dance" of excited anticipation, "full of gesture and swift motion" continues "till the crowning of the cock" (283–85), a dawn that heralds the opening of the gates of this bright Palace to reveal Prince Henry as Oberon leading the "ceremony due to Arthur's chair." The boisterous saltations of the Satyrs "give place and silence" (319) to the "nation of Faies" (291) surrounding the symbol of British power and legitimacy. The ensuing ceremony centers on the King, who "in his own true circle, still doth run; / And holds the course, certain as the sun" (352–53). Circling him like ancillary stars, the masquers

> let [their] nimble feet
> Tread subtle circles, that may always meet
> In point to him; and figures to express
> The grace of him, and his great empress.
>   (361–64)

Drawn into the light of Albion, the dark Satyrs are silenced and stilled, replaced by courtiers who revolve like heavenly bodies, expanding Arthurian light concentrically outward through the extensive space of the hall in figures of Brittanic grace.

The Jonsonian other, like black Nymphs and Morris dances, progressively lightened, and in *The Irish Masque at Court* (1613), the Irish footmen are dark only by linguistic proxy.[56] Rarely did a court masque deal as explicitly with England's colonial investiture as did this one. The plantation of Ireland to which the masque refers was in many senses an Old World parallel to the settlement of the New World: a governing hierarchy was installed, estates were bought cheaply from impoverished landlords by English investors and homesteaders, and land that was "not properly cultivated" was enclosed and planted. The enterprise was also an example of the potential disruptions of the colonial endeavor, for the project did not proceed without difficulty. Soldiers sent to dominate the populace defected, the colonizers themselves were dangerously unstable, the Irish were fractious. The Anglo-Irish ruling class was more or less loyal to England and despised the Gaelic Irish but were in turn despised by the English. Language was a prominent site of struggle; significantly, the incorporation of Ireland into the kingdom was accomplished discursively by proclamation and not by military conquest, with hierarchies and loyalties determined by language as much as by religion.[57]

Appropriately enough, in *The Irish Masque at Court,* alterity is defined by linguistic paradigms; however, the transformation of alien to royal subject is effected kinetically, through courtly dancing. In this way, as the antimasque is cleared from the court, history is swept clean as well, for the masque appears to address problematic incidents and developments in the English occupation of Ireland as recounted by Sir John Davies in *A Discoverie of the True Causes why Ireland was never entirely Subdued.*[58] Under Edward III, he writes, English lords taxed the English freeholders so mercilessly that they gave up their lands and returned home. The English lords then placed Irish tenants on the lands, "and with them they married . . . and within one age, the English, both lords and freeholders, became degenerate and most Irish in their language and their apparel . . . and in all customs of life whatsoever."[59] In a more recent embarrassment, Richard II was badly deceived when he attempted to enlist the Irish lords (49). They seemed to be willing to submit themselves to enrollment, and "satisfied the young King . . . with their bowing and bending," but broke their agreement when he returned to England, "and so brake the army that was prepared to brake them."[60]

The central action of the masque is that of *Queens* and *Oberon:* the barbarian who makes rude noises is silenced by the light of Albion and incorporated into the court. The Irishmen are a nexus of social, generic, and theatrical codes of barbarity: the Irish footmen dance "to the bagpipe and other rude music" (135–37), and introduce the Irish Gentlemen with the familiar cry of itinerant players—"Room, for our mayshters" (139)—tacitly equating their gentry with English vagabonds. As in *The Masque of Queens,* language is a crucial marker of difference, and the humor of the antimasque relies heavily on the linguistic barbarism of the footmen: "[The Gentlemen] shit like poor men i' the porsh yonder" (130), one of them observes. The boundaries of the antimasque and masque are defined by sounds and silence, with the raucous bagpipes, "unlettered" speech, and "deafening drum" of the "country's most unnatural broils" erased by the melodious harps, the Gentlemen's silence, and the "music of [James's] peace." In the antimasque, the thick-speaking Irish footmen[61] make and dance to "rude music" (136), before giving way to

the "mayshters," who "dance to a solemn music of harps" and introduce "J A M E S . . . [who] Should end our countries most unnatural
broils" (156–57).

The Anglo-Irish Gentlemen are both transitional and instrumental in the "conversion" of the common Irish to English subjects.
Rude and gentle Irishmen briefly share the floor in an image of general Irish subjugation, then the Gentlemen reveal their inward "En-
glishness" in the same way that the black Nymphs revealed their
"lightness," by performing the universal dances of the European elite
(140–41). Their outward transformation is precipitated when they
perform their capitulation in the courtly "honor," (one that, additionally, undoes the dishonor suffered by Richard II). Promised salvation from "servitude," "barbarism," and "want" (162–3), they are
instructed by a Bard[62] to

> Bow both your heads at once, and hearts,
>   Obedience doth not well in parts.
> It is but standing in his eye,
>   You'll feel yourselves changed by and by.
> (175–78)

Warmed by the "gladding face of the great king" (154), their molt
is completed, and they "discover" under a dark chrysalis of "Irish
mantles," emblem of rebellion and fluidity,[63] the light and stability
of their full English "masquing apparel" (183). As in earlier
masques, the monarch is furnished with generative capacities that
are biologically female: the king has powers of "quickening" that
surpass those of nature herself, his light breaking "earth's rugged
chains, / wherein rude winter bound her veins" (187–88).

> Few live, that know, how quick a spring
>   Works in the presence of a king:
> "Tis done by this; your slough let fall,
>   And come forth new-born creatures all.
> (179–82)

These newborn creatures, though, are emphatically not the progeny
of English-gone-native, and Ireland's rebirth as English is celebrated
with dances that laud the fecundity of English patriarchy: "All get
vigor, youth, and spright, / That are but looked on by his light"
(193–94).

If in the *Irish Masque,* colonization was linguistic, *Pleasure Reconciled to Virtue* (1618) is a spectacle of bodily imperialism. Of course, this masque functioned on many levels, and discourses of rank, gender, and race were co-implicated as in other masques, but one of its projects was the formulation and circulation of an image of the perfect body. The politico-moral argument of *Pleasure Reconciled* figures alterity and identity chiefly in terms of corporeal shape and size, with the morphological extremes of portly Bottle and dwarfish Pygmy displaced by a fit, trim courtier "bred / within the hill / of skill" (230–32). Excess and insufficiency are defeated, and by the end of the play, the shape of a modulated Virtue[64] has been revealed. Not surprisingly, this shape (as the configuration of verse on page additionally emphasizes for the reader) is tall, slender, and enclosed. Prodigality is unambiguously embodied in the carnival antics of paunchy Comus and his Bottles, ultimately replaced by the refined excellence of upward-trained masquers; and as in the earlier masques, the denizens of the antimasque are identified by skillfully deployed social and misogynist tropes.

The entrance of Comus, "the god of cheer, or the belly" (6), is announced by the cry of mummers and Morris dancers[65] that links Comus with the Irish footmen in *The Irish Masque at Court:* "Room, room, make room for the bouncing belly" (13). Associated with appetite and excrement—"first father of sauce" (14) and "father of farts" (61)—Comus is also a generator of monstrous births as his belly expands to the bursting point: "eating and drinking, until thou dost nod / thou break'st all thy girdles, and breakst forth a god." Comus's "liquidity" visibly emasculates, "a pleasure, to extinguish man . . . or so quite change him in his figure" (108). The first antimasque dances of Bottles and Tun, "moving measures of drink" (78–79), celebrate the transformative powers of dancing, but the transformation is not the refinement of courtly dancing that "maketh the beholder wise" (271). Instead of training body and spirit upward to the heights of masculine virtue, the jigging of the weakening vessels articulates a decline into a grotesquely feminine amorphity (211) of appetite and disorder.

The hero Hercules, paradigm of strength, ingenuity, and tidiness, clears this unruly species from the preserves of the court, banishing the noxious creatures who "transform themselves, and do every day, to Bottles or Tuns" (57–77) by eliminating their terrain: "here must be no shelter nor no shroud / for such. Sink, Grove, or vanish into cloud" (113–14).[66] In the second antimasque of Pygmies, moral defect is defined not only dimensionally but racially, drawing on the colonizer's fable of native treachery that justified assault. Decisively smaller than the European giant, the dark Pygmies plot against the sleeping hero, but when he wakes, bringing to light their dark plots, they cravenly scurry back into their shadowy holes (135–59). Dispersing them with a signifying glance, Hercules' triumph is practically effortless:

> Wake, Hercules, awake! but heave up thy black eye,
> 'tis only asked of thee to look,
>   and these will die, or fly.
> Already they are fled,
> Whom scorn had else left dead.
>
> (160–64)

In the service of the light, the "active friend of Virtue" Hercules (168) detonates black looks that instantly dispel the threat of savagery, tactically appropriating advantageous features of the "other" as the King appropriated feminine nurturance in *The Irish Masque*. With the Pygmies having defeated themselves by an ignominious if timely retreat, the memory of Comus' bursting femininity, also, is erased by the appearance of a "measured" Virtue. Her behavior is laudibly deferential: Penelope-like, she weaves Hercules a garland of "choicest herbiage" (127–30) and then sits "looking on" (213).[67]

Virtue need no longer fear that the masquers "should grow soft, or wax effeminate here" (211). The "downward" transformation in the antimasques to woman, drunk, or pigmy is contrasted with the ennobling transformation figured in the theatrical masque dances of classical bodies "instructed to the heightening sense / of dignity, and reverence" (285–86). These dances are

> an exercise
> not only shows the mover's wit,
> but maketh the beholder wise,
> as he hath power to rise to it.
>
> (269–72)

They function both to inspire and to facilitate ascent; the appetites that dragged the body down are contained by an exercise that con-

trols and closes it in an impermeable image of nobility, with its compact symmetry and erect posture proclaiming the power of the
bearer, and the "wit" of the dance revealing an "internal grace of
virtue and excellence."[68] Fortified by their regimen of Platonic exercises, the dancers are immune to degradation, and robust enough to
colonize the lower regions:

> Descend,
> descend,
> though pleasure lead,
> fear not to follow;
> they who are bred
> within the hill
> of skill
> may safely tread
> what path they will:
> no ground of good is hollow.
> (226–35)

The Masquers descend onto the space whence the debased have recently been erased, reassured that they need not fear the pleasures of
expansion, for this ground is not "hollow" like that of the Witches,
but simply "newer" (284).

On this newly cleared ground, the masquers inscribe a "mysteri-
ous map" for "men" to "read" of the "lines, and signs / of royal education, and the right" (220–24). They "put themselves in form" (250),
"interweav[ing] the curious knot," composing themselves into exemplary figures of "all aptness . . . that proportion / or color can dis-
close" (279–80). They trace their designs over the floor of the hall,
so that "men may read each act [they] do / And when they see the
Graces meet, admire the wisdom of [their] feet" (266–86). When
"English letters" have been irrefutably imprinted over the prospect
of the court, the masquers return to the light and fruitful mount of
Atlas,[69] there to survey the scene of their success, and prepare to

> advance
> with labor, and inhabit still
> that height, and crown
> from whence [they] ever may look down
> upon triumphed Chance.
> [Virtue] it is, in darkness shines.
> 'tis she it still herself refines,

> by her own light to every eye
> more seen, more known, when Vice stands by.
>
> (331–42)

With power mystified by verses that emphasize the courtiers' arduous obligation,[70] the threat of female unruliness contained in the person of Virtue (passive friend of Hercules), and the masquers safely inside the hill of skill, the Mount of Atlas "closes, and is a Mountain again, as before," an image of stable and lasting patriarchal dominance.

In the court masques that followed *Pleasure Reconciled to Virtue,* antimasques proliferated, the borders between antimasque and masque became less distinct, and the oppositional form broke down. But for a time, the dances of the court masque both confirmed a desire for expansion and supremacy, and allayed the anxieties the desire evoked. As an association of culturally reproductive practices, the masque circulated the paradigms of form and dominance of the age, embodying the impulses that fueled English expansion. In the early seventeenth century, masque dances brought the "removed mysteries" of the New World into the court, and through stage machinery, sartorial inventions, and choreographic delights, the "threatening other"—woman, witch, barbarian, player, settler— was vanquished in an instant. In spectacles of the effortless subordination of an alien barbarism to European "letters," the masque both moralized expansion and affirmed courtly control over a distant venture—accomplished, in fact, by those who at home would have been confined in an antimasque.

Mischiefs Masking
in Expected Pleasures:

Anti-Courtly Dancing in Two Plays
by Thomas Middleton

If the dancing in the early Jonsonian masque enacted the containment and erasure of an overflowing popular body by a fortified
courtly figure, that of Thomas Middleton's later plays reciprocally
perform the infiltration of the closed patriarchal body by a swelling
female one,[1] an inversion unsettling to the hierarchical assumptions
that secured court power.[2] Middleton has been critically recognized
for his incisive portrayals of the "middling sort" and for vivid representations of disorderly women, but his skillful satires of courtly
dancing, related to both, are less-frequently admired. The music and
dancing in his plays are usually explained as a relic of his association
with the children's companies, or the consequence of his tenure as
pageant director for the City of London. However, if these elements
were merely a habit or an obligation, it is strange that in his city
masques there is only one dance, and that dancing takes center stage
not in the children's plays but in the late comedies and tragedies for
the adult companies.[3] Far from being an incidental ornament or a
benign amusement, Middleton's satiric courtly dances were a visual
discourse that, like antidance writing, expressed an urban challenge
to court power and policy.

COMPETING INTERESTS

Middleton's career was a varied one: he began as a verse satirist, then
turned to the stage, writing for the boy companies and after their

decline, for the public stage. He collaborated with Thomas Dekker on *The Roaring Girl,* and with William Rowley on *The Changeling;* the latter was followed, it is believed, by *Women Beware Women,* and, in 1624, by the political satire for which Middleton was best known in his day, *A Game at Chess.* In 1613, he began to write for civic celebrations with apparent success, and was appointed city chronologer in 1620. His political and religious views are unclear: London-born, he married into a more affluent family with Puritan sympathies, but there is no indication that he shared them; in fact, the depiction of Puritans in *The Family of Love* (1602–5) and *A Chaste Maid in Cheapside* (1611) suggests the opposite. A change of tone in his work has been noted around the time when he began to work for his "Parliamentary Puritan patrons" on the city masques, and *A Game at Chess,* a caustic portrayal of the English alliance with Papist Spain, was a Puritan favorite. However, his views were probably not determined by his associations with city interests, but rather the reverse.[4]

The London of Middleton's day might have inspired his image of the exploding patriarchal body, for the city itself was inflamed with conflicting concerns.[5] Extremes of wealth and poverty congregated in London, which expanded outward as its population grew. The second half of James's reign was a time of rapid population and economic shifts, with a growing and prospering class of professionals, a merchant class whose wealth increased as a result of expanding manufacturing and trade, and a depression that intensified suffering among the poor. Populations of masterless "men" increased in the city as well as in the countryside. Some were hardworking, itinerant craftsmen, or urban Protestant sectaries, well organized and an ideological threat to the established order; others were economic rejects of a changing society: the unemployed, squatters, free craftsmen, and an underworld of gypsies, tramps, and thieves who threatened civic peace.

As the number and hardship of the poor increased, their discontent and disruptive potential engendered in the city fathers a profound fear of disorder and a need to assert their control. Established merchants dependent on royal patents supported the Crown, but among the rising entrepreneurs, the Court lost popularity over royal profligacy, favoritism, and pro-Spanish sympathies. James, however, continued to claim absolutist rights and privileges, spending lavishly, and elevating his supporters regardless of merit. It was a time of competing interests and rising anxieties, and the playhouse responded, the diversity of "world pictures" and the conflicts between them informing the staging of cultural practices.

Dancing was an optimal means of staging subversion in an era of political censorship of the stage, for nonlinguistic elements such as intonation, gesture, and movement had the advantage of appearing on the page in an innocuous and nearly uncensorable form. A stage direction calling for a dance might not be cause for alarm, but the nature of the dance when performed could give much provocation.[6] Numerous offenses might be inserted into a theatrical performance after the official approval of a script by the Master of Revels, and with physical practice as a metonym of political practice, a critique of the ruling elite could be promulgated by means of a parody of their dances and festive customs without changing a word of the licensed playtext. Whether or not Middleton intended to do so, in repeatedly mocking a set of courtly practices in his plays, he circulated images that challenged the power structures they supported.

DANCING: MIDDLETON AND HIS CONTEMPORARIES

Middleton's satiric vision of courtly dancing was different from that of his contemporaries, yet he used a common language. One of his targets, the French dancing master, was a dramatic joke familiar enough to appear with notable stage characters including Falstaff (Fig. 20).[7] In the plays of his Jacobean colleagues, though, courtly norms are for the most part operative and unquestioned. In Beaumont and Fletcher's *The Maid's Tragedy,* the decorous measures of the wedding masque mimed an ideal of marriage that disintegrated over the course of the play. In John Ford's *The Broken Heart,* the restraints of a courtly dance reflected and heightened the heroine's nobility at the news of tragic loss. In *The Duchess of Malfi,* a popular round was danced by madmen as they howled "hideous noise" and "dismal music."[8] Although some of these dances may function as an ironic comment on the action, they are not, as they are in Middleton's plays, performed ironically, by the wrong sort of people, or with stylistic quirks that render them comic or sinister. Middleton, however, inverts generic expectations: it is courtly dancing, not popular, that is played for comedy. Where in *The Duchess of Malfi,* madmen dance an

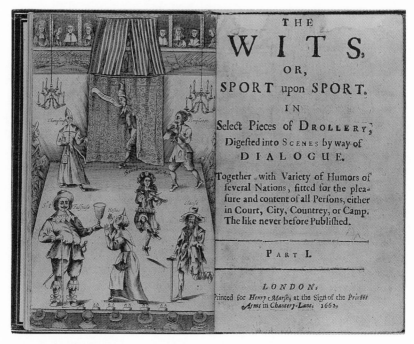

20. French Dancing Master. *The Wits,* 1632. W3218. By permission of The Folger Shakespeare Library.

old, popular round, in *The Changeling* (4.3.89–140), they execute ill-made figures, honors, and capers, questioning by association the lucidity of those who customarily perform them.

Middleton's use of dancing differed radically from Shakespeare's, who drew on both elite and popular traditions—courtly measures in *Much Ado About Nothing, A Midsummer Night's Dream, Romeo and Juliet, Cymbeline,* and *Henry VIII,* and popular dances in *A Midsummer Night's Dream, The Tempest,* and *Macbeth.* However, courtly or popular, the dances were usually performed by appropriate characters according to traditional norms, with courtly dances executed by the lofty, in heterosexual couples, with grace and gravity, and popular dances by mixed groups of servants, clowns, or witches. Satiric intimations subtly introduced by Shakespeare, however, come to full flower in Middleton's works: Shakespeare fleetingly invoked the disparity between the putative elegance of courtly dancing and Sir Toby's piss-elegance, and between the fiery spirit of the *galliard* and the palsied sinkapacer, but then moved quickly away from the harshness of these discrepancies, and their political implications. It is these discrepancies upon which Middleton expands.

Two scenes recur with ritualistic regularity in Middleton's plays: the scene of courtly self-affirmation undone, and the scene of courtly self-fashioning unachieved. The first of these, the masque gone awry, satirizes the self-mythologizing practices of the elite; the second, the dancing lesson that fails, targets the urban aspirants who supported court power by aping its cultural practices. There are masques manquées in *The Old Law, Your Five Gallants, No Wit, No Help Like a Woman's, More Dissemblers Besides Women, Hengist, King of Kent, A Game at Chess,* and *Women Beware Women,* and there are scenes of dancing mastery, most notably in *The Old Law,* and pointed references to its neglect as in *A Chaste Maid in Cheapside.* Both of these typical scenes play a prominent part in Middleton's tragedy *Women Beware Women* and in the little-known comedy printed with it, *More Dissemblers Besides Women.* In both plays, moreover, disruptive dancing is linked with the transgressive women onto whom social anxieties were traditionally displaced.

Both masque and dancing lesson were targeted in *The Old Law* (c. 1616), a collaborative effort by Massinger, Middleton, and Rowley that caricatured the avarice of the propertied and professional classes. The Old Law, recently rediscovered, legislated the termination of life for men at eighty and women at sixty to ensure their heirs a timely prosperity (2:1.1.130–59). In a dancing lesson that mocks the humanist defense of courtly dancing as the young man's means of moral and social advancement, the elderly Lysander attempts to restore his lost youth, and thus prolong his life, by honing his dancing skills (3.2), and the dancing duel that he foolishly provokes ridicules the deadly competitiveness of courtly self-fashioning. The masque in *The Old Law* (4.1) features singularly unattractive old women who diverge far from the feminine ideal of the court masque. Perhaps they are not even ladies, for the vizarded "men or women, or between both" of the masque (4.1.83) not only "take out" the men to dance, the men then depart "every one [with] his wench to his several room" (98). Since the court masque celebrated the youth, beauty, and virtue of the courtly ladies who danced in it, the incongruity of the old, dancing, defines courtly dancing, now decades old, as the exhausted social practice of a tottering elite.

WOMEN BEWARE WOMEN

If in *The Old Law,* courtly dancing is mocked as the expended practice of a degenerate elite, in the banquet scene of *Women Beware Women,* it is arraigned for the perpetuation of pernicious illusions among the urban gentry. A central issue of the play is the commodification of women in a mercantile society.[9] The play begins as a romantic comedy of multiple courtships that go astray.[10] The two young women whose marriages are at issue prefer the *senex* as romantic partner: the new bride, Bianca, leaves her hardworking young husband for an elderly duke of "[a]bout some fifty-five" (1.3.92), and Isabella finds erotic satisfaction with her uncle. Bianca is described by her doting husband Leantio as a curio to be collected: "As often as I look upon that treasure," he exults, "[I] know it to be mine . . . here's my masterpiece. Do you now behold her! / Look on her well, she's mine" (1.1.15–16, 41–42). Leantio can only enjoy his wife at night because he must go to work in the morning (155), but while away, he cases up his jewel from all men's eyes (170). The Duke, though, happens to look up as he progresses past Bianca's balcony and glimpses her (1.3.106); enchanted, he promises "better in exchange—wealth, honor" (2.2.370). "[Y]'have cast away your life / Upon necessities," he counsels, "Come, play the wise wench, and provide forever" (376 and 383). Bianca's subsequent ruin, however, is shown as simply another event in a convivial city evening, accomplished as her mother-in-law plays chess with the bawd Livia (2.2); afterwards, all proceed to dinner.[11]

Isabella, meanwhile, agrees to an arranged marriage with the pimply Ward in order to continue her secret affair with her uncle: "this marriage shall go forward. . . . T'would be ill for us else," she assures Hippolito (2.1.206–7). In the banquet scene, as Bianca's "womanly perfections" are proudly exhibited by her new lover, Isabella's "good parts" are put on display before her intended husband, who has been well advised by his man Sordido the qualities to seek:

> The wife your guardiner ought to tender,
> Should be pretty, straight, and slender;
> Her hair not short, her foot not long,
> Her hand not huge, nor too loud in her tongue;
> No pearl in eye nor ruby in her nose,

No burn or cut but what the catalogue shows,
She must have teeth, and no black ones,
And kiss most sweet when she doth smack once:
Her skin must be both white and plump,
Her body straight, not hopper-rumped,
Or wriggle sideways like a crab,
She must be neither slut nor drab,
Nor go splay-footed with her shoes
To make her smock lick up the dews.
And two things more which I forgot to tell ye:
She neither must have bump in back or belly.
                                        (2.2.100–116)

This paragon of femininity is constructed from familiar tropes of patriarchal and mercantile discourses of dancing. Her posture should
be an erect emblem of upward aspiration, "straight and slender," not
grotesquely "hopper-rumped" or bumpy fore or aft. She should be an
icon of symmetry and measure, hair not short, foot not long, hand
not huge, nor loud of tongue; and she must walk in equal paces, not
wriggle sideways or go splay-footed. She should also be an unblemished product with no imperfection of eye, nose, tooth that reveals
disease, and no cuts or burns from overuse. She must be agreeable to
touch and savor, plump and firm, and sweet to kiss.

Fabritio has cannily attended to his daughter's shaping, having
given the "dear child" ("dear to my purse, I mean") all the
advantages.

> She has the full qualities of a gentlewoman;
> I have brought her up to music, dancing, and what not,
> That may commend her sex and stir her husband.
>   (3.2.11–13)

Conflating terpsichorean discourses by appropriating the inflammatory powers credited to dancing in moralistic discourse as a market-
ing tool, he smirks officiously, "How like you her breast, my lord?"
(159). And ever the eager merchant, he further inquires, "May it
please your grace / To give her leave to show another quality?" (165–
66). The Ward puritanically refuses to dance with Isabella on the
grounds that dancing with a woman not his wife would precipitously
and sinfully signify matrimony (179–82). Instead, he chooses Hippolito to display the wares, as Hippolito notes ironically:

> I have a strange office on't here!
> 'Tis some man's luck to keep the joys he likes
> Concealed for his own bosom; but my fortune
> To set 'em out now for another's liking.
>
> (195–98)

Isabella and Hippolito dance together quite correctly, observing all the proprieties to the letter: "making honors before the Duke and curtsy to themselves, both before and after," as Fabritio crows, "she wins both prick and praise where'er she comes" (207).

The Ward, however, persistently demurs, ponderously joking that he will "venture but a hornpipe with her . . . Or some such married man's dance" (212–13), little realizing how accurate his jest will prove; and in case anyone misses his attempt at humor, he repeats it in leaden verse:

> Plain men dance the measures, the cinquapace the gay
> Cuckolds dance the hornpipe, and farmers dance the hay;
> Your soldiers dance the round, and maidens that grow big,
> Your drunkards the canaries, your whore and bawd, the jig.
>
> (217–19)

Finally, though, the Ward does dance with Isabella in a ridiculous imitation of Hippolito, as the Duke and Bianca mock him *sotto voce* (223–36). Presumably aroused by this endeavor, the Ward attempts to evaluate the sweetness of her kisses (3.3.55), the genuineness of her hair (64), the soundness of her teeth (76), and the integrity of her lower limbs (103–10). Although nether limbs prove acceptable, the Ward's attempts to examine her teeth are foiled, for Isabella refuses to open her mouth widely enough for him to inspect them (96).

While Isabella possesses the approved shape and accomplishments, and smells good, these qualities are completely unrelated to her marital suitability, as the Ward ultimately discovers: "This is she brought up so courtly! can sing and dance—and tumble too, methinks. I'll never marry wife again that has so many qualities" (4.2.103–5). Isabella has kept her mouth closed, but her inchastity has confuted patriarchal ideology that equated silence with virtue and an open mouth with sexual license. In the banquet scene, Middleton shatters the icons of dancing structured around the misogynist icons of femininity of wife, virgin, and whore:[12] the humanist image of the chaste married dancer, the urban fantasy of the sweet-

140

smelling and well-dowered bride, and the Puritan nightmare of the gaping, lascivious trollop. By means of the discourses of dancing, the scene deconstructs inherited assumptions of all sorts about women, value, and dancing—including the "Puritan opposition" to it. The landed but moronic Ward (3.2.118) improbably voices the "Puritan" position on the sinfulness of dancing, which is discredited by an incessant prurience that shows him less moral than timid, and by his use of dancing—a damnable evil practice—in a jigging rhyme to display his mother wit (217–19). As no subject-position in the play is untainted, neither are any discourses of dancing; and the banquet scene, which might simultaneously be cited for anticourt sentiments, anti-Puritan portrayals, anti-mercantile critique, and anti-misogynist satire, evokes through images of dancing a changing society in which inherited assumptions of all kinds were increasingly called into question.

If in the banquet scene, the discourses of self-fashioning fail in myriad ways, the unruly nuptial masque that ends the play demolishes the festive forms of courtly self-congratulation. The conventions of court masque were not unfamiliar to Middleton. *The Inner Temple Masque* ("Or Masque of Heroes"), presented by the King's Men, follows the Jonsonian model, with two antimasques of "ridiculous figures" replaced at a chord of loud music with three conventional masque dances, and culminating in the commoning of masquers and spectators.[13] Middleton and Rowley's *A World Tost at Tennis* ("A Courtly Masque") is also marked with many of the features of Jonsonian masque, building to a descent of pairs of Nine Muses and Nine Worthies who dance to a song that emphasizes their tidy coupling:

> Muses, usher in these states,
> And amongst 'em choose your mates;
> There wants not one, nor one to spare,
> For thrice three both your numbers are.
>   (266–69)

Both of these masques testify to Middleton's mastery of courtly conventions, and bear witness to a mischievous intent on the more frequent occasions when he does them wrong.

Staged ostensibly in celebration of the marriage of the Duke and Bianca, the masque is actually an occasion for Livia to avenge the murder of her young lover, Leantio, former husband of the bride. This is accomplished, and much more: with the deaths of Hippolito, Isabella, Livia, Guardiano, Bianca, and the Duke, the court is not self-acclaimed, it is self-eliminated. The argument distributed to the courtly spectators recounts the plot of a love triangle referred to Juno for arbitration, with the traditional cast of classical deities and nymphs of court masque. However, as the Duke repeatedly notes, the argument is inaccurate. The masque forthwith inverts courtly custom: three masquers (a disruptively asymmetrical number), dance instantly upon their arrival, then address the spectators, presenting cups of nectar to the Duke and the Cardinal (5.2.50–59) in a breach of the decorum that disallowed contact between masquers and spectators until the revels. The Duke is puzzled:

> But soft! here's no such persons in the argument
> As these three, Hymen, Hebe, Ganymede;
> The actors that this model here discovers
> Are only four—Juno, nymph, two lovers.
>
> (65–69)

However, Bianca, believing that her enemy the Cardinal has been poisoned to her satisfaction, reassures the Duke that this deviation is most likely merely an antimasque.

The masque proceeds with the entrance of Isabella accompanied by two nymphs, and Hippolito and Guardiano dressed as shepherds, who offer incense on the altar of Juno, portrayed by Livia. Juno descends, promising a sign that their amatory requests will be granted, but just when it seems as if the masque is returning to the promised plotline, Livia deflects its course:

> —Now for a sign of wealth and golden days,
> Bright-eyed prosperity which all couples love,
> Aye, and makes love—take that!
> [*Throws flaming gold on Isabella, who falls dead.*]
>
> (111–14)

Fabritio continues to smirk—"Too much prosperity overjoys us all, / And she has her lapful, it seems, my lord" (119–20)—but the Duke is querulous ("This swerves a little from the argument, though"). The disorderly masque continues apace: Guardiano, attempting to set off a trap, captures and kills himself (122), Livia is overcome with Isabella's poisonous incense (132), and the Duke murmurs, "I have

142

lost myself in this quite" (140), his repeated comments on the departure of the masque from its published scenario demonstrating deep anxiety over his progressive loss of control. Cupids appear and shoot poisoned arrows at Hippolito, who runs on a guard's sword to end his suffering; the Duke, still unaware that he has been mistakenly poisoned by his bride-to-be, worriedly orders the bodies removed:

> Upon the first night of our nuptial honors
> Destruction play her triumph, and great mischiefs
> Mask in expected pleasures! 'tis prodigious!
> They're things most frightfully ominous: I like 'em not.
> Remove these ruined bodies from our eyes.
>
> (168–72)

Their hasty disposal, though, does not slow the momentum of mischief, error, and revenge that soon unites the Duke and Bianca in a shroud instead of a marriage bed, bringing the play to a close.

Like many dramatic revenge masques, this one considerably reduces the dancing of the court masque, and replaces it with a revels of death. Although the masque seems disorganized, it concludes the action with an extended emblem of poetic justice[14]—Livia dies in the role of the erotic matchmaker in which she did so much harm, Isabella is extinguished by the fire in her lap, Guardiano is impaled in his lower parts, and Hippolito shot by Cupid's arrow. In fact, this masque of a court out of control is as tightly controlled as the masque form it parodied, with deadly devices of traps, tapers, and leaping flames satirizing the sensational spectacles of the court masque, and a corps de ballet that reduces both principal players and audience to corpses. Dying, the Duke is a paradigm of patriarchal form "colonized" by woman: "My heart swells bigger yet; help here, break't ope! / My breast flies open next" (186–87). The masque has been invaded by an antimasque in which mischief masks in courtly pleasures and Destruction has her triumph, a prodigious spectacle of ruined courtly bodies that circulates images of a moribund court, and reveals the insufficiency of courtly practices in an urban world.

MORE DISSEMBLERS BESIDES WOMEN

Printed with *Women Beware Women*,[15] *More Dissemblers Besides Women*, is different in tone, but similar in other important ways. Both employ and distort the conventions of romantic comedy, take place in a mercantile world that revolves around issues of marriage, depict unruly women as more decisive than men, and demythologize dancing practices. Little attention, critical or theatrical, has been paid to *More Dissemblers Besides Women,* a congealing dish of Italianate comic devices and hoary theatrical set pieces: mismatched and deceptive lovers, forced marriage, tenuous chastity, multiple disguises, sudden discoveries, and fatigued sexual puns. The sprightliness of this play, in fact, resides almost totally in the ingenious dancing scenes that structure its plot. The play takes place in Milan, the intersection of a courtly past and an urban present: Milan was a rising city like London, but located in close proximity to the Florentine cradle of early modern festivity. Over the course of the play, hierarchies of court and country, elite and popular, male and female, truth and dissemblance, are destabilized in disruptive representations of courtly dancing, and the birthplace of the patriarchal body becomes, in another instance of poetic justice, the scene of its demise.

Devoted to the widowed Duchess of Milan, the Lord Cardinal plans to test her unparalleled chastity; bound by a vow of fidelity to her departed husband, she has led a life of exemplary continence for seven years (1.2). Such restraint is far from customary: Lactantio, nephew and heir to the Lord Cardinal, though pretending a peerless frigidity, is immediately discovered in the illicit and successful courtship of Aurelia (1.1). She enthusiastically welcomes Lactantio's pursuit, since her father has betrothed her to the elderly Governor of the Fort. In an attempt to thwart her father's plans, she assumes the identity of a gentleman's servant, but her vigilant father soon penetrates this disguise (1.2). The return of General Andrugio from his successful campaign inspires great excitement. The chaste Duchess, appearing at his ceremonial welcome in order to present an uplifting spectacle of chastity, falls in love with him at first glance (1.3). The General, however, has a long-standing, clandestine attachment to Aurelia. Now enamored of Lactantio, she proposes to evade her former lover as well as her future husband (2.3). Meanwhile, the Duchess leads the Cardinal to believe that she has fallen in love with Lactantio; after an initial *frisson* of dismay, the Cardinal decides to arrange a match between the chaste duchess and his chaste nephew (2.1). An additional complication, however, is revealed to the audience: Lactantio has impregnated the Page, a young woman who has disguised herself as a boy in order to stay close to him (1.2); but unaware of her disguise, the Cardinal reassigns the Page to the Duchess's household for the perfection of "his" social refinements (3.1).

Andrugio waits for Aurelia to keep their rendezvous at a gypsy camp; Lactantio kidnaps Andrugio, and Aurelia joins the gypsies to avoid her pursuing father (4.1). The Duchess has tricked Lactantio into writing a love letter to her, supposedly from Andrugio (3.2), then tricks Andrugio into reading it, providing herself with the occasion to return his amorous sentiments (4.2). To placate the Cardinal, the Duchess arranges to sponsor the courtly training of the Page in the form of singing and dancing lessons (4.2). However, the vigorous exercises to which the Page is subjected by the dancing master Sinquapace precipitate the birth of her child, revealing her identity and Lactantio's treachery once and for all (5.1). The play ends with appropriate matches remade, and "dissemblances" put right: the Duchess withdraws from Andrugio's affections in favor of his age-appropriate marriage with Aurelia to which she pledges her support in the face of parental opposition, and engineers the marriage of Lactantio and the Page, sweetening Lactantio's initial displeasure with a generous dowry for the girl.

Virtually the only commentary on the play, George Rowe's generic reading, acknowledges the centrality to the play of the intersecting discourses of femininity and dancing.[16] Each of three dancing scenes centers on one of the female characters: the masque in act 1 provides the occasion for the Duchess's temptation, the gypsies' dance of act 4 celebrates the "masterlessness" of Aurelia, and the Page's dancing lesson results in the apocalypse of fertility that leaves the courtly body in ruins. As the title implies, each of the three scenes unsettles patriarchal hierarchies by leveling or inverting hierarchical oppositions.[17] In *More Dissemblers Besides Women,* representations of both women and men are disruptive, with men failing to meet patriarchal expectations, and women rewarded for flouting them. None of the men whose strictures necessitate feminine strategies of dissemblance justify a claim of masculine supremacy. The Cardinal, who proposes to test female chastity is easily deceived by the Duchess; Andrugio, the war hero, is easily betrayed by Aurelia; Lactantio, the rake, is sentenced by the Duchess to marry the mother of his child; Aurelia's father has his plans for her advantageous marriage thwarted. On the other hand, the women, seemingly dependent, are neither chaste nor obedient, but fulfill their desires through their own actions, and are rewarded with chastity in the process: the Page and Aurelia advance from whore to wife, the Duchess from wife to virgin, moving fluidly along the patriarchal "virgin-wife-whore" continuum.[18] At the play's end, Aurelia and the Page enjoy the agreeable prospect of desired children within a desired marriage, while the Duchess regains her virtue and enjoys sublimated parenthood.

THE MASQUE

Disruptive representations of femininity are abetted by equally disruptive representations of the courtly practices that subordinated women. The court masque ostensibly confirmed masculine control and enforced feminine chastity with glorifying images of both, but the masque in *More Dissemblers Besides Women* incites lust in the Duchess and displays the weakness of the General. Staged for his victorious return, the masque affords the Duchess, urged out of her accustomed solitude by the Cardinal, the fatal glance at masculine splendor that precipitates her fall from virtue. Honored for some unspecified triumph, the General Andrugio enters attended by the nobility and senators. Masquers serenade him:

> Laurel is a victor's due,
>   I give it you,
>   I give it you;
> Thy name with praise,
> Thy brows with bays
>   We circle round
> All men rejoice
> With cheerful voice,
>   To see thee like a conqueror crowned.
>   (1.3.68–76)

The court masque celebrated female silence and subordination, for although women appeared as dancing masquers, they were not permitted to speak the epideictic verses, and the fashionable dances that they performed reinforced male dominance. At first, it seems as if this masque subordinates the Duchess to a spectacle of masculine prowess. However, the spectacle is extremely thin, with simplistic rhyme, perfunctory song, and pallid dance that, the verses suggest, meagerly consists of lodging a wreath on the conqueror's head and circling funereally around him. Furthermore, the song slyly insinuates the artificiality of the occasion, because the General is crowned not "as" but "like" a conqueror.

Traditionally, the master of ceremonies of the court masque personified some heroic virtue, and descended into the court to unify it in preparation for the Platonic ascent articulated in courtly dances. Here, however, Cupid, in an ironic echo of the masquers in *Pleasure Reconciled,* descends while advertising his destructive powers:

> I am a little conqueror too;
>> For wreaths of bays,
>> There's arms of cross
> And that's my due:
> I give the flaming heart,
>> It is my crest;
> And by my mother's side,
>> The weeping eye,
>> The sighing breast.
> It is not power in you, fair beauties;
> If I command love, 'tis your duties. [*Ascends*]
>> (77–86)

Ominously, Cupid replaces "wreaths of bays" with "arms of cross," and dismembers the body in a blazon of flaming heart, mother's side, weeping eye, and sighing breast, a fragmentation emphasized by his untidy rhymes. Unlike the conventional speaker of the masque, Cupid does not unite the court, but, challenging the hero and dooming the fair beauties, threatens it with dismemberment. The honored Andrugio, instead of playing the part of a hero, or even paying attention, occupies himself by miserably searching the crowd for a glimpse of his faithless beloved (92–94). Oblivious to his gloom and inattention, the masquers end with an anemic refrain: "Welcome, welcome, son of fame, / Honor triumphs in thy name" (89–90), while the manifest anxiety of the honored hero further undermines a form already in precarious shape.

THE GYPSY CAMP

The masque seems even more constricted in contrast with the jolly revels of the gypsy camp that follow, a world of mobility, appetite, and indeterminacy, where oppositions of rank and gender further crumble. Dondolo, Lactantio's servant, disappointed by the uncollegiality of the Page who refuses to bed down or swim with him familiarly" (3.1.83, 93), decides to flee to the countryside and turn gypsy (115). He is lured by their merriment and purloined booty (110–20); most important, however, he seeks sexual satisfactionwith the "dantiest knave / That ever mother's son took journey to" (108–9). The image of the Page pregnant by her "master" and Dondolo's simultaneous pursuit of this "fellow" servant activates the eroticism of border-crossing relations,[19] although Dondolo is cheerfully unaware that his homoerotic desire for the Page is actually a heterosexual one, and blandly ambiguous concerning the gender of the dainty knave whom he hopes to encounter in the gypsy camp.

With the help of Andrugio, Aurelia has plotted to evade her father and her future husband, the Governor of the Fortress, of her chastity and has escaped to the countryside. Transgressively mobile, dressed as a gypsy, complexion darkened to confuse the pesky Andrugio (4.1.45–50), she is triply "fluid." Encountering Dondolo outside the gypsy camp, she recognizes him as Lactantio's servant, but he, too, rejects his former social roles: "I serve Lactantio! I scorn to serve anybody; I am more gypsy-minded than so: though my face look of a Christian color, if my belly were ripped up you shall find my heart as black as any patch about you" (79–82). Like Aurelia, he has descended down the social hierarchy to the cellar of masterless men who welcome insubordinate servants and disobedient women alike.

Life on the bottom, however, looks highly appealing. The carefree Gypsy Captain leads an unexpectedly prosperous and friendly "company of Gypsies, male and female, carrying booties" (85–87) who sing of the pleasures of the cony-catching life.[20]

G. CAP.	Come my dainty doxies,
	My dells, my dells most dear;
	We have neither house nor land,
	You never want good cheer.
CHORUS.	We never want good cheer.

G . CAP.	We take no care for candle rents.
SEC. GYP.	We lie.
TH. GYP.	We snort.
G . CAP.	We sport in tents.
	Then rise betimes and steal our dinners.

. . . .

At wakes and fairs we cozen
Poor country folk by the dozen;
If one have money, he disburses;
　Whilst some tell fortunes, some pick purses;
　Rather than be out of use,
　We'll steal garters, hose, and shoes,

. . . .

Come live with us, come live with us,
All you that love your eases;
　he's a gypsy may be drunk or tipsy
At what hour he pleases.

CHORUS.　　　We laugh, we quaff, we roar, we scuffle;
　　　　We cheat, we drab, we filch, we shuffle.

(88–114)

This is an unruly society, appetitic and fluid, conspicuously dismissive of the urban institutions of private property, sobriety, moral rectitude, and good manners. The Gypsies have no "candle rents," and they gratify their needs as they arise, sporting in tents and sleeping until time to steal their dinners. Their pleasures are perpetual, for a gypsy may be drunk or tipsy at what hour he pleases. Their property is held in common: "If one have money, he disburses"; and each contributes according to his ability: "Whilst some tell fortunes, some pick purses." They are free from polite taboos against snorting, roaring, and scuffling, and they do not assume courtly poses, they "shuffle." Expectedly, Dondolo responds to this paradigm of festive inversion with an hyperbole of sexual pleasure: "oh, sweet! they deserve to be hanged for the ravishing of me" (114).

The topsy-turvy private language of the gypsies (115–22) is the conclusive marker of their difference. The gypsy lexicon of bodily apertures open the closed orifices of the courtly body and invert traditional hierarchies: the nose is called *arsinio,* the woman's bottom, *nosario.*[21] Related hierarchies are also overturned: the Gypsy Captain darkens Dondolo's face with stolen bacon (introducing the possibility that he, too, has selected a dark complexion over a light), and makes a socially disruptive match between servant and young lady, giving Aurelia to Dondolo "[to] lie by [his] sweet side and swell" (197–98). Aurelia quickly masters the gypsy way of speaking in incantatory tetrameters (240–41), deceiving both her father and the Governor with her darkened face and new language. Pretending to by a gypsy fortune-teller, she warns the Governor that he should give her up as hopelessly unmanageable.

> Let her go, and be the gladder;
> She'd but shame you, if you had her;
> Ten councillors could never school her;
> She's so wild you could not rule her.
>   (286–89)

Although the Governor reluctantly agrees with this advice, he nevertheless goes in pursuit of Aurelia, following her wrong directions.

The gypsies compliment Aurelia on her successful dissemblance, and all celebrate her revolution with an exhilarating song and dance.

G. CAP.	Our wealth swells high, my boys.
DON.	Our wealth swells high, my boys.
G. CAP.	Let every gypsy Dance with his doxy, And then drink, drink for joy.
DON.	Let every gypsy Dance with his doxy, And then drink, drink for joy.
CHORUS.	And then drink, drink for joy. [*Exeunt with a strange wild-fashioned dance to the hautboys or cornets.*]

                                                          (301–12)

In an amorphic and ever-increasing tumult, bodies and voices swirl together, accompanied by loud blasts from instruments associated with marches, antimasques, and country weddings.[22] This celebration provides a distinct and devastating comparison with the formal debility of the masque, and one of the jokes, presumably, is that the gypsies make the martial noises of the conqueror, where the celebration of the supposed conqueror, Andrugio, was effetely sedate. The Gypsies swell with images of pregnancy and drink, celebrating an unregulated and "martial" female fluidity. They dance out of the scene rather than into the center of the stage, but their "strange wild-fashioned dance" further undermines the structures that the masque was supposed to confirm, but weakened instead.

THE DANCING LESSON

Abruptly, the revolutionary world of the gypsies resubmerges beneath the increasingly thin veneer of court and city, and the next scene between the Cardinal and the Duchess seems to reinstate ideologies of femininity that oppose "will" and "virtue" (4.11.1–2). The Cardinal, however, has reversed his earlier advocacy of female continence, and in order to persuade the Duchess to marry Lactantio, employes a discourse of chastity to argue against celibacy (25–30). With his departure, the Duchess puts off her dissemblance of hesitant restraint, avidly reading to Andrugio the letter that she has dictated in his name, a bold efflorescence of blunt references to the sharpness of desire (168–80). Andrugio demurs, puzzled by her strange language (196), but the Duchess cuts him off and ruthlessly orders Lactantio taken prisoner, since "the time's not ripe for . . . nuptial solace" (202). With the Cardinal opposing chastity, the General struck dumb, and the Duchess speaking in strange tongues, the fixed world visibly dissolves.

The Page, meanwhile, attending her lesson with the music master Crochet under the supervision of the waiting-woman Celia, is likewise overwhelmed with strange appetites.

> In troth methink's I've a great longing in me
> To bite a piece of the musician's nose off;
>
> . . . .
>
> The very tip will serve my turn, methinks,
> If I could get it; that he might well spare,
> His nose is of the longest.
>
> (9–14)

151

Her preoccupation with masculine protuberances, apparently related to the beginning of her labor (14), echoes that of the Duchess, and is accompanied by a helpless and horrified surveillance of orifices whose operations are beyond her control.

CROT.   How many cliffs be there?

PAGE.   One cliff, sir.[23]

CROT.   . . . do you know but one cliff?

PAGE.   No more indeed, I, sir.
                 [*Aside*]—and at this time I know too much of
                 that . . .

CROT.   Will you repeat your notes then?

PAGE.   . . . Never trust me
                 If I've not lost my wind with naming of 'em.

                                              (24–36)

The Page's "openness" (against which dancing masters fervently warned) replicates her gaping womb,[24] and at the same time continues the pattern of anatomical inversion that the gypsies began with their *arsinios*. Crochet and the Page sing prick-song, Celia noting approvingly that the Page "will do well in time, being kept under . . . [a]nd that's the way to bring a boy to goodness, sir" (45–47), settling once and for all the Page's status as polymorphous prey.

The backstairs enclosures of the Duchess's house resemble more and more the sexually disruptive spaces of the gypsy camp. The dancing master Sinquapace bursts into the scene with an unintelligible tale about the loss of his fiddle. Since "fiddle" denoted both a musical instrument and the action of playing with "the woman's part,"[25] the dancing master's loss has sexual overtones—or undertones, since, like Dondolo, his virility is diversely engaged by Celia (98), Nicolao, and, apparently, the Page. While the Page huddles obedient and silent, Crochet invites Sinquapace to "use his own tool" and "dilate" (63–64), and Sinquapace responds with reminiscences of his beginnings in service as a "pumper" (78), until the "dandiprat usher" Nicholao (149) rushes in with the replacement viol that finally enables Sinquapace to "violate" the Page—that is, to give him his dancing lesson.[26] "Come, my young scholar," calls Sinquapace, "I'm ready for you now" (156–57). "Enter him, Nicholao; / For the fool's bashful, as they are all at first, / Till they be once well entered" (163–64).

The untoward exertions to which this endeavor subjects the Page precipitate the birth of her child, an event that both conclusively reveals her masculine disguise, and pronounces on the diminishing efficacy of patriarchal self-fashioning. The hectic ambiance of this dancing lesson marks a distinct decline from the hushed solemnity traditionally surrounding art-and-nature debates; but, representing the former as ridiculous and the latter as implacable, serves to dismiss the issue. Neither the Page's disguise nor the dancing master's instruction has the power to transform a woman's body in the advanced stages of parturition into a trim and dexterous male one, and both costume and poses fall helplessly away as an incontrovertible baby bursts forth.

One reason that courtly dancing is impotent as a strategy of self-fashioning is that it is considerably out-of-date. In the person of Sinquapace, courtly dancing is defined as superannuated: he is not only an exhausted satiric convention, he is a relic. The affected French dancing master was by this time an old object of dramatic satire, and the "sink-a-pace" had long been discarded by the arbiters of fashion and replaced by the *coranto*. That Sinquapace is hardly au courant is firmly established when he airily describes his horse galloping in a *"coranto*-pace" (75), but tries to transform the Page into a fashionable gentleman by means of the antiquated *galliard*. But Sinquapace undermines hierarchies in more important ways than simple incompetence. Although paid to "fix" the dancing body in a classical form, Sinquapace is himself disturbingly fluid. His eroticism is migratory at best, aroused by a variety of sexual objects; sadly, Sinquapace, whose profession it is to position others in society, has no place of his own. Unlike the fifteenth-century Italian dancing-masters who were valued members of princely households, the teachers who served the urban classes were part of an itinerant population for whom physical mobility was a precondition of the trade. Sinquapace plaintively praises Nicholao's "springals" as

> The glory of Dancer's Hall, if they had any!
> And of all professions they'd most need of one,
> For room to practice in, yet they have none.

. . . .

Why should the leaden-heeled plumber have his hall,
And the light-footed dancer have none at all?

. . . .

We're born to teach in back-houses and nooks,
Garrets sometimes, where it rains on our books.
(168–77)

Like the gypsies, Sinquapace is a landless man. Poignantly, the essential material of his profession is the space he does not have, and the commodity that he sells is obsolete.

In the ideal, courtly dancing facilitated upward mobility, morally, physically, and socially, a certain way to "eradicate the bad actions which a negligent upbringing has ingrained . . . [and] raise [the dancer] to perfection . . . [ensuring] an illustrious admission into the acquaintance of his Court and Society."[27] However, in *More Dissemblers Besides Women,* dancing is not the exercise of aspiring gentles, but the onerous duty of the common sort. Sinquapace is not a fashioner of "courtly servants," but a trainer for chambermaids and ushers, and his instruction is designed, not to uplift them into fashionable society, but to keep them in their places by teaching them a few tricks to entertain their masters and mistresses. Moreover, dancing does not appear to promote moral restraint, but the reverse: the *sortie* of Celia's mother and the Duke of Florence (119–21) had the precise result foreseen in Puritan warnings about lascivious dancing. Relations between all of those who dance in the play—Sinquapace, Celia, Nicholao, the Page—are erotically charged, and Celia even hints that the Duchess has arranged dancing lessons for the Page to make him a more enticing sexual partner (143–44).

Sinquapace begins his instruction of the Page quite conventionally with the *honor* with which dances began and ended. In the seventeenth century the *honor* was to be executed, according to the French dancing master De Lauze, as follows:

After having removed the hat with the right hand, which [the dancer] will hold negligently—not on the thigh as was formerly the custom, but in front of the busk . . . by the left hand in order to leave the other free, he advances toward the company, looking at them with a smiling countenance, albeit with slow steps, without awkwardness. . . . [W]ithout bending his knees, he gently slides the right leg in front till it nearly touches the left. Then, without stopping . . . except but a little, in gently bending both knees, the toes well turned out, he will disengage the left, as it were, insensible, and will thus continue until he has joined [his hosts]. (85–87)

De Lauze describes a minutely regulated body, whose well-rehearsed "negligence" diligently displays the flag of *sprezzatura*. This dancer's body is firmly closed, and emphatically distanced from grotesque lumpiness by the hat positioned modestly "in front of the busk." Body parts are isolated from one another, one leg disengages insensibly, "nearly" but not quite touching the other, and the dancer's smiling countenance disembodiedly hovers over the rest of him like the Cheshire Cat as he "advances toward the company." The Page, though, cannot accomplish this virtuosic exploit, but in desperation "makes a curtsy like a chambermaid" (182), bobbing like a little cork in an effort to avoid the possibility that "toes well turned out" might provide just the opportunity that her body seeks.

Ironically, the Page badly needs to keep her apertures closed, but Sinquapace, ostensible monitor of closure,[28] fantasizes scenarios involving picklocks, screws, and vises, while attempting to force them open.

SIN.   Now begin, boy.—O,O,O,O!&c. Open thy knees; wider, wider, wider, wider: did you ever see a boy dance clenched up? he needs a picklock: out upon thee for an arrant ass! an arrant ass! I shall lose my credit by thee; a pestilence on thee! . . . let me come to him; I shall get more disgrace by this little monkey now than by all the ladies I ever taught.—Come on, sir, now; cast thy leg out from thee; lift it up aloft, boy: a pox, his knees are soldered together, they're sewed together, canst not stride? O, I could eat thee up, I could eat thee up, and begin upon thy hinder quarter, thy hinder quarter! I shall never teach this boy without a screw; his knees must be opened with a vice, or there's no good to be done upon him. . . . You can turn above the ground boy?

PAGE.   Not I, sir; my turn's rather under ground.

SIN.	Show him a close trick, Nicholao.
	Ha, dainty stripling!—Come, boy.
PAGE.	'Las, not I, sir; I'm not for lofty tricks, indeed I am not, sir.

(190–210)

"What a beastly leg / Has made there now! it would vex one's heart out," the dancing master complains, disappointed with the Page's imperfectly phallicized *révérence*.[29] "Come on, sir, now; cast thy leg out from thee; lift it up aloft, boy: a pox, his knees are soldered together, they're sewed together, canst not stride?" Sinquapace sings and dances orificial encouragements around the hapless Page: "Now begin, boy.—O,O,O,O!&c. Open thy knees; wider, wider, wider, wider." The dainty stripling is much too tight for the dancing master's purposes—"an arrant ass, an arrant ass"—and arouses the erotically carniverous impulses earlier noted in the Page: "I could eat thee up, I could eat thee up, and begin upon thy hinder quarter, thy hinder quarter!" Closed, the Page's body is an irresistible lure: "let me come to him; I shall get more disgrace by this little monkey now than by all the ladies I ever taught."

Temporarily, the Page manages both to resist the intrusions of Sinquapace and contain her own increasing span, talking her way out of the lofty turns and tricks that could precipitate an abrupt decline. But faced with the ultimate threat of exposure, she abandons herself to the rigors of courtly dancing, and attempts the high caper of masculine performance. Instead of ascending, however, she collapses.

PAGE.	I'm not for lofty tricks, indeed I am not, sir.
SIN.	How? such another word and down goes your hose, boy.
PAGE.	Alas, tis time for me to do anything, then.
	[*Attempts to dance and falls down.*]

. . . .

SIN.	I ne'er knew one die with a lofty trick before.

. . . .

PAGE.	A midwife! run for a midwife!
SIN.	A midwife? by this light, the boy's with child!

A miracle! some woman is the father.
The world's turned upside-down; sure if
men breed,
Women must get; one never could do both
yet.—
No marvel you danced close-knee'd the
sinquapace.—
Put up my fiddle, here's a stranger case.
(188–228)

The unmasking that threatens the Page is not the usual disclosure of facial features or feminine coiffeur concealed beneath a cloak or hat, but an unmasking that turns her body upside down and identifies the Page by her bare *nosario*. Nicholao, horrified, gasps that the boy is dead, but Sinquapace is skeptical: "Dead? I ne'er knew one die with a lofty trick before," he scoffs, the man of experience.

The Page need not have worried, though, about the penetration of her disguise, for it seems impossible for Sinquapace to grasp that the Page is, underneath, female: "the boy's with child! / A miracle! some woman is the father." Sinquapace is so committed to his sexual fantasies and his patriarchal practices that he transforms a normal birth into a prodigy, correctly perceiving—but for the wrong reasons—that the world has been turned upside-down. Although Sinquapace tenaciously credits a miracle of masculine generativity, he no longer marvels that the Page resisted his instructions and "danced close-knee'd the sinquapace." With this observation, Sinquapace does a little disrobing of his own, revealing what the audience has known all along, that he is culture personified, simultaneously the shape of the cinquapace and the shaper. But with the explosion of the Page's dancing body right under his nose, Sinquapace is a cultural authority out of work, and with no more courtly subjects to fashion, packs up his fiddling.

The ending of the play seems contradictory. On the one hand, it achieves a trim closure that Sinquapace might envy, were he still around. The patriarchal family appears to have been reinstated, unruly eroticism to have dissolved into a female fertility appropriated in the interests of patrilineal reproduction.[30] The Duchess yields to a "younger, fairer" rival (5.1.128), and the play predicts a future of multiple marriages and incessant procreation, with the three mobile and disruptive women firmly fixed in motherhood. But the fertility into which disruptive sexuality fades is more abstract than biology; in supplying comedic closure, it is defined as a cultural artifact. So the tidy ending of the play is, in fact, a paradigm of the too-neat ending of the prerevolutionary tragicomedy that advertises its self-subversion.[31]

Therefore, the nuptial ending of the play is far from a recuperation in which the woman is colonized and female resources absorbed into patriarchal power.[32] Rather the reverse, since patriarchal formations have themselves been disrupted and colonized: a lovesick hero subverts the harmony of the courtly masque, the transgressive popular dances and the unsanctioned sexuality of free spaces spread into city and court, a new life bursts through the old techniques of courtly self-fashioning. Hierarchical oppositions of status and gender have been leveled, and patriarchal forms breached by the "belly [that] cannot be confined in a waistband" (5.2.249–51). In the figure of the dancing body, patriarchal power has been repeatedly invaded and ruptured by a swelling feminine presence, and Nicholao tolls its requiem: "I fear me [this event] will bring dancing out of request, / And hinder our profession for a time" (5.2.231–32).

If patriarchy was performative in courtly dancing, as multiple repetitions and images of socially coded movements supported a gendered power structure, then images that systematically and repeatedly inverted elite norms may have helped to destabilize it. Middleton's parodic dances were an ingenious response to an increasing urban disaffection with the court and its practices, manifested in the wild popularity of A Game at Chess. The English revolution was a long way off, and many of the radical ideas and alliances that propelled it had yet to be formalized. But by overturning hierarchies in miniature and by proxy, the dancing in Middleton's plays functioned as an anticourt discourse that reflected and perhaps even shaped the "revolutionary mentality" articulated in the more explicitly political resistances of the time, measurably questioning the authority of the courtly ideal.

Notes

INTRODUCTION

1. Engraving by Thomas De Bry (1561–1623) from a Behan woodcut, in F. W. H. Holstein, *Dutch and Flemish Etchings, Engravings, and Woodcuts, c. 1450–1700*, 46 vols. (Amsterdam: N. Hertzberger, 1949–), 4:17–21. I am indebted to two decades of scholarship on the body, particularly to Mikhail Bakhtin, *Rabelais and His World*, trans. Helene Iswolsky (Bloomington: Indiana University Press, 1984), on the two bodily canons; Michel Foucault, *Discipline and Punish: The Birth of the Prison*, trans. Alan Sheridan (New York: Vintage, 1979), on the "docile body"; Norbert Elias, *The Civilizing Process*, vol. 1, *The History of Manners*, vol. 2, *Power and Civility*, trans. Edmund Jephcott, notes and revisions by the author (New York: Pantheon, 1978, 1982), and Frank Whigham, *Ambition and Privilege: The Social Tropes of Elizabethan Courtesy Theory* (Berkeley and Los Angeles: University of California, 1984), on the physical practices of "civility"; Peter Stallybrass, "Patriarchal Territories: The Body Enclosed," in *Rewriting the Renaissance: The Discourses of Sexual Difference in Early Modern Europe*, ed. Margaret W. Ferguson, Maureen Quilligan, and Nancy J. Vickers (Chicago: University of Chicago Press, 1986), on gendered bodily paradigms; and Gail Kern Paster, *The Body Embarrassed: Drama and the Disciplines of Shame in Early Modern England* (Ithaca: Cornell University Press, 1993), on the material body that was contained by the rigors of civility.

2. Helkiah Crooke, *Microcosmographia* (London, 1615), 4, echoes the medieval commonplace that man's body is the measure of all others, "the frame and composition which is upright, mounting toward heaven." See Georges Vigarello, "The Upward Training of the Body from the Age of Chivalry to Courtly Civility," in *Fragments for a History of the Human Body, Part Two*, ed. Michel Feher, with Ramona Neddaff and Nadia Tazi (New York: Zone, 1989), on the moralization of posture.

3. Alan Brissenden's translation in *Shakespeare and the Dance* (Atlantic Highlands, N.J.: Humanities Press, 1981), 37, an invaluable discussion of early modern English dancing, and the only full-length examination of dancing and its metaphors in Shakespeare's plays. Keith Moxey, *Peasants, Warriors, and Wives: Popular Imagery in the Reformation* (Chicago: University of Chicago Press, 1989), translates the caption in a way that emphasizes peasant unruliness: "As far as the court is from the sheepfold, so is the courtier from the peasants. This bawdy round dance will soon teach you that" (49–50). Moxey argues that as "components in the mechanized production of cultural commodities" (33), woodcuts such as the Behans' circulated the views of their elite consumers.

4. Sir Thomas Elyot's *The Boke named the Governour* (London: Thomas Bertheleti, 1531, 1564), Facsimile Reprint, English Linguistics, 1500–1800, No. 246, ed. R. C. Alston (Menston, Eng.: Scholar, 1970), and Sir John Davies' *"Orchestra, or a Poeme of Dauncing,"* in *The Poems of Sir John Davies*, ed. Robert Krueger (Oxford: Clarendon, 1975), are the recognized "literary" authorities on English dancing. E. M. W. Tillyard, *The Elizabethan World Picture: A Study of the Idea of Order in the Age of Shakespeare, Donne, and Milton* (New York: Macmillan, 1943, Vintage Books),

did acknowledge (106) that *"Orchestra"* served as "pure didacticism" and the "perfect illustration of a general doctrine," but, consistent with the thought of his day, assumed that this doctrine was universally accepted, not an elite ideology. On the cosmic dance, see John Meagher's *Method and Meaning in Jonson's Masques* (Notre Dame: University of Notre Dame, 1966), chaps. 3 and 4, and James Miller's *Measures of Wisdom: The Cosmic Dance in Classical and Christian Antiquity* (Toronto: University of Toronto Press, 1986).

5. Stephen Greenblatt, in *Renaissance Self-Fashioning: From More to Shakespeare* (Chicago: University of Chicago Press, 1980) emphasizes the importance in self-fashioning of the "repetition of the self-constitutive act" (201); Greenblatt refers to action rather than movement, but as Elyot and many others argued, dancing was imagined as self-constituting in a variety of ways.

6. Similarly, Judith Butler, *Gender Trouble: Feminism and the Subversion of Identity* (London: Routledge, 1991), has rejected generalizations of "the body" that do not account for "political forces with strategic interests in keeping that body bounded and constituted" (129).

7. Julia Sutton, in the introduction to Fabritio Caroso's *Nobilità di Dame* (Venice, 1600), trans. Sutton, music transcribed and edited F. Marian Walker (Oxford: Oxford University Press, 1986), 29, and Ingrid Brainard, *The Art of Courtly Dancing in the Early Renaissance, Part II: The Practice of Courtly Dances* (West Newton, Mass., 1st preliminary ed., 1981), 4, both acknowledge the interaction of popular and courtly dancing. See also Michael D. Bristol, *Carnival and Theatre: Plebean Culture and the Structure of Authority in Renaissance England* (New York: Methuen, 1985), on the "carnival" infiltration of official culture (21–23), and Carlo Ginzburg, *The Cheese and the Worms: The Cosmos of a Sixteenth-Century Miller,* trans. John Tedeschi and Anne Tedeschi (Baltimore: Johns Hopkins University Press, 1980), on "hidden but fruitful exchanges, moving in both directions between high and popular cultures," followed by "an increasingly rigid distinction between the culture of the dominant classes and artisan and peasant cultures" (126); I am indebted to Peter Herman for the latter reference.

8. Peter Burke, *Popular Culture in Early Modern Europe* (New York: Harper and Row, 1978), 28.

9. Mark Franko, *The Dancing Body in Renaissance Choreography (1416–1589)* (Birmingham, Ala.: Summa Publications, 1986), asserts (4) that a model of dancing as "a systematic and generalizable perspective on movement quality within choreographic descriptions" may be assumed for critical purposes. He notes, however, that even dancing texts do not provide a text of the dance, but simply a text *on* the dance: "We may, in fact, reasonably ask whether treatises . . . represent the dance of their day . . . or a utopian ideal of what the dance should have been" (7).

10. Annabel Patterson, *Shakespeare and the Popular Voice* (Oxford: Basil Blackwell, 1989) notes that knowledge of the "little" tradition is "distorted by our necessary dependence on texts *selected* for wide dissemination, whether printed ballads, almanacs or chapbooks, or on the references to festival morris dances, May games, etc., that can be painstakingly collated from other texts, usually in the dominant culture" (33). Similarly, Moxey argues (33) that even the woodcut, once believed a paradigm of "popular art," reproduced elite perspectives in highly conventional-

ized representations that revealed more about the workshop and the consumer than the details of common life.

11. Investigation of "folk" dance beginning in the late nineteenth century relied on observations of dances presumed similar, performed centuries later, and in distant lands: see Curt Sachs, *World History of the Dance* (Berlin, 1933), trans. Bessie Schoenberg (New York: Norton, 1937), who suggests that in the absence of direct evidence of some medieval dances, the "indirect evidence, today's dance of . . . Iceland and the Faroes, fills the gap" (262); and studies on the Morris such as Cecil Sharp, *The Morris Book* (1912–24), repr. (Yorkshire: EP Publishing, 1974).

12. *The English Dancing Master, or, Plaine and Easie Rules for the Dancing of Country Dances, with the Tune to each Dance,* printed by John Playford in 1651, ed. Hugh Mellor and Leslie Bridgewater (London: Dance Books, 1984); some of the dances Playford included were traditional, but others, like the *pavane,* were of courtly origin.

13. *The maner of dauncynge of bace daunces after the use of fraunce and other places* (1521), trans. Robert Coplande, Facsimile (Sussex: Pear Tree, 1937), repr. in Mabel Dolmetsch, *Dances of England and France from 1450 to 1600* (London: Routledge and Kegan Paul, 1949; New York: Da Capo, 1976), 2–4, was originally appended to a French grammar. The best-known commonplace manuscripts, both seventeenth-century, are John Ramsey's "Practice for Dancing" from his *Commonplace Book* (Bod. Dou., fols. 66a–66b), reprinted in *Four Hundred Songs and Dances from the Stuart Masque,* ed. Andrew J. Sabol (Providence: Brown University Press, 1978, 1982), app. C, 546–48, and Elias Ashmole's "copy of the old measures" (MS Rawl. D 864, f.199–199v), cited in *Elias Ashmole (1617–1692),* ed. C. H. Josten, 5 vols. (Oxford: Clarendon, 1966), 2:313.

14. See Gordon Kipling, *The Triumph of Honour: Burgundian Origins of the Elizabethan Renaissance* (The Hague: Leyden University Press, 1977), 97–115; Stephen Orgel, "The Spectacles of State," in *Persons in Groups: Social Behavior as Identity Formation in Medieval and Renaissance Europe,* ed. Richard C. Trexler (Binghamton: Medieval and Renaissance Texts and Studies, 1985), 101–21; Roy Strong, *Art and Power: Renaissance Festivals, 1450–1650* (Woodbridge: Boydell, 1973, 1984), and *Henry VIII: A European Court in England,* ed. David Starkey (London: Collins and Brown, 1991).

15. Roger Ascham, *The Scholemaster, or plaine and perfite way of teachyng children the Latin Tong* (London, 1570), ed. Edward Arber (Westminster: A. Constable, 1895), Biiv. Ascham also praises "comely dancing" as one of the "courtly exercises, and gentlemanlike pastimes" that "young men should use, and delight in" (Giiiv). Spelling and punctuation of early texts have been normalized throughout, titles in original spelling or as in editions cited.

16. In *Henry V,* 3.4.33, dancing masters and French gentlemen are linked in effeminacy: "[Our ladies] bid us to the English dancing schools," rails a French courtier, "And teach lavoltas high and swift corantos, / Saying our grace is only in our heels, / And that we are most lofty runaways." Citations to *The Riverside Shakespeare* (Boston: Houghton Mifflin, 1974). R. E. G. Kirk and Ernest Kirk, *Returns of Aliens Dwelling in the City and Suburbs of London from the Reign of Henry VIII to that of James I,* 3 vols. (Aberdeen: Huguenot Society, 1902), suggest that musicians

(dancing masters were often fiddlers or tabor players) were frequently French or Italian; see 2:427, No. 10, 1590, a list of the Queen's [alien] musicians.

17. Many musicians and dancing masters of the Italian Courts were Jewish, notes Otto Kinkeldy in *A Jewish Dancing Master of the Renaissance: Guglielmo Ebreo* (New York: Dance Horizons, 1966), reprinted from *Studies in Jewish Bibliography and Related Subjects in Memory of Solomon Friedus* (New York, 1929); Guglielmo Ebreo da Pesaro, dancing master for the Sforzas and Medicis, is the best known. Roger Prior, in "Jewish Musicians at the Tudor Court," *Musical Quarterly* 69, no. 2 (Spring 1983): 253–65, claims that a "high proportion" of the Italian musicians at the Tudor Court were Jews, nineteen members of the King's Music alone. Some of these may have taught dancing: Muriel St. Clare Byrne, ed., *The Lisle Letters*, 6 vols. (Chicago: University of Chicago Press, 1981), notes a disbursement in the accounts of the Rutland family to the "king's minstrels to teach my Lord Roos (the heir) to dance" (4:488), and another to "Monsieur Simon, a drummer, who taught [Lord Roos] to dance for the second time in a space of two months" (517); Prior identifies Simon as a Jewish Italian name.

18. In the *Calendar of Patent Rolls,* Elizabeth I, 6:1572–75 (London: Her Majesty's Stationery Office, 1973), 258, an entry for 26 February 1574: "Appointment of 21 years of Richard Frythe, Robert Warren and William Warren to be the only teachers of dancing within the City of London and suburbs; the teaching to be conducted within their dwelling houses; other persons forbidden to teach under pain, for every day's teaching, of 10 days of imprisonment and forfeiture of 40s."

19. An entry in the *Register of Freemen of the City of London in the Reigns of Henry VIII and Edward IV,* ed. Charles Welch (London: Archaeological Society, 1908), 20, names Thomas Hall, a brickmaker's son, as an "apprentice [in minstrelsy] of Richard Frythe." The Rutland accounts for 1556, *The Manuscripts of the Duke of Rutland,* (London: Her Magesty's Stationery Office, 1905), 4:382, records a "reward to Frythe that teacheth my Lord Roos to dance, xls." In the *Calendar of State Papers, Domestic Series, Elizabeth 1595–97* (London: Longman, Green, Reader, and Dyer, 1869), for 1596, 271: "Grant to Wm. Warren, in place of Ambrose Lupo, deceased, of the office of musician for the violins." Were the patented dancing masters long-lived, members of a dynasty, or did they simply have common names? William Ingram, "Minstrels in Elizabethan London: Who Were They, What Did They Do?" *English Literary Renaissance* 14 (1984):29–54, may provide some clues.

20. Baldesar Castiglione, *The Booke of the Courtyer,* "done into English" by Sir Thomas Hoby (1561), (London: David Nutt, 1900), 115. Whigham, *Ambition and Privilege* (15), and many others emphasize the influence of Castiglione on the formation of the English gentleman. On the separation of elite and popular dancing, see Burke, *Popular Culture,* 270–71, and Curt Sachs, *Dance* 299–301.

21. Calendar, British Library Add. MS 24098 f. 19b, reproduces virtually the same scene from an earlier German calendar; the major difference, aside from clothing, is that the lower border of the latter shows a city street with more prosperous citizens going about their business past the prominently barred window of the lower part of the palace. Manuscript illuminations, drawings, and engravings from printed books were decorative and conventional rather than representational, as Ruth Samson Luborsky explains in "Connections and Disconnections between

Images and Text: The Case of Secular Book Illustration," *Word and Image* 3, no. 1 (January–March, 1987):74–85. Therefore, the illustrations represent expectations or fantasies of dancing—its shape, settings, relations, and mythology—rather than actual physical practices.

22. John Stow, *Survey of London,* ed. Valerie Pearl (London: J. M. Dent, 1987), 85. Interestingly enough, the present tense is used to describe pastimes "now suppressed," a manifestation of Stow's longing for a simple, bucolic past engendered by a changing London, as Ian Archer explains in "The Nostalgia of John Stow," in *The Theatrical City: Culture, Theatre, and Politics in London, 1576–1649,* ed. David L. Smith, Richard Strier, and David Bevington (Cambridge: Cambridge University Press, 1995), 17–34.

23. Lawrence Stone, "Social Mobility in England, 1500–1700," *Past and Present* 33, (1966): 8, defines the fundamental social distinction in terms of manual labor. Another relevant distinction was between those who could write and those who could not.

24. Franko, *Dancing Body,* 46.

25. In practice, neither the separation of popular and courtly dancing nor the development of the latter was rigidly structured, for the "medieval round" and the "popular Morris" were performed at court throughout the early modern era; see Raymond Williams in *Marxism and Literature* (Oxford: Oxford University Press, 1977), 121–27, on dominant, emergent, and residual culture.

26. Sachs, *Dance,* 124–31, 147. The connection of dancing with the medieval church is shown in a French book of hours, c. 1445, M. 287, fol. 64v, Pierpont Morgan Library; such representations perhaps justified the persistent association of dancing with popery by English Puritans.

27. On the ideology of pastoral imagery associated with the Queen, see Louis Adrian Montrose, "'Eliza, Queene of Shepheardes,' and the Pastoral of Power," in *Renaissance Historicism,* ed. Arthur F. Kinney and Dan S. Collins (Amherst: University of Massachusetts Press, 1987), 34–63; John N. King, "Queen Elizabeth I: Representations of the Virgin Queen," *Renaissance Quarterly* 43, no. 1 (Spring 1990): 30–74; Roy Strong, *The Cult of Elizabeth: Elizabethan Portraiture and Pageantry* (Berkeley and Los Angeles: University of California Press, 1977); and Frances Yates, *Astraea: The Imperial Theme in the Sixteenth Century* (London: Routledge and Kegan Paul, 1975). Louis Montrose, *The Purpose of Playing: Shakespeare and the Cultural Politics of the Elizabethan Theatre* (Chicago: University of Chicago Press, 1996), suggests that the inclusion of festive customs in court festivity functioned to establish social difference as well as nationality: "[t]he presentation of such quaint shows within the context of . . . spectacular courtly pageants suggests that they were being framed and displayed for the amusement of an elite that was already in the process of withdrawing itself from direct participation in the popular" (183).

28. Edmund Spenser, *The Shepheardes Calendar,* 2d ed. (London, 1581), Pierpont Morgan M. 78109, fol. 16, "May."

29. "Dance Scene in a Public Square," French book of hours, Bourges, c. 1473, Jean Colombe and workshop. Pierpont Morgan Library, M. 677, fol. 137.

30. A drawing of an "Ancient Window in the House of George Tollet, Esq., at

Henley in Staffordshire," Folger Shakespeare Library, a charming fantasy of the traditional personages of the Morris neatly contained in individual panels, including (in the center) Morris dancer with bells, Maypole, hobbyhorse, and Maid Marian. On dancing and seasonal festivals in England, see especially E. K. Chambers, *The Mediaeval Stage* (London: Oxford University Press, 1903, 1951), 1:117–29 and 160–79; C. L. Barber, *Shakespeare's Festive Comedy: A Study of Dramatic Form in Relation to Social Custom* (Princeton: Princeton University Press, 1959, 1972); Charles Read Baskervill, *The Elizabethan Jig and Related Song Dramas* (Chicago: University of Chicago, 1929); John Brand, *Observations on Popular Antiquities,* ed. Henry Ellis (London, 1841–42); and Robert Chambers, *The Book of Days, A Miscellany of Popular Antiquities in Connection with the Calendar* (London, 1863). Sharp, *Morris Book,* makes the distinction between "spectacular" dances performed for an audience and participatory "social" ones (1:21).

31. On the *estampie* and the pre-Tudor Provençal connection, see Frances Rust, *Dance in Society* (London: Routledge and Kegan Paul, 1969), 34.

32. Guillaume de Machaut, *La Remède de Fortune,* M S Fr. 1586, fol. 51, Bibliothèque Nationale, Paris; commentary in François Avril, *Manuscript Painting at the Court of France: The Fourteenth Century,* trans. Ursule Molinaro and Bruce Benderson (New York: Braziller, 1978), 26–28 and 86. Elias, *Power and Civility,* 258–59, writes that the "inner pacification of a society" was part of the process in the transition from warriors to courtiers.

33. Fifteenth-century French-Flemish manuscript, M S Lat. 1173 fol. 20v, Bibliothèque Nationale, Paris.

34. "[D]espite the differences in choreography from region to region," Franko, *Dancing Body,* asserts, "[it] is reducible to an identity which was exemplary for the Renaissance" (5).

35. Henri de Ferrières, *Livre de Roi Modus et de Royne Racio,* c. 1465, Brittany or Anjou, M 820, f. 105, Pierpont Morgan Library. The *basse* dance embodied the paradox that has yet to be theorized of "upward training" solidly anchored by "low" movements.

36. Toinot Arbeau [Jehan Tabourot], *Orchésographie* (1588, 1589, and reprints), trans. as *Orchesography,* by Mary Stewart Evans; intro. and notes by Julia Sutton (New York: Dover, 1967), 52. He describes the *basse* dance at length, 77–83, even though in France it had been "out of date for some forty or fifty years" (51). Citations are to Evans's translation.

37. See James L. Jackman, *Fifteenth-Century Basse Dances* (Wellesley: Wellesley College, 1964), iii, and Dolmetsch, *England and France,* 4.

38. In texts, the dance steps are usually listed in the bottom line, below the notes and the words of the song to which it was danced.

39. Italian treatises date from 1425, and include Domenico da Piacenza, *De arte saltanj & choreas ducendj,* Paris, Bibliothèque Nationale, fonds.it.972, trans. Mabel Dolmetsch, in her *Dances of Spain and Italy from 1400 to 1600* (London: Routledge and Kegan Paul, 1954), 2–3; Guglielmo Ebreo, *Guglielmo hebraei pisaurensis de practica seu arte tripudii vulghare opusculum,* Milan, Paganus Rhaudensis, scribe, 1463, copy in the Cia Fornaroli Collection of the New York City Public Library; and Antonio Cornazano, *Libro dell'arte del danzare,* c. 1455, Vatican Li-

brary, cod. Capponiano No. 203, translated as *The Art of Dancing* by Madeleine Inglehearn and Peggy Forsyth (London: Dance Books, 1981). Evidently, the dancing masters borrowed categories from other disciplines: compare with Cicero's components of oratory, *inventio, collacatio, elocutio, actio,* and *memoria;* or Vasari's *regola, ordine, misura, disegno,* and *maniera.*

40. Cornazano's requisites are slightly different: *memoria, misura, maniera, aere, diversità di cose,* and *compartimento di terreno* (18–19). My interpretation is based on the commentary of Kinkeldy, *Jewish Dancing Master,* 8–12, and Dolmetsch, *Spain and Italy,* 2–5, the translations of Dolmetsch, 2–3, and Inglehearn (in Cornazano, *Art of Dancing,* 18), and the discussion of Franko, *Dancing Bodies,* 60–66. Franko objects to Kinkeldy's explanation of "measure" as "the dancer's ability to keep time" as an oversimplification (60–63) and redefines it as a transitional category that balances polarities of movement and suspension, and of rise and fall.

41. On the development of a modern sense of time, see David Landes, *Revolution in Time: Clocks and the Making of the Modern World* (Cambridge: Harvard University Press, 1984), reference in Phyllis Rackin, *Stages of History: English Chronicles* (Ithaca: Cornell University Press, 1990), 16. Burgundian texts are believed to postdate the Italians, and include *Le Livre dit les Basses Danses* (the "Brussels manuscript") Brussels Bibliothèque Royale M S 9085, Facsimile; Ernest Closson, *Le Manuscrit dit les Basses Danses de la Bibliothèque de Bourgogne* (Brussels: Société des Bibliophiles et Iconophiles de Belgique, 1912; repr., 1975); and *L'art et instruction de bien dancer* printed by Michel Toulouze, Paris, c. 1488, facsimile with notes by Victor Scholderer, transcription by Richard Rastell (London: Royal College of Physicians, 1936). Studies include Jackman's *Fifteenth-Century Basse Dance* and Raymond Meyland's *L'énigme de la musique des basses danses du quinzième siècle,* Publication de la société de musicologie (Berne: Paul Haupt, 1968).

42. In the Brussels manuscript, musical notes, step sequences, and song are attractively recorded but not linked in any intelligible way. Reconstructionists often "solve" the "problem" by adding either music or dance steps: Jackman, *Fifteenth-Century Basse Dance,* notes that in his collation "editorial attention has devoted itself to correcting and matching the choreography with the music, and . . . supplying sequences that are at least theoretically proper" (iii).

43. Elias's compelling image of the early modern era as a whole, (*History of Manners,* 83).

44. Arbeau, *Orchesography,* 59. "The Ball," c. 1500, a German engraving by Matthaus Zasinger, shows a dance that is probably a *pavane* performed by kings, princes, and great noblemen displaying themselves in their fine mantles, and their ladies in their sweeping trains, to the admiration of onlookers.

45. Thomas Morley, *A Plaine and Easie Introduction to Practicall Musicke* (London: Peter Short, 1597) Shakespeare Association Facsimile 14 (London: Oxford University Press, 1937), 181. The mournful kind of *pavane* has endured in the literary imagination, but in fact, as Baskervill observes, the dance became livelier and developed variations like the Spanish *pavane* as "high" dances became the fashion, and the distinction between the *pavane* and the *galliard* became blurred (*Elizabethan Jig,* 347).

46. Arbeau describes the *galliard,* as a lively dance in triple time, with two

"measures" for each set of five steps and a pause on the sixth beat (*Orchesography*, 77–88).

47. Ibid., 77.

48. Cesare Negri, *Le Gratie d'Amore* (Milan, 1602), Monuments of Music and Music Literature in Facsimile, 2d ser., CXLI (New York: Bronde Bros., 1969), F2v, F3v, F4v, G1v. The pictures in this volume are decorative, not only illustrating the text to which they seem to refer, but recurring at intervals throughout, perhaps implying that the same principles obtained in all dances. In her introduction to *Nobilità di Dame*, Sutton lists sixty-eight dance steps and twenty-four notes on etiquette.

49. Breu the Younger, "The Garden Festival in Venice" (1539), woodcut by Jost Amman 1570, British Library.

50. Often, one or two couples performed for the assembly, as in Figure 13.

51. Morley, *A Plaine and Easie Introduction*, 181; the manual of F. de Lauze, *Apologie de la Danse*, French, with English translation and introduction by Joan Wildeblood (London: Frederick Muller, 1952), demonstrates, with a plethora of *corantos* and a paucity of *galliards*, that the *coranto* had replaced the *galliard* by the early seventeenth century.

52. On figured dancing, see especially Mark Franko, *Dance as Text: Ideologies of the Baroque Body* (Cambridge: Cambridge University Press, 1993), 15–51, and Roy Strong, *Art and Power*, 58–60.

53. "Le Balet des Polonais," presented at the French court in 1573, in Jean Dorat, *Magnificentissimi spectaculi* (Paris: Frederick Morel, 1573), shows embodied writing centered, fixed, and framed in the banquet hall. As Strong writes: "dancers were meant to be read by the onlooking audience, who looked down on the patterns from above" (*Art and Power*, 60); this representation honors the reader of the book with a vantage point higher than the courtly audience, and even than the royal spectator.

54. Franko, *Dance as Text*, 30–31.

55. For discussion of the links among political, economic, and related cultural practices, see Jonathan Goldberg, *Writing Matter: From the Hands of the English Renaissance* (Stanford: Stanford University Press, 1990); Patricia Parker, *Literary Fat Ladies: Rhetoric, Gender, Property* (London: Methuen, 1987); and Rosemary Kegl, *The Rhetoric of Concealment: Figuring Gender and Class in Renaissance Literature* (Ithaca: Cornell University Press, 1994).

56. *Il libro del cortegiano* in 1528, Hoby's English translation of 1561, and *La civile conversation del Sig. Stephan Guazzo* of 1574 followed the early dancing manuals by a century.

57. Whigham, *Ambition and Privilege*, xii.

58. Caroso, *Nobilità di Dame*, 242–44.

59. See Meagher, *Jonson's Masques*, on humanist influence of Caroso and his "attempt to unite dance with poetry" in the *contrapasso* (93–94). Caroso explains the *dattile* (dactylic step) as a spring followed by two rapid steps (*Nobilità di Dame*, 129–31). The metrical effect was to be achieved by a sequence of two dactylics and a spondaic; the sequence was then repeated, starting with the other foot. Unfortu-

nately, this alternation is impossible for dancers possessing an even number of legs, so Caroso halves the second spondee.

60. Morley, *Practicall Musicke*, 181.

61. Richard Sherry, *A Treatise of Schemes and Tropes* (London, 1550), fol. 9, cited by Kier Elam, *Shakespeare's Universe of Discourse* (Cambridge: Cambridge University Press, 1984), 257; also see Franko's discussion of figure and scheme in *Dance as Text*, 16.

62. Davies, "Orchestra," stanzas 92–94.

63. Peter Herman's formulation, private conversation.

64. Arbeau, *Orchesography*, 16. Readers will no doubt observe that in my discussion, I generally use masculine pronouns rather than nonsexist "he and she" formulations. I find this exclusion of women inherently objectional; however, the dancing texts of the time (as Arbeau in the passage quoted) were addressed primarily to men, whose power to fashion a social identity was assumed. Women were expected to fashion themselves according to masculine standards, and the masculine pronoun, therefore, serves to emphasize their effective exclusion from the agency that dancing promised the gentleman.

65. Whigham, *Ambition and Privilege*, classifies courtesy literature with heraldry as "lost specializations" (3), and cites Michel Foucault, *Power/Knowledge: Selected Interviews and Other Writings, 1972–1977*, ed. Colin Gordon (New York: Pantheon, 1980), 83, on the "buried, subjugated knowledges" that were "concerned with a *historical knowledge of struggles.*"

66. Catherine Belsey, "Disrupting Sexual Differences: Meaning and Gender in the Comedies," in *Alternative Shakespeares*, ed. John Drakakis (London: Methuen, 1985), defines discourses as "sets of terms and relations between terms in which a specific meaning is inscribed" (166).

67. Hayden White, *Tropics of Discourse: Essays in Cultural Criticism* (Baltimore: Johns Hopkins University Press, 1978), 3.

68. Courtly dancing functioned like a "state apparatus," as described by Louis Althusser, "Ideology and Ideological State Apparatuses (Notes towards an Investigation)," in *Lenin and Philosophy, and Other Essays*, trans. Ben Brewster (London: New Left Books, 1971), 170–73, constructing subjectivity within a context of power relations.

69. Mark Franko, "Renaissance Conduct Literature and the Kinesis of *Bonne Grace*," in *Persons in Groups: Social Behavior as Identity Formation in Medieval and Renaissance Europe*, ed. Richard C. Trexler (Binghamton: Medieval and Renaissance Texts and Studies, 1985), 55.

70. Michel Foucault, *Discipline and Punish: The Birth of the Prison*, trans. Alan Sheridan (New York: Vintage, 1979), 136.

71. Foucault, *Discipline and Punish*, argues for the historical specificity of this development, linking the docile body with the rise of capitalism by opposing the unified body ("wholesale") with its individual parts ("retail"). By the same token, the docile body may well have been emergent in early modern England. However, the point at which the docile and dancing bodies part company lies in "the object of control" of the docile body: "no longer the signifying elements or the language

of the body, but . . . the efficiency of movements, their internal organization" (137); the dancing body was, foremost, a signifier. For a discussion of Foucault in relation to the performance of gender, see Butler, *Gender Trouble*, 134–36.

72. Foucault, *Discipline and Punish*, 137.

73. Foucault, *Power/Knowledge*, 56.

74. Louis Adrian Montrose, "'Shaping Fantasies': Figurations of Gender and Power in Elizabethan Culture," in *Representing the English Renaissance*, ed. Stephen Greenblatt (Berkeley and Los Angeles: University of California Press, 1988), an exemplary statement of the relationship of society and culture.

ONE. ASCENDING THE RICH MOUNT

1. Edward Hall, *The Union of the Two Noble and Illustrious Families of Lancaster and York*, 1548, 1550; facsimile reprint, *Hall's Chronicle*, London, 1809 (New York, 1965), 631. Spelling, punctuation, and dates have been normalized, cited as *Hall's Chronicle*.

2. The Great Hall of Hampton Court Palace, which dates from the latter part of the reign is vertically divided into an enclosed, windowless base and an open clerestoried ceiling; horizontally it is symmetrical in both structure and ornament moldings. For the most part, the festivities cited were held in the banqueting houses at Richmond, Greenwich, or Whitehall, but the major features of the Great Hall show an archetectural realization of evolving social divisions. On the royal palaces, see E. K. Chambers, *The Elizabethan Stage* (Oxford: Oxford University Press, 1928), 1:8–9, and Starkey's collection on the archeology of Greenwich (*Henry VIII*).

3. The opposition of gentle and base is Whigham's (*Ambition and Privilege*) and aptly links social and spatial structures.

4. Hall, *Chronicle*, 526.

5. Enid Welsford's observation in *The Court Masque* (New York: Russell and Russell, 1927, 1962), 166, that "the *raison d'être* of the whole performance [of the early court masque] was the arrival of noble personages disguised and masqued to dance a specially prepared dance," is often cited, as by Stephen Orgel in *The Jonsonian Masque* (New York: Columbia University Press, 1965, 1981), 5. Other important studies with material on the early English masque include Kipling, *Triumph of Honour*; Sabol, *Four Hundred Songs and Dances from the Stuart Masque*; Sidney Anglo, *Spectacle, Pageantry, and Early Tudor Policy* (Oxford: Clarendon, 1969); Paul Reyher, *Les Masques Anglais* (New York: Benjamin Blom, 1909, 1964); E. K. Chambers, *The Elizabethan Stage*, vol. 1 and *The Mediaeval Stage*, vol. 1 (London: Oxford University Press, 1903, 1951); and Glynne Wickham, *Early English Stages*, vol. 1, *1300–1576* (London: Routledge and Kegan Paul, 1959) and *The Medieval Theatre* (Cambridge: Cambridge University Press, 1974, 1987).

6. As Peter Herman argues in the introduction to his ground-breaking collection *Rethinking the Henrician Era* (Urbana: Illinois University Press, 1994), the Henrician era anticipates many of the developments previously attributed to the Elizabethan.

7. Orgel has formulated the influential critical paradigm: "what the spectator watched he ultimately became. The most common method of effecting this trans-

formation was to have the production culminate, literally and dramatically, in the revels, the dance between the masquers and members of the audience" (*Jonsonian Masque*, 7).

8. Henry VIII was, in practical terms, an absolutist monarch, asserts Perry Anderson, *Lineages of the Absolutist State* (London: New Left Books, 1974), 122: "Within the inherited framework of the English feudal polity . . . a national Absolutism was in the making that in practice seemed to bear comparison with that of any of its continental counterparts."

9. *Pleasure Reconciled to Virtue, Ben Jonson*, ed. C. H. Hereford, Percy Simpson, and Evelyn Simpson (Oxford: Clarendon, 1941), 7:489, 269–73.

10. On Elyot's *Governour*, see Goldberg, *Writing Matter*, 43, and G. R. Elton, *Reform and Reformation: England, 1509–1558* (Cambridge: Harvard University Press, 1977), who observes, 161, that the *Governour* "expounds a programme for the education of the ruling elite derived from Italian exemplars to which Elyot added a short defence of monarchic rule." A letter to his protector Cromwell, in Henry Ellis, *Original Letters Illustrative of English History*, 5 vols. (London, 1824), 2:113–19, reveals an anxious, plaintive Elyot, preoccupied with the precarious condition of his fortune and property.

11. On changing educational practices, including tutors, schools, and foreign travel, and a curriculum that included dancing as part of humanist studies, see Lawrence Stone, *The Crisis of the Aristocracy, 1558–1641* (Oxford: Oxford University Press, 1965), 672–702; on the political and social functions of education and writing, Goldberg, *Writing Matter*, 28–55.

12. On the transition from warrior to courtier society, see Whigham's excellent discussion in relation to "civility" (*Ambition and Privilege*, 6–18); Elias, *Power and Civility*, esp. 247–73; Wallace MacCaffrey, "Place and Patronage in Elizabethan Politics," in *Elizabethan Government and Society: Essays Presented to Sir John Neale*, ed. S. T. Bindoff, Joel Hurstfield, and C. H. Williams (London: Athalone, 1961), who emphasizes the centralization of political life and the gentler qualifications for a political career; Mervyn James, *Society, Politics and Culture: Studies in Early Modern England* (Cambridge: Cambridge University Press, 1986), 308–20, on the changing concept of honor; Lawrence Stone, "Social Mobility in England, 1500–1700," *Past and Present* 33 (1966):16–55; John Guy, *Tudor England* (Oxford: Oxford University Press, 1988); and G. R. Elton, *England Under the Tudors*, 3d ed. (London: Routledge, 1955, 1991).

13. The importance of the regulated body *to* the state was articulated in tropical analogies of regulated body *and* state, as in "An Homily of Obedience," in *Certain Sermons*, 1582: "Almighty God hath created and appointed all things in heaven, earth, and waters, in a most excellent and perfect order. In Heaven, he hath appointed distinct and several orders and states of Archangels and Angels. In earth he hath assigned and appointed kings, princes, with other governors under them, in all good and necessary order. . . . A man himself also hath all his parts both within and without, as soul, heart, mind, memory, understanding, reason, speech, with all and singular corporal members of his body, in a profitable, necessary, and pleasant order; every degree of people in their vocation, calling and office, hath appointed to them their duty and order."

14. See Elton, *Reform and Reformation*, 25, on the "network of patronage."

15. Elias, *History of Manners*, 55, writes of an "outward bodily propriety," and links personal and social structure, 201.

16. Eric A. Havelock, *Preface to Plato* (Cambridge: Belknap Press of Harvard University Press, 1963), 151, suggests that dancing served as a mnemonic device in the oral culture of Greece, with the physical motions that conventionally accompanied a speech strengthened by associated patterns of danced movement. Whigham cites as an epigraph to *Ambition and Privilege* the suggestion of Pierre Bourdieu, *Outline of a Theory of Practice*, trans. Richard Nice (Cambridge: Cambridge University Press, 1977), that movement functions as an abbreviated cultural reminder.

17. Judith Butler, "Performative Acts and Gender Constitution: An Essay on Phenomenology and Feminist Theory," in *Performing Feminisms*, ed. Sue-Ellen Case (Baltimore: Johns Hopkins University Press, 1990), 271–78, contends that gender is performative in a "stylized repetition of acts" (271), which are "renewed, revised, and consolidated over time" (274); Elyot assumes a similar process in terms of both rank and gender. Stephen Merriam Foley, "Coming to Terms: Thomas Elyot's Definitions and the Particularity of Human Letters," *ELR* 61 (1994): 211–30, makes the parallel assertion that "Elyot's *Dictionary* finds in linguistic stratification a means of encoding social hierarchy" (211).

18. See Vigarello, "Upward Training," esp. 153–54, on the platonizing of posture.

19. Arbeau's *Orchesography* is helpful in many ways: it contains descriptions of and notation of dances, suggestions on correct deportment, music, and drawings, of which the *révérence*, 54 and 80, and the *capriole*, 91, are the most relevant.

20. On respectful gestures that strengthened the hierarchy, see Lawrence Stone, *The Family, Sex and Marriage in England, 1500–1800* (London: Weidenfeld and Nicolson, 1977), 177; on dancing and hierarchy, Judith Lynne Hanna, *To Dance is Human: A Theory of Non-Verbal Communication* (Chicago: University of Chicago Press, 1979), 25: dancing "is part of those networks of social stratification that organize the interconnected activities of members of a society." On Elyot's moralized "honor," see James, "English Politics and the Concept of Honour," in *Society, Politics, and Culture*: "Sir Thomas Elyot restat[ed] the honour code in terms of the popularized humanism of the age. In *The Boke named the Governour* . . . he attempted to do for honour what the church had once attempted for chivalry: to incorporate its values into a universalized moral system, and to relate it to religion" (338).

21. Feminine enclosure and dependence was much emphasized in homilies, conduct books, and marriage tracts; see, for example, John Dod and Robert Cleaver, *A Godly Form of Household Government* (London, 1598), "the good wife keeps her house . . . chastity careth to please but one, and therefore she keeps her closet as if she were still at prayer," sig.J4, and "A Homily of the State of Matrimony," *The Second Tome* (London, 1563): "as Saint Paul expresseth it in this form of words: 'Let women be subject to their husbands as to the Lord; for the husband is the head of the woman, as Christ is the head of the church' . . . as for their

husbands, [wives] must obey, and cease from commanding, and perform subjection."

22. Judith Lynne Hanna, *Dance, Sex, and Gender: Signs of Identity, Dominance, Defiance, and Desire* (Chicago: University of Chicago Press, 1988), 12, observes that dancing "offers models of gender attitudes and behavior," and that the "array of dance messages of sexuality and gender may lead to reinforcing ongoing models [or] acquiring new responses."

23. Elton, *Tudors*, 70, characterizes the diplomacy of Henry VII as a "foreign policy based on matrimony rather than war."

24. Stone, *Aristocracy*, argues that in the absence of a police force and during a period of religious transition, the family was the guarantor of order and morality (591–92); and in *Family*, that the power of the state was strengthened by "a deliberately fostered increase in the power of the husband and father within the conjugal unit, that is to say, a strengthening of patriarchy" (135). The vision of a monolithic "patriarchal family," especially *Family* (132–42), has been challenged with an emphasis on the variety and change in family formations over time and among social ranks; see Susan Dwyer Amussen, "Gender, Family, and the Social Order, 1560–1725," in *Order and Disorder in Early Modern England*, ed. Anthony Fletcher and John Stevenson (Cambridge: Cambridge University Press, 1985), and *An Ordered Society: Gender and Class in Early Modern England* (London: Basil Blackwell, 1988); and Keith Wrightson, *English Society, 1580–1680* (Rutgers: Rutgers University Press, 1982).

25. In Richard Hyrde's translation of *De institutio feominae christianae*, 1523, *The Instruction of a Christian Woman* (1540), "Of the virtues of a woman and examples that she should follow," "shamefastness and sobriety be the inseparable companions of chastity, insomuch as she cannot be chaste that is not ashamed, for that is a cover and veil of her face" (Sig. 33r). Ian Maclean, *The Renaissance Notion of Woman: A Study in the Fortunes of Scholasticism and Medical Science in European Intellectual Life* (Cambridge: Cambridge University Press, 1980), discusses Aristotelian dualities of gender (hot-cold, active-passive, completion-incompletion) in relation to biblical texts: the woman is the "weaker vessel" (1 Peter 3:7), the woman's salvation lies in the procreation of males (1 Tim. 2:15), 8–13.

26. Fol. 83r. While it might be argued that Elyot's combination of masculine and feminine qualities is a "companionate" dance that dignifies the woman with a unique and necessary contribution to the emblem of "concord," it is likely that the dance itself and Elyot's representation functioned, as Rosemary Kegl, *Rhetoric of Concealment*, suggests that conduct books did (67), by disguising feminine subordination with the language of complementarity; as Butler observes, "Gender is . . . a construction that regularly conceals its genesis" ("Performative Acts," 273).

27. The society under construction in the Henrician era was the subject of admiring analyses of which William Harrison's, in his *Description of England* (1577), ed. F. J. Furnivall, 4 parts (London: New Shakspeare Society, 1877–1908), is perhaps the best known: "We in England divide our people commonly into four sorts, as gentlemen, citizens or burgesses, yeomen, and artificers or laborers" (1:105). On social structure and social change, see David Cressy, "Describing the Social Order

in Elizabethan and Stuart England," *Literature and History,* no. 3 (March 1976): 29–34, and Stone, "Social Mobility."

28. Stow, *Survey,* 88–89; see Chambers, *Medieval Stage,* 1:394–95, for the description in manuscript that Stow paraphrased.

29. Wickham, *Early English Stages,* 207.

30. Welsford, *Court Masque,* 118–19, suggests that the *morisco* was one of the Continental fashions brought to court by Henry VII. It was best known as a sixteenth-century dance, but there may have been a fourteenth-century equivalent; nevertheless, one hundred and thirty dancers is a pretty big Morris.

31. Stallybrass, in "Patriarchal Territories," remarks upon the assumption of an "ungendered" male body by writers as diverse as Bakhtin and Elias, following "early Elizabethan proclamations on apparel that legislate men's dress but are silent on women's" (125) until 1574. Early commentators on this passage, including Chambers, Reyher, Welsford, and Wickham, have made the same assumption.

32. In his chapter on the northern influences on the early Tudor masque, "Upon the Rich Mount of England: Burgundian Pageants and Tudor Disguisings," to which I owe a titular debt, Gordon Kipling questions the literary myth of the Italianate origins of the Jacobean masque: "While the English masque thus stands indebted to Italy for its name, it owes its basic structure and spectacular form to Burgundy" (115). Local festive customs as well as Continental figured in court festivities, as least early in the reign: Hall reports that "on May day . . . in the second year of his reign, his grace being young and willing not to be idle, rose in the morning very early to fetch May or green bows" (*Chronicle,* 515), and with his courtiers went forth to the wood to shoot.

33. Hall, *Chronicle,* 526.

34. Chambers, *Elizabethan Stage,* 151–52.

35. Welsford, *Court Masque,* 137.

36. Not—as Stephen Orgel observes in *Illusion of Power: Political Theater in the English Renaissance* (Berkeley and Los Angeles: University of California Press, 1975)—as James was, part of the spectacle as spectator (16).

37. Welsford, *Court Masque,* 122.

38. Reyher, *Masques Anglais,* 500–502, reprints the descriptions of the wedding celebrations from Harleian M S 69, fols. 29–31.

39. Hall, *Chronicle,* 619; noted in Welsford, *Court Masque,* 143.

40. Wilfred Hooper, in "The Tudor Sumptuary Laws," *English Historical Review* 30 (1915): 433–49, observes that Henry VIII's first Parliament (1510) passed a sumptuary law continuing earlier restrictions, but imposed forfeiture of offending apparel, outlined measures for its recovery, and gave the sovereign the right to make exemptions (433).

41. Hall, *Chronicle,* 518–19.

42. Ibid., 535; see Sabol's discussion of this masque (*Four Hundred Songs,* 9–10).

43. Hall, *Chronicle,* 631.

44. Ibid., 723–24.

45. David Scott Kastan, "Proud Majesty Made a Subject: Shakespeare and the Spectacle of Rule," *Shakespeare Quarterly* 37, no. 4 (Winter 1986): 458–75. Kastan rightly suggests that representations of proud kingship on the public stage may

have "weakened the structure of authority" (461); however, within the Henrician court, the representation of an ideal of masculine "gentility" by the king may have served to enforce its authority.

46. As Orgel has observed, "no one could refuse [to dance] for long, knowing that beneath the disguise danced the king," and no one could refuse to emulate him, for "when the monarch has moved into the masque world, the court is obliged to follow" (*Illusion of Power*, 27).

47. Hall, *Chronicle*, 513.

48. In a proleptic divestment at Arthur's marriage celebrations, "last came down the Duke of York having with him the Lady Margaret, his sister, in his hand, and dances two base dances, and afterwards, he perceiving himself to be encumbered with his clothes suddenly cast off his gown and danced in his jacket . . . in so goodly and pleasant manner that it was to the King and Queen right great and singular pleasure" (Harleian M S 69, in Reyher, *Masques Anglais*, 502).

49. Hall, *Chronicle*, 535.

50. Brissenden, *Shakespeare and the Dance*, 103.

51. Wickham, *Medieval Theater*, 165–66.

52. Wickham suggests that the words spoken on these occasions were "super-fluous" (*Early English Stages*, 221).

53. Jean E. Howard, "Scripts and/versus Playhouses: Ideological Production and the Renaissance Public Stage," in *Renaissance Drama as Cultural History*, ed. Mary Beth Rose (Evanston: Northwestern University Press, 1989), 37.

TWO. IMITATING THE STARS CELESTIAL

1. On the controversy over dancing, see Mary Pennino-Baskerville, "Terpsi-chore Reviled: Antidance Tracts in Elizabethan England," *Sixteenth-Century Journal* 22, no. 3 (1991): 475–93, and Sarah Thesiger, "The *Orchestra* of Sir John Davies and the Image of the Dance," *Journal of the Warburg and Courtauld Institutes* 36 (1973): 277–304. On antitheatricality, see Jonas Barish, *The Antitheatrical Prejudice* (Berkeley and Los Angeles: University of California Press, 1981), Jean E. Howard, *The Stage and Social Struggle in Early Modern England* (London: Routledge, 1994), and Levine, *Men in Women's Clothing*. On antipoetics, see Peter Herman, *Squitter-wits and Muse-haters: Sidney, Spenser, Milton and Renaissance Antipoetic Sentiment* (Detroit: Wayne State University Press, 1996). Herman observes that antipoetic and antitheatrical traditions overlap, and antitheatrical and antidancing traditions do as well, with the same texts supplying ammunition for both stage- and dancing-haters (15).

2. Phillip Stubbes, *The Anatomie of Abuses* (London, 1583), ed. Frederick J. Furnivall as *Phillip Stubbes's Anatomy of the Abuses in England in Shakspere's Youth*, The New Shakspere Society (London: N. Trubner, 1877–79), 154.

3. Lucian's "The Dance" (*Saltatio*), c. 162–165 A . D . in *Lucian*, vol. 5, trans. A. M. Harmon, Loeb Classical Library (Cambridge: Harvard University Press, 1936, 1962), from which both Renaissance defenses and attacks borrowed liberally, was framed as a refutation: "Well, Crato," begins Lycinus, the champion of dancing, "this is truly a forceful indictment that you have brought . . . against dances and the dancer's art [as] something unworthy and effeminate" (211). Lucian

defends dancing as "a thing of utter harmony, putting a fine edge on the soul, disciplining the body, delighting the beholders and teaching them much that happened of old" (275), and links it with "the concord of the heavenly spheres" (221). Elyot's Proteus is strongly reminiscent of Lucian's, 231–33: "the ancient myth about Proteus the Egyptian means nothing else than that he was a dancer, an imitative fellow, able to shape himself and change himself into anything, so that he could imitate even the liquidity of water and the sharpness of fire in the liveliness of his movements" (231–33).

4. Elyot's position on the nature of women, whom he defended elsewhere, is complex. However, the characterization of his discourse of dancing is characterized as "patriarchal" to emphasize the importance of social difference to elite dancing and to his defense, which privileges the gentleman in a context of marital relations.

5. Lucian, "Dance," 227.

6. Ibid., 271–73.

7. See John M. Major, "The Moralization of the Dance in Elyot's *Governor*," *Studies in the Renaissance* 5 (1958): 26–36.

8. Elyot, *Governour*, fols. 77v–78r. Krueger, in his commentary on Davies' "*Orchestra*" (*Poems*, 360), notes that Elyot and Davies both borrow and also expand the cosmic metaphor in Lucian.

9. Vigarello observes ("Upward Training," 167), that the function of dancing was purgative, not expressive, with excess humors contained and dried up by exercise. For relevant discussions of "classical" and "grotesque" bodies and class-coded bodily canons, see the introduction to Bakhtin's *Rabelais and His World*, esp. 18–30, Stallybrass's "Patriarchal Territories," and Vigarello, 179–81. Gail Kern Paster, in *The Body Embarrassed*, conceives the "two bodily canons" somewhat differently, not as "high" and "low," but as outer ("civilized") and inner (experienced, humoral).

10. Antonius de Arena, *Ad suos compagnones studiantes qui sunt de persona friantes, bassas dansas in gallanti stilo bisogatas . . .* Avignon, 1517, facs. of 1572 (Lion: Benoist Rigaud), trans. John Guthrie and Mario Zorzi as *Rules of Dancing*, in *Dance Research* 4, no. 2 (1986): 3–52; Guthrie and Zorzi, 3, note the popularity of this treatise: forty-two editions were printed between 1529 and 1770.

11. Arena, "*Rules*," 26.

12. Stubbes, *Anatomy of Abuses*, 155.

13. Defining the boundaries of kinetic, oral, and written discourses is tricky, but the insistence with which written texts on dancing (both adversarial and commendatory) overlap suggests that all the texts probably had a relatively greater component of orally transmitted material and a smaller proportion of "the work of one man." As Brissenden observes, the most complete dance instructions in English before Playford's *Dancing Master* were to be found in the manuscripts of six men who had been students at the Inns of Court, and adds that "[w]hat is remarkable is that even though at least fifty years, and probably more lie between the writing of the earliest [1570] and latest of these . . . they all have the names of six dances in common, copied down in the same order" (*Shakespeare and the Dance*, 6). This seems to suggest that a pedagogy of dancing circulated orally and was written

down from time to time, rather than a universal familiarity with a master dancing treatise.

14. Thomas Middleton's *A Chaste Maid in Cheapside* opens with Maudlin reprimanding her phlegmatic daughter Moll for neglecting the dancing lessons that might improve her personality and marital prospects (1.1.12–24). The Puritan Stubbes rails against this proliferation, "Yea, they are not ashamed to erect schools of dancing, thinking it an ornament to their children to be expert in this noble science of heathen deviltry" (154–55). On the regulation of dancing schools, see Pennino-Baskerville, 479, and Ian W. Archer, *The Pursuit of Stability: Social Relations in Elizabethan London* (Cambridge: Cambridge University Press, 1971), 242–43, and 255.

15. Arena, *Ad suos compagnones studiantes,* 1572, D2r, after an anonymous translation given to me by William Burdick; hereafter, I cite Guthrie's *Rules of Dancing,* an engaging rendition of Arena's Latin macaronic verse.

16. Arena, "*Rules,*" 26–38, passim.

17. Gail Kern Paster, *Body Embarrassed,* 14–15, emphasizes the similarities in "corporeal flux and openness" between the humoral and "grotesque" bodies, with its stress on the "body's thresholds and its sites of pleasure—anus, mouth, genitalia," and Stallybrass, "Patriarchal Territories," 124, bodily differentiation along class lines, with classical and grotesque bodies constructed in opposition to one another, but each "formed by the redrawing of the boundaries of the other." Arena details the process of civilizing the vulgar body that was presumed necessary for upward mobility, but in the process, he emphasizes the bodily openness to the degree that the bodily canons are almost inverted, as Stallybrass, "Reading the Body: *The Revenger's Tragedy* and the Jacobean Theater of Consumption," *Renaissance Drama XVIII,* ed. Mary Beth Rose (Evanston: Northwestern University Press, 1987), 137, observes in *The Revenger's Tragedy.*

18. Arbeau, *Orchesography,* 12.

19. John Northbrooke, *A treatise wherein dicing, dancing, vaine playes or enterludes . . . are reproved,* Shakespeare Society reprint from the earliest edition, 1577 (London, 1843), 159. The antidancing tracts used a common vocabulary of biblical references (King David), arguments (dancing incites lust), and images (the Golden Calf); therefore, Northbrooke's treatise may be cited as typical of the genre. Others include Stubbes's *Anatomie of Abuses;* Stephen Gosson, "The horrible Vice of pestiferous dancing," in *The Shoole of Abuse, containing a pleasaunt invective against poets, pipers, plaiers, jesters and such like caterpillers of a commonwealth* (1579); the anonymous *A Treatise of Daunces, wherin it is showed, that they are as it were accessories and dependents . . . to whoredom* (1581), ed. Arthur Freeman (repr., New York: Garland, 1974); and Christopher Fetherstone, *A dialogue against light, lewd, and lascivious dancing* (London, 1582).

20. Fetherstone, *A dialogue,* C74–C8r.

21. Stubbes, *Anatomy of Abuses,* 157–64.

22. Ibid., 155.

23. On the subversion of patriarchal categories of gender and rank and the appropriation of the techniques of self-fashioning, see Jean E. Howard, in "Renais-

sance Antitheatricality and the Politics of Gender and Rank in *Much Ado About Nothing*," in *Shakespeare Reproduced*, ed. Jean E. Howard and Marian F. O'Connor (London: Methuen, 1987), 165–67.

24. For a nuanced analysis of London populations, see Theodore B. Leinwand, "Shakespeare and the Middling Sort," *Shakespeare Quarterly* 4, no. 3 (1993): 284–304. Conrad Russell, *The Crisis of Parliaments: English History, 1509–1660* (Oxford: Oxford University Press, 1971), discusses the difficulties in defining the "typical Puritan" in terms of religious beliefs, social attitudes or behavior (167–78); on the complexities of Puritan attitudes toward dancing, see Rick Bowers "John Lowin's Conclusions Upon Dances: Puritan Conclusions of a Godly Player," in *Renaissance and Reformation / Renaissance et Réforme*, n.s., 9, no. 2 (1987): 163–73.

25. An entry in the *Diary of Henry Machyn, Citizen of London, 1550–1563*, ed. John Gough Nichols (London: Camden Society, 1849), 20, shows traditional festivity under attack in the 1550s, when the "lord mayor by counsel" ordered a "godly Maypole" to be taken down and broken. The Records of Early English Drama series is a trove of prosecutions; *Herefordshire/Worcestershire*, ed. David N. Klausner (Toronto: University of Toronto Press, 1990), for example, lists multiple indictments and excommunications of both men and women for dancing on the Sabbath (150–54, 159, 160, 163–64); dancing the Morris on the Sabbath (176–77); and playing the fiddle for dancing on the Sabbath (180).

26. John Milton, *A Masque Presented at Ludlow Castle*, 1634, printed by Henry Lawes, 1637. Baskervill observes (*Elizabethan Jig*, 351) that country dances were becoming a fad of the elite; and see Michael Wilding, "Milton's 'A Masque Presented at Ludlow Castle, 1634': Theatre and Politics at the Border," *Trivium* 20 (May 1985): 147–79.

27. Northbrooke, *Treatise*, 165.

28. Ibid., 148.

29. Fetherstone, too, associates dancing with festered sores, Sig.4r, notes Pennino-Baskerville, 481, following Vives' *Instruction*, Sig.D3r. Constance Jordan, in *Renaissance Feminism* (Ithaca: Cornell University Press, 1990), 119, observes that Elyot's *Defense of Good Women* (1540) "functions (whether intentionally or not) as a refutation of Vives' *Instruction*," and possibly his defense of dancing also responded to the original Vives.

30. Northbrooke, *Treatise*, 154.

31. Ibid., 146.

32. Ibid., 146, 153, and 171.

33. Heavenly bodies were often referred to as "wandering stars," but as the *OED* confirms, "wandering" more often resonated with vagrancy and unruliness. Dancing was long criticized as feminizing: Lucian's adversary, Crato, asks the defender Lycinus how he can sit "watching a girlish fellow play the wanton with dainty clothing" (211), and early modern stage- and dancing-haters frequently linked dancing with effeminacy, as Stubbes rails, "in [England], both men, women, and children are so skillful in [dancing] as they may be thought nothing inferior to Cynoedus, the prostitute ribauld, or Sardanapalus, that effeminate varlet" (*Anatomy of Abuses*, 154–55).

34. Northbrooke, *Treatise*, 155–56.

35. Ibid., 150.

36. Ibid., 170–71.

37. "Of leapings and dances and fools that pass their time in such vanity," engraving by Albrecht Dürer, 1494, reprinted in the Alexander Barclay translation of Sebastian Brant's *Ship of Fools* (1509), STC 3545, Folger Shakespeare Library. Antidance writers frequently invoked this biblical occasion of blasphemy to condemn all dancing.

38. "[The queen] takes great pleasure in dancing and music. She told me that she entertained at least sixty musicians; in her youth she danced very well, and composed measures, and had played them herself and danced to them," wrote the French ambassador, in *A Journal of All That Was Accomplished by Monsieur de Maisse Ambassador in England from Henri IV to Queen Elizabeth* (1597), trans. G. B. Harrison and R. A. Jones (London: Nonesuch, 1931), 95.

39. Northbrooke, *Treatise,* 166.

40. Ibid., 167.

41. De Maisse, *Journal,* 95.

42. The painting, c. 1574, was supposed to show Queen Elizabeth dancing the *volta* with the earl of Leicester, as does an illustration in Frances Rust, *Dance in Society,* pl. IV. Northbrooke's assumption of the de facto lewdness of any woman who hops high strays dangerously into political territory by implicitly threatening the ideological center of the monarch's natural body. As Marie Axton notes in *The Queen's Two Bodies: Drama and the Elizabethan Succession* (London: Royal Historical Society, 1977), 17, chastity was closely linked with inheritance and succession.

43. Richard Mulcaster, *Positions, Wherein Those Primitive Circumstances Be Examined, Which Are necessarie for the Training up of children, either for skill in their booke or health in their bodie.* London, 1581 (New York: Da Capo, 1971), chap. 16.

44. Richard L. Molen, "Richard Mulcaster and Elizabethan Pageantry," *Studies in English Literature* 14 (1974): 209–21, notes that Mulcaster composed a summary of the Royal Entry sponsored by the city companies for the coronation of Elizabeth (printed 1559), Latin verses for the Kenilworth entertainments of 1575, speeches for the Lord Mayor's pageants of 1561 and 1568, and a Latin oration for the Royal Entry of James I.

45. Mulcaster, *Positions,* 71.

46. Ibid., 71.

47. Ibid., 72.

48. See Levinus Lemnius, *The Touchstone of Complexions,* London, 1576, STC 15456, 51v–52r, and William Vaughn, *Approved Directions for Health . . . ,* 4th ed., London, 1612, STC 24615, 64.

49. John Jones, *The Arte and Science of preserving Bodie and Soule in al Health, Wisdome, and Catholicke Religion: Physically, Philosophically, and Divinely* (London: Ralph Newberie, 1579), STC 14724a, 24 and 22. The treatise is dedicated to the Queen but recommended as "[r]ight profitable for all persons . . . chiefly for Princes, Rulers, Nobles, Bishops, Preachers, Parents, and them of the Parliament house."

50. Mulcaster, *Positions,* 72.

51. Northbrooke, *Treatise,* 156.

52. Ibid.

53. Philip Barrough, *The Method of Physick Containing the Causes, Signs, and Cures of inward Diseases in man's bodie*, 7th edition (London: George Miller, 1634), STC 1515, M1r–v,M4r–v.

54. *Positions*, 73. Also see William Bullein, *Bullein's Bulwark of Defense against all Sickness, Soreness, and Wounds that doe dayly assault mankinde*, 1562, printed 1579, STC 4034, who warns, fol. 17b, that "[t]he counsel of Galen must be observed . . . there is no meat but it will corrupt or stink, if the body be cast in a sudden heat by strong travail soon after meat," or the result will be "sudden great blushing of your face, veins swelled and puffed up, red eyes, and gross skin, extended and stretched out with fullness, like to a blown bladder."

55. Mulcaster, *Positions*, 72.

56. Barrough, *Method of Physic*, C2r–v.

57. As Gail Paster has established in *The Body Embarrassed*, the "embarrassed" body was a humoral, feminized one; Mulcaster's injudicious dancer is both leaky and diminutive.

58. Stubbes, *Anatomy of Abuses*, 156.

59. Mulcaster, *Positions*, 72.

60. Ibid., 74.

61. Ibid., 75.

62. Richard Helgerson, in *Forms of Nationhood: The Elizabethan Writing of England* (Chicago: University of Chicago Press, 1992) writes, that "early modern self-representation . . . based its claim to cultural legitimacy on removing itself from popular culture and aligning itself with standard of order and civility that transcended national boundaries, but enforced boundaries of class" (10–11), as Mulcaster does through the absent gesture. Also see Goldberg, *Writing Matter*, 30–37, on Mulcaster and the "right writing" that served the state.

63. Citations to Sir John Davies' "*Orchestra*, or a Poeme of Dauncing," in *The Poems of Sir John Davies*, ed. Robert Krueger. Sources on Davies and his poem include Krueger's introduction and commentary, Thesiger's "*Orchestra*," James Sanderson, *Sir John Davies* (Boston: Twayne, 1975), and J. R. Brink's essays "Sir John Davies's Orchestra: Political Symbolism and Textual Revisions," *Durham University Journal* 72 (1980): 195–202, and "The 1622 Edition of John Davies's Orchestra," *The Library: A Quarterly Journal of Bibliography* 30 (1975): 25–33. In his introduction, lxiv–lxvi, Krueger suggests that Davies first wrote "*Orchestra*" as a "mock-encomium" for his friend Richard Martin, an attractive and accomplished dancer, and after their estrangement revised it, perhaps as an entertainment for Elizabeth. The poem was registered in 1594, copied in 1595, printed in 1596 with additional stanzas, and reprinted with an amended ending and a hopeful dedication to Prince Charles in 1622; my reading cites the stanzas common to both printings. The poem has been profitably considered on many levels, but my discussion will be restricted to the ways in which Davies represents and codes dance movement.

64. Thesiger observes that in the poem, "dancing becomes a literal acting out of the social order" ("*Orchestra*," 303).

65. Philip J. Finkelpearl, *John Marston of the Middle Temple: An Elizabethan Dramatist in His Social Setting* (Cambridge: Harvard University Press, 1969), 76–79,

cited by Krueger, *Poems,* 358; Brink "Political Symbolism," 196 n. 7, questions this supposition.

66. Davies makes liberal use of the civility tropes—the hierarchy of gentle and base and the elite pose of self-sacrifice—that Whigham identifies in *Ambition and Privilege.*

67. Another acquisition from Lucian, "Dance," 221, also noted by Thesiger (*"Orchestra"*); Krueger suggests (*Poems,* 365 n. 29), that Davies borrowed Plato's vision of creation whereby the creator imposes order on chaos in the form of circular motion from the *Timaeus.*

68. In the measures, the *honor* moved up and down, the *singles* and *double* forward, the *reprise* back, and the *branle* from side to side.

69. See Crooke, "Why Men Are Hotter Than Women" (in *Microcosmographia*), in which he endeavors, not always successfully, to explain the hot behaviors in women, and Maclean, *Renaissance Notion,* 19, on the solar analogy in Luther's sermon on Genesis. In *The Body Embarrassed,* Gail Paster argues that "the materials of early modern humoral theory encode a completely articulated hierarchy of physical differences paralleling and replicating structures of social difference" (16); given Davies' fusion of redundant associations, the gendering of his dances is somewhat overdetermined.

70. See John N. King, "Queen Elizabeth I: Representations of the Virgin Queen," *Renaissance Quarterly* 43, no. 1 (Spring 1990): 30–74, 55, on the androgynous imagery of the April eclogue in Spenser's *Shepheardes Calendar,* with which "Elizabeth's lunar qualities both as a woman and a queen are overlaid with the solar symbolism that iconographical tradition accorded to kings as males."

71. Arbeau describes the *lavolta* as a lively dance with whirling lifts in which the woman is supported by the partner's hand under the busk in front, and his knee beneath under the buttocks in back, concluding with a warning: "I leave it to you to judge whether it is a becoming thing for a young girl to take long strides and separations of the legs, and whether in this lavolta both honor and health are not involved and at stake" (119–21).

THREE. HANDS, FEET, AND BOTTOMS

1. As Brissenden, *Shakespeare and the Dance,* restates the humanist commonplace, many of the comedies end with a dance because "most of them move from initial disorder to happy resolution and the dance offers such a strong visual image of concord" (34).

2. On the diversity of populations and cultures in London and their interactions in relation to the stage, see Peter Burke, "Popular Culture in Seventeenth Century London," in *Popular Culture in Seventeenth-Century England,* ed. Barry Reay (London: Croom Helm, 1985), and Reay's introduction, esp. 13–14; David Underdown's, *Revel, Riot and Rebellion: Popular Politics and Culture in England, 1603–1660.* (Oxford: Clarendon, 1985); Robert Weimann, *Shakespeare and the Popular Tradition in the Theater: Studies in the Social Dimension of Dramatic Form and Function,* ed. Robert Schwartz (Baltimore: Johns Hopkins University Press, 1978); and Walter Cohen, *Drama of a Nation: Public Theater in Renaissance England and Spain* (Ithaca: Cornell University Press, 1985).

3. Walter Sorell, "Shakespeare and the Dance," in *Shakespeare Quarterly* 8 (1957): 367–71, notes that Shakespeare calls for or refers to a dance on some fifty occasions in his plays, specifying twelve different dances; Brissenden lists the dances to which the plays refer, and speculates on those performed (*Shakespeare and the Dance,* 135–36).

4. Robert Weimann's formulation in "Towards a Literary Theory of Ideology: Mimesis, Representation, Authority," in *Shakespeare Reproduced: The Text in History and Ideology* ed. Jean E. Howard and Marian F. O'Connor (London: Methuen, 1987), 268, cited by Howard, 183, in her essay on *Much Ado* in the same volume.

5. See Brissenden's (*Shakespeare and the Dance*) discussion, 41–45, citations to 43, 41, and 45.

6. Harold F. Brooks, introduction to the Arden edition of *A Midsummer Night's Dream* (London: Methuen, 1979), cxxiv.

7. Leonard Tennenhouse, *Power on Display: The Politics of Shakespearean Genres* (London: Methuen, 1986), 43–44, suggests that dancing serves a simple hegemonic function in the play, asserting that though the play shows the interaction of popular and elite bodies, the final dance "incorporates the whole range of social elements within a celebration of state power."

8. Louis Montrose, "Shaping Fantasies," as well as his "A Kingdom of Shadows," in *The Theatrical City: Culture, Theatre, and Politics in London, 1576–1649,* ed. David L. Smith, Richard Strier, and David Bevington (Cambridge: Cambridge University Press, 1995), and *The Purpose of Playing;* Theodore Leinwand, "I believe we must leave the killing out": Deference and Accommodation in *A Midsummer Night's Dream,* in *Renaissance Papers* (1986):11–30. Annabel Patterson in *Shakespeare and the Popular Voice* (Cambridge: Basil Blackwell, 1989); C. L. Barber, *Shakespeare's Festive Comedy: A Study of Dramatic Form and Its Relation to Social Custom* (Princeton: Princeton University Press Press, 1959, 1972), and Patricia Parker, *Shakespeare from the Margins: Language, Culture, Context* (Chicago: University of Chicago Press, 1995.

9. Barber suggests (*Shakespeare's Festive Comedy,* 138), that Titania and the fairies dance a popular round, but Inge Leimberg in "'Give me thy hand': Some Notes on the Phrase in Shakespeare's Comedies and Tragedies," in *Shakespeare: Text, Language, Criticism,* ed. Bernard Fabian and Kurt Tetzeli von Rosador (Hildesheim; Olms, 1987), 126, proposes that Shakespeare alludes to the round dance of Botticelli's Three Graces, that is, to a courtly tradition.

10. Montrose, "Shaping Fantasies" 44.

11. Titania is not Queen Elizabeth, of course, but it is perhaps more than a coincidence that the queen was imaginatively associated with popular festive customs and outdoor entertainments, Henry and James with Continental dancing and court masques. In several summer entertainments, she was saluted by a Fairy Queen and her maidens: see, for example, A. W. Pollard, *The Queen's Majesty: Entertainment at Woodstock, 1575* (Oxford: H. Dorrel and H. Hart, 1903, 1910); and Jean Wilson, *Entertainments for Elizabeth I* (Woodbridge, Eng.: D. S. Brewer, 1980): "The Fourth Days Entertainment: 'the Fairy Queen came into the garden, dancing with her maids about her'" (115). For an evocative discussion of these entertain-

ments, see Bruce Smith's "Landscape with Figures: The Three Realms of Queen Elizabeth's Country-house Revels," in *Renaissance Drama*, n.s., 8 (1966): 57–109.

12. See Patterson, *Shakespeare* 33, and Burke, *Popular Culture*, 91, on popular oral culture.

13. See Arbeau on the many different versions of the *branle* (*Orchesography*, 128–75), a linked couple dance in which the chain of dancers moved back and forth from side to side, danced in France, by young and old, polished and inept, in the court and in the country; and Baskervill, *Elizabethan Jig*, 347–51.

14. In French colloquial usage, *branler* has an autoerotic sense. According to the *OED*, "branle" or "branler" was in use in England in the sense of "moving from side to side" or "moving to and fro"—the respectable French meaning—until the middle of the fifteenth century, and may have had the less polite sense as well.

15. Baskervill, *Elizabethan Jig*, 338. Titania's final round is an example of the old carole that combined dance and sung accompaniment. Arbeau emphasizes the exoticism of the *canary*, 66, a late-sixteenth-century courtly dance.

16. John Marston, *The Malcontent*, in *Elizabethan Plays*, ed. Arthur H. Nethercot, Charles R. Baskervill, and Virgil B. Heltzel, rev. Arthur H. Nethercot (New York: Holt, Rinehart and Winston, 1971), 4.1.1–12. While Marston was a satirist and may have exaggerated, a satiric description assumes there is something to satirize.

17. *Twelfth Night*, 1.3.115–31. Carole Levin has called to my attention an anecdote recounted by David Underdown in *Fire from Heaven: Life in an English Town in the Seventeenth Century* (New Haven: Yale University Press Press, 1992), 61–62, that connects terpsichorean display with an ill-fated exposure of masculine endowments. In Dorchester in 1634, a party was held at which there was much "drinking and merriment"; one man, "obviously far gone in drink," was given a loaf of bread in return for the entertainment of a dance; when asked "if he were well-provided," he "showed forth his privy members." Straining to get a good look in the dark room, some of the women approached him with a candle—too closely, it turned out: he died a few weeks later.

18. On female leakiness, see Gail Kern Paster, "Leaky Vessels: The Incontinent Women of City Comedy," in *Renaissance Drama as Cultural History*, ed. Mary Beth Rose (Evanston: Northwestern University Press, 1990); in *Body Embarrassed*, she observes that water was identified with male potency as well as female leaking, 58.

19. "[W]hen you have entered the place where the company is assembled, you will choose some comely damsel who takes your fancy, and . . . proffer her [hand] to lead her out to dance. She, being sensible and well brought up, will offer you her left hand and rise to accompany you" (Arbeau, *Orchesography*, 52).

20. Davies, *"Orchestra,"* stanza 111.

21. See Arbeau, *Orchesography*, on the *tourdion*, 57, and the *almain*, 125. Brissenden, *Shakespeare and the Dance*, 136, opts for an *almain* or a courtly pavan.

22. Brooks, *Midsummer Night's Dream*, cxxiii.

23. Ibid., cxviii.

24. Montrose, "Shaping Fantasies," 55.

25. Patterson, *Shakespeare*, 63.

26. Brissenden, *Shakespeare and the Dance*, 45.

27. Brooks, *Midsummer Night's Dream*, cxx.

28. William A. Ringler Jr., "The Number of Actors in Shakespeare's Early Plays," in *The Seventeenth-Century Stage: A Collection of Critical Essays*, ed. G. E. Bentley (Chicago: University of Chicago Press, 1968), 131–33.

29. Sachs describes the dance as "a procession in a circle, then . . . a waltz in couples, then a procession again" (278), in the *Dictionary of the Dance*, comp., written, and ed. by W. G. Raffe, assisted by M. E. Purdom (New York: A. S. Barnes, 1964), 63, as a quick dance in double time for two couples or a larger group, in which men and women move in two circles in opposite directions, then embrace and continue in couples. Sabol, *Four Hundred Songs*, 15, observes that the Bergamask was linked with the Morris.

30. On theatrical cross-dressing, see Tracey Sedinger, "'If Sight and Shape be True': The Epistemology of Cross-Dressing on the London Stage," *Shakespeare Quarterly* 48, no. 1 (Spring 1997): 63–79; Laura Levine, *Men in Women's Clothing: Anti-theatricality and Effeminization, 1579–1642* (Cambridge: Cambridge University Press, 1994); Stephen Orgel, "Nobody's Perfect: or, Why Did the English Stage Take Boys for Women?" *South Atlantic Quarterly*, 88 (1989): 7–30; Jean E. Howard, "Crossdressing, the Theatre, and Gender Struggle in Early Modern England," *Shakespeare Quarterly* 39, no. 4 (1988): 419–40; Phyllis Rackin, "Androgyny, Mimesis, and the Marriage of the Boy Heroine on the English Renaissance Stage," *PMLA* 102 (1987): 29–41; and Lisa Jardine, *Still Harping on Daughters*. On the erotic potentials of the pantomined version of the Morris, linked to the Bergomask in the person of Kempe, see Bruce Smith, *Homosexual Desire in Shakespeare's England: A Cultural Poetics* (Chicago: University of Chicago Press, 1991), 122–25.

31. Brooks, *Midsummer Night's Dream*, lxxxii; see Kempe's account of his twenty-seven-day dance in *Kempas nine daies wonder, performed in a dance from London to Norwich* (London, 1600), STC 14923. The Morris, like the French *branle*, took many forms, and spanned elite and popular sites, notes Weimann, *Shakespeare*, 25. It was originally probably a weapons dance involving a group of men, and later, "contaminated" by its performance during the May Games, developed into a pantomime involving hobbyhorse and Maid Marian; it was also performed as a male solo dance with handkerchief, bells, and high capers to ring them, and finally gained respectability as the "English national dance." See Arbeau, *Orchesography*, 177–81, and Baskerville, *Elizabethan Jig*, 352–57.

32. Baskervill, *Elizabethan Jig*, 109–10.

33. "Since Kempe created the role of Bottom, "we can well imagine that, being the comedian that he was, and an excellent dancer as well, he probably put in the Bergomask acrobatic [as well as] clownish features," Sorell, *Dance*, 30.

34. Baskervill, *Elizabethan Jig*, 353.

35. As Richard Helgerson, *Forms of Nationhood: The Elizabethan Writing of England* (Chicago: University of Chicago Press, 1992), 258–59, Kempe's nine days' wonder was, in fact, no longer a "popular" form: "Kemp takes over the popular to make it a ground for a new kind of popularity, that of the popular celebrity, the famous entertainer. His morris does not depend on any communal festivity. . . . Instead of expressing holiday merriment . . . Kemp's morris is a measured and

certified . . . athletic accomplishment, widely advertised in advance to draw large and generous crowds."

36. Barber, *Shakespeare's Festive Comedy*, 138, suggests that two distinct dances are involved here, a round and a procession. Titania "seems to start a circling dance [for] by contrast with Oberon's 'after me,' she calls for 'hand in hand.'" Oberon, however, proposes that the fairies dance the processional form of the early linked dance, for he instructs "each fairy" to "stray" through the house "until the break of day" (5.1.401–2).

37. See Jean-Christophe Agnew, *Worlds Apart: The Market and the Theatre in Anglo-American Thought, 1550–1750* (Cambridge: Cambridge University Press, 1986), on the oral contracts of the medieval marketplace, esp. 29, and the transactions in the early modern playhouse, 110–11.

38. Leimberg notes ("Give me thy hand," 126), that the sense of Titania's gesture is "confirmed as well as slightly persiflaged when Puck as Chorus wants to establish friendship across the footlights."

39. Agnew, *Worlds Apart*, 37.

40. Patterson, *Shakespeare*, 69.

41. The epilogue of *Henry IV, Part II* promises the audience to "dance out of your debt" (5.5); see Baskervill, *Elizabethan Jig*, esp. 3–6 and 106–7, on the stage jig as afterpiece.

42. On the dancing in *Much Ado*, see Harry Berger Jr., in "Against the Sink-a-Pace: Sexual and Family Politics in *Much Ado About Nothing*," *Shakespeare Quarterly* 33 (1982): 302–13; and Harold Jenkins, "The Ball Scene in *Much Ado About Nothing*," in *Shakespeare: Text, Language, Criticism*, ed. Bernard Fabian and Kurt Tetzeli von Rosador (Hildesheim; Olms, 1987). On issues of gender, see Jean E. Howard, "Renaissance Antitheatricality and the Politics of Gender and Rank in *Much Ado About Nothing*," in *Shakespeare Reproduced*, ed. Jean E. Howard and Marion F. O'Connor (London: Methuen, 1987); Carol Cook, "The Sign and Semblance of Her Honor," *PMLA* 101 (1986), 186–202; Carol Thomas Neely, *Broken Nuptials in Shakespeare's Plays* (New Haven: Yale University Press, 1985); and Janice Hays, "Those 'Soft and Delicate Desires': *Much Ado* and the Distrust of Women," *The Woman's Part: Feminist Criticism of Shakespeare*, ed. Carolyn Ruth Swift Lenz, Gayle Greene, and Carol Thomas Neely (Urbana: University of Illinois Press, 1980).

43. Brissenden, *Shakespeare and the Dance*, 50–51.

44. See Berger, "Against the Sink-a-Pace," 312–13 and Brissenden, *Shakespeare and the Dance*, 52.

45. Harry Berger Jr., "Against the Sink-a-Pace," reads the passage as an admonition against the circumstances and effects of patriarchal marriage, "[t]he state and ancientry of the wedding indicate the influence of the older generation, the father's interest in and control of the alliance that seals his daughter's future," which concludes in the "decelerating sink-a-pace of the yoke of boredom" (302).

46. See Baskervill, *Elizabethan Jig*, 12, and "The New Scotch-Jigg: or, The Bonny Cravat," 398–401.

47. Davies, "*Orchestra*," stanza 83.

48. Ibid., stanza 112.

49. Jean Howard observes ("Renaissance Antitheatricality," 173) that the play

"seems to dramatize the social consequences of staging lies," an observation as relevant to the staging of dancing as to the issue of antitheatricality.

50. Jenkins suggests that in its "disguisings and impersonations [the dance is] the symbol of the play's larger action in which the characters move or are steered towards or away from a union in marriage" ("Ball Scene," 98).

51. Brissenden notes that the dialogue falls into four sections of four lines each and a concluding line, the length of a "measure" of dance music, spoken in turn as each couple dances: "The scene is structured so that the dialogue fits the movements of a dance, most conveniently one that is relatively slow, in duple time, and with four or eight figures. A pavan is the obvious choice . . . for in that elegant perambulation the couples can be side by side with hands linked at arms length and the steps involve turns back and forth, retreats and advances, so that it is ideal for highlighting dramatic conversation" (*Shakespeare and the Dance,* 49).

52. Brissenden (ibid.) sees the dance as enacting the dialogue, with Hero walking alongside Don Pedro when she says "I am yours for the walk" and pulling away when she says "and especially when I walk away." Jenkins agrees that "[i]t seems clear that the play envisages a correspondance between steps and speech that will enhance the effect of both" ("Ball Scene," 106).

53. Berger suggests that Hero's conditions constitute a "self-description" ("Against the Sink-a-Pace," 303).

54. Jenkins, "Ball Scene," 109–10.

55. Ibid., 110–11.

56. Jenkins points out that "with three of the four couples the point of the dialogue lies in the man' concealment of his identity and the woman's attempt to detect it" ("Ball Scene," 103).

57. Brissenden (*Shakespeare and the Dance,* 50) observes that "they," not Beatrice, became "engrossed with each other, stopped dancing and just talked (or rather, Beatrice has)"; Jenkins cites Brissenden's supposition that "this couple actually stop dancing" ("Ball Scene," 112).

58. Arbeau, *Orchesography,* 52 and 57.

59. There is an opening for a few dance steps here, and a cue: Margaret's "I scorn that with my heels" (51), Margaret's proposal of a lively dance is sufficient to make the point. In the Riverside edition, "Light 'o Love" is glossed as "a popular song."

60. "Why, how now, cousin, wherefore sink you down," asks Beatrice with alarm as Hero faints (4.1.110).

61. Jenkins, "Ball Scene," 112.

62. Berger, "Against the Sink-a-Pace," 312.

63. For another view, see Carol Thomas Neely, *Broken Nuptials,* 56, who sees Beatrice as one of the "strong, articulate women [who] are subdued at the ends of their comedies."

FOUR. THE NERVY LIMBS OF ELIZABETH CARY

1. Elizabeth Cary, Lady Falkland, *The Tragedy of Mariam, The Fair Queen of Jewry, with The Lady Falkland: Her Life,* ed. Barry Weller and Margaret W. Ferguson (Berkeley and Los Angeles: University of California Press, 1994), and *The Tragedy*

of Mariam, the Faire Queen of Jewry, Malone Society Reprints, ed. A. C. Dunstan and W. W. Greg (Oxford: Oxford University Press, 1914); citations to Weller and Ferguson. Elizabeth Cary and her writing have engendered much splendid scholarship to which I am indebted, especially to Margaret W. Ferguson's introduction to the play, "Running On With Almost Public Voice: The Case of 'E.C.,'" in *Tradition and the Talents of Women,* ed. Florence Howe (Urbana: University of Illinois Press, 1991), 37–67, "A Room Not Their Own: Renaissance Women as Readers and Writers," in *The Comparative Perspective on Literary Approaches to Theory and Practice,* ed. Clayton Koelb and Susan Noakes (Ithaca: Cornell University Press, 1985), and "The Spectre of Resistance," in *Staging the Renaissance: Reinterpretations of Elizabethan and Jacobean Drama,* ed. David Scott Kastan and Peter Stallybrass (New York: Routledge, 1991); Barbara Lewalski, *Writing Women in Jacobean England* (Cambridge: Harvard University Press, 1993); Betty S. Travitsky, "The *Feme Covert* in Elizabeth Cary's *Mariam,*" in *Ambiguous Realities: Women in the Middle Ages and Renaissance,* ed. Carole Levin and Jeanie Watson (Detroit: Wayne State University Press, 1987); Nancy Cotton Pearse, "Elizabeth Cary, Renaissance Playwright," *Texas Studies in Literature and Language* 18, no. 4 (1977); Sandra K. Fischer in "Elizabeth Cary and Tyranny, Domestic and Religious," in *Silent But for the Word,* ed. Margaret Patterson Hannay (Kent: Kent State University Press, 1985); Elaine V. Beilin in "Elizabeth Cary and *The Tragedy of Mariam,*" *Papers on Language and Literature* 16, no. 1 (1980), 45–64; Donald W. Foster, "Resurrecting the Author: Elizabeth Tanfield Cary," in *Privileging Gender in Early Modern England;* and Catherine Belsey, *The Subject of Tragedy: Identity and Difference in Renaissance Tragedy* (London: Methuen, 1985).

2. In a relevant analysis, Ann Rosalind Jones, "Nets and Bridles: Early Modern Conduct Books and Sixteenth-Century Women's Lyrics," in *The Ideology of Conduct,* ed. Nancy Armstrong and Leonard Tennenhouse (London: Methuen, 1987), links changing social formations to the conflicting prescriptions for female behavior presented in Continental conduct books, and examines the ways in which these contradictory dictates were negotiated in women's lyric poetry. Patricia Parker, in *Literary Fat Ladies: Rhetoric, Gender, Property* (London: Methuen, 1987), 7 and 8, refers to the applicable concept of "mimicry," formulated by Luce Irigaray, *This Sex Which Is Not One,* translated by Catherine Porter (Ithaca: Cornell University Press, 1977, 1985), 76–77, as a way of making the invisible become visible, and of converting subordination into affirmation.

3. On Cary's life, see *The Lady Falkland* and Ferguson's introduction, 1–8, Beilin, "Elizabeth Cary," 49–52, Pearse, "Elizabeth Cary," 601–2, and Fischer, "Elizabeth Cary," 225–28.

4. Lady Fanshawe, for example, records in her diary that she was educated "with all the advantages that time afforded, both for working all sorts of fine work with my needle, and learning French, singing, [the] lute, the virginals, and dancing," in *The Memoirs of Ann Lady Fanshawe, 1600–1672* (1676), printed from manuscript (London: John Lane, 1907), 22.

5. On Cary's friendship with the Duke and Duchess of Buckingham, see Ferguson's introduction, 15, and *The Lady Falkland,* 211; Fischer, "Elizabeth Cary," 230, notes Cary's enjoyment of Sir Henry's appearance in a court masque in 1612.

6. Joan Kelly, "Did Women Have a Renaissance?" in *Women, History, and Theory: The Essays of Joan Kelly* (Chicago: University of Chicago Press, 1984), 35, notes that Renaissance humanist education placed girls as well as boys under a "male cultural authority" who promoted classical culture "with all its patriarchal and misogynous bias."

7. Judith Fetterly, *The Resisting Reader: A Feminist Approach to American Fiction* (Bloomington: Indiana University Press, 1978), xx, writes of "the *immasculation* of women by men. As readers and teachers and scholars, women are taught to think as men, to identify with a male point of view, and to accept as normal and legitimate a male system of values, one of whose central principles is misogyny."

8. Clifford's letter is reprinted in G. C. Williamson's *George, Third Earl of Cumberland (1558–1605), His Life and Voyages* (Cambridge: Cambridge University Press, 1920), 285–88; the reference to dancing is also noted by Lewalski, *Writing Women*, 136. Clifford's invocation of the movements of the measures as a formal paradigm is similar to Cary's, though Cary's references are more specific.

9. Margaret Cavendish, duchess of Newcastle, *The World's OLIO*, STC 1658; I thank Kim Hall for the reference.

10. John Davies, *The Muses Sacrifice or Divine Meditations* (London: for George Norton, 1612), quoted in Dunstan's introduction to Elizabeth Cary, *The Tragedy*, xvi–ii, who asserts that the poem's dedication "proves conclusively that Lady Falkland is the author of the play," xvi. Davies of Hereford was a poet and writing master, not the author of "*Orchestra.*"

11. Ferguson, "Running On," 44–45, suggests that the poem is problematic in that "by praising a member of a class at the expense of that class ('the weaker Sexe') he implicitly places the woman in the double-bind situation: achievement is bought at the price of dissociation from what the culture considers to be one's nature. . . . Davies further complicates his exhortation to female publication by suggesting that it may involve a derogation of noble status, and, in particular, a danger to female chastity . . . [his] phrasing surround[ing] publication with an aura of unseemly sexual importunity."

12. Elaine V. Beilin, *Redeeming Eve: Women Writers of the English Renaissance* (Princeton: Princeton University Press, 1987), 157, among many others. Barbara Lewalski suggests that "[a]n inner conflict between domestic subservience and intellectual independence offers itself readily enough as an explanation for her periods of depression, manifested in long spells of sleeping" (*Writing Women*, 184). Significantly, Cary's heroine dies by decapitation: "Her body is divided from her head" (5.90).

13. For important discussions of the play in relation to the issue of the woman's voice, see especially Ferguson, "Resistance," 236–39, "Running," 47–49, and "Room," 107; Beilin, "Elizabeth Cary," 53; Foster, "Resurrecting the Author," 154–57, and Belsey, *Subject of Tragedy*, 171–75.

14. Lewalski, *Writing Women*, 181.

15. On the morality-like triangulation of female speakers in the play, with Mariam confronted with the options of Graphina as Virtue and Salome as Vice, see Ferguson, "Running On," 47, and Beilin, "Elizabeth Cary," 55 and 57.

16. My analysis of the opening soliloquy is profoundly indebted to the discus-

sions of Ferguson, "Resistance," 238, "Running On," 48–49, "Room," 106–7, and Foster, "Resurrecting the Author," 149–51.

17. See Vigarello, "Upward Training," 150, 152, and 154; and Alice Jardine, "Death Sentences: Writing Couples and Ideology," in *The Female Body in Western Culture: Contemporary Perspectives* (Cambridge: Harvard University Press, 1985, 1986), 85–86, who suggests that the couple is a model for all Western metaphysical systems.

18. Dunstan, introduction to Elizabeth Cary, *The Tragedy*, vi–vii.

19. *Regola IV*, "On Asking a Lady to Dance," *Le Gratie d'Amore* (1602), D3v, 42.

20. See Chapter 1, n. 21 on the middle-class homebound woman (Dod and Cleaver, *Household Government*), and Arbeau on the *galliard* (*Orchesography*, 77). Even when the lady was permitted to perform some of the same steps as the gentleman in a *balletto*, invariably she performed them after him in a kind of echo, and, of course, in miniature, as the dances in Caroso's *Nobilità di Dame*, especially "*Forza d'Amore*," 230–31, *Le Gratie d'Amore*, and *Apologie de la Danse*, attest.

21. *Regola V*, "Warning a Lady Not to Touch Her Skirt While Dancing," D4v, 45.

22. On these details of women's deportment, see especially de Lauze, *Apologie de la Danse*, 131, 133, and 137, and Caroso, *Nobilità di Dame*, 144.

23. Earlier garments followed the outline of the body, but by the middle of the sixteenth century, notes Vigarello ("Upward Training," 155), corsets and whalebone stays imposed onto the body a conventional shape. The bodies of children were "shaped" by means of swaddling clothes and corrective iron corsets, and of those of adult women by the addition of cotton and the constriction of laces (168–76).

24. The lady's chopines peek out from under her dress in "Asking a Lady to Dance." Caroso is concerned with the management of chopines (*Nobilità di Dame*, 141). "Now in order to walk nicely, and to wear chopines properly on one's feet, so that they do not twist or go awry (for if one is ignorant of how to wear them, one may splinter them, or fall frequently) . . . it is better for [the lady] to raise the toe of the foot she moves when she takes a step, for by raising thus, she straightens the knee of that foot, and this extension keeps her body attractive and erect, besides which her chopine will not fall off that foot. . . . In this way, and by observing [this rule], she may move entirely with grace, seemliness, and beauty, better than the way one walked before; for a natural step is one thing, but a well-ordered step is another. By walking this way, therefore, even if the lady's chopines are more than a handbreadth-and-a-half high, she will seem to be on chopines only three fingerbreadths high, and will be able to dance *flourishes* and galliard variations at a ball." In *The Lady Falkland*, 248, Cary is reported to have given up wearing chopines after the death of her husband.

25. Arbeau, *Orchesography*, 18.

26. See Donna Wilshire on the "hierarchical dualisms," legacy of Aristotle and Aquinas, "The Uses of Myth, Image, and the Female Body in Re-visioning Knowledge," in *Gender/Body/Knowledge*, ed. Jaggar and Bordo, 95.

27. See Arbeau, *Orchesography*, 7, and Caroso, *Nobilità di Dame*, 96–97.

28. Caroso, *Nobilità di Dame*, 88–89.

29. Arbeau, *Orchesography,* 16; see also 7, and Caroso, *Nobilità di Dame,* 96–97.

30. Except for Arena's, of course. Franko notes the absence of the body from the treatises, *Dancing Body,* 9–10, and its replacement by a stylized image; choreographic movement as effect was substituted for body movement as process; in dancing, as in civility, the courtier was always already flawless. The *sprezzatura* of Castiglione, which Whigham calls "the master trope of the courtier" (*Ambition and Privilege,* 93), also emphasized the appearance of effortlessness, and similarly privileged effect over process.

31. Foster suggests ("Resurrecting the Author," 159) that Miriam's face is a silent text that is not her own.

32. See Ferguson, "Resistance," 242, and "Room," 109, on verbal license.

33. Ferguson, "Running On," 53, observes that the image "rewrites Mariam's fault as one of double excess or 'openness,' whereas what the play actually shows is that Mariam's verbal openness is a sign of sexual closure."

34. George Chapman, *Bussy D'Ambois,* ed. Nicholas Brooke, Revels Plays (Cambridge: Harvard University Press, 1964). However, unlike Cary, Chapman did presume the presence of a paying audience.

35. Josephus, *Jewish Antiquities,* trans. Ralph Marcus, vol. 8, books 15–17 (Cambridge: Harvard University Press, 1963). In Josephus, more than a year passes between Herod's return and the Salome's gift of the love-potion, 105–7. In the introduction to the Malone Society edition, A. C. Dunstan acknowledges alterations "to simplify the story and to observe the unities" (introduction to Elizabeth Cary, *The Tragedy,* xiii); Beilin, "Elizabeth Cary," 53, notes Cary's compression of events to maintain the unity of time, and discusses similarities to the morality play, 62.

36. See *The Writings of Fulke Greville,* ed. Joan Rees (London: Athlone, 1973), introduction (6) and *Mustapha, Chorus Quintus, Tartarurum* and *Chorus Sacerdotum* in *Poems and Dramas of Fulke Greville first lord Brooke,* ed. Geoffrey Bullough (Edinburgh: Oliver and Boyd, 1939) (137–38). Pearse ("Elizabeth Cary," 606), Fischer ("Elizabeth Cary," 228), and many others note the connection between Cary and the Duchess.

37. Pearse, "Elizabeth Cary," 64.

38. Elam, *Shakespeare's Universe,* discusses the schematic connections between poetry and dancing in his chapter on "Figures," noting the potential of "phonemic iteration" to "materialize the form of expression . . . crucial in an oral art like the theatre," and suggesting that it may also function to "order and segment the very form of the content" (244).

39. Elam, *Shakespeare's Universe,* 254.

40. See Carol Cook's remarks on the textualization of the body in "Unbodied Figures of Desire" in *Performing Feminism: Feminist Critical Theory and Theory,* ed. Sue-Ellen Case (Baltimore: Johns Hopkins University Press, 1990), 192–93.

FIVE. REHEARSING FOR EMPIRE

1. References to Jonson's masques are from C. H. Hereford, Percy Simpson, and Evelyn Simpson, *Ben Jonson,* 11 vols. (Oxford: Clarendon, 1925–52); *The Masque of Queens,* 7:354–62.

2. Welsford, *Court Masque,* observes that "[t]he *Masque of Queens* fixed the norm of the masque for some years. From 1609 to 1617 [the masques showed] the same careful structure and unity of design" (188); see also Orgel's *Jonsonian Masque,* 14, 35, 72–73, and 117, and Sabol's *Songs and Dances from the Stuart Masque,* 11–14. The city masque was structured differently, and eliminated the interludes of courtly dancing.

3. On the implications of female impersonation in the antimasque, see Suzanne Gossett, "'Man-Maid, Begone!': Women in Masques," *English Literary Renaissance* 18 (Winter 1988): 96–113.

4. Orgel's *Jonsonian Masque* and *The Illusion of Power: Political Theater in the English Renaissance* (Berkeley and Los Angeles: University of California Press, 1975), Roy Strong's *Art and Power,* D. J. Gordon, *The Renaissance Imagination: Essays and Lectures,* collected and ed. Stephen Orgel (Berkeley and Los Angeles: University of California Press, 1975), and Jonathan Goldberg, *James I and the Politics of Literature* (Stanford: Stanford University Press, 1989).

5. See especially Leah Sinanoglou Marcus, "'Present Occasions' and the Shaping of Ben Jonson's Masques," *ELH* 45 (1978): 201–25, *The Politics of Mirth: Jonson, Herrick, Milton, Marvell, and the Defense of Old Holiday Pastimes* (Chicago: University of Chicago Press, 1978), and "Masquing Occasions and Masque Structure," *Research Opportunities in Renaissance Drama* 24 (1981): 7–16. Stephen Orgel, "Jonson and the Amazons," in *Soliciting Interpretation: Literary Theory and Seventeenth-Century Poetry,* ed. Elizabeth D. Harvey and Katherine Eisaman Maus (Chicago: University of Chicago Press, 1991); and the essays in *The Court Masque,* ed. David Lindley (Manchester: Manchester University Press, 1984). The strains of masque criticism often overlap: in *Politics of Mirth,* Marcus argues that the masque was not merely a simple celebration of the monarch, but allowed the expression of subversive impulses which were inevitably "quelled by the intervention of some reforming energy associated with the policy and person of the king" (9–10), related to the royal policy, articulated in the statutes that became known as the *Book of Sports* (1618, 1633), of harnessing the energies of popular festivity in the interests of state power.

6. Marion Wynne-Davies, "The Queen's Masque: Renaissance Women and the Seventeenth-Century Court Masque," in *Gloriana's Face: Women, Public and Private, in the English Renaissance,* ed. S. P. Cerasano and Marion Wynne-Davies (Detroit: Wayne State University Press, 1992), argues that the "court masque was a cultural construct which allowed the women of the court, and specifically the Queen, access to a politically resonant discourse. Their penetration into this exclusively masculine field . . . questioned the legitimacy of absolute male power as symbolized by the Stuart King" (80). In *Writing Women,* Barbara Keifer Lewalski likewise sees certain early Jonsonian masques as an expression of feminine opposition to the patriarchal court.

7. On the court masque as colonial practice, see Kim Hall, "Sexual Politics and Cultural Identity in *The Masque of Blackness,*" in *The Performance of Power: Theatrical Discourse and Politics,* ed. Sue-Ellen Case and Janelle Reinelt (Iowa City: University of Iowa Press, 1991), and *Things of Darkness: Economies of Race and Gender in Early Modern England* (Ithaca: Cornell University Press, 1995); Yumna Siddiqui, "Dark Incontinents: The Discourses of Race and Gender in Three Renaissance Masques,"

Renaissance Drama 23, ed. Mary Beth Rose (Evanston: Northwestern University Press, 1992); and Anthony Gerard Barthelemy's *Black Face, Maligned Race* (Baton Rouge: Louisiana State University Press, 1987).

8. Historical sources include Peter Hulme, *Colonial Encounters: Europe and the Native Carribean, 1492–1797* (London: Methuen, 1986); K. R. Andrews, N. P. Canny, and P. E. H. Hair, eds., *The Westward Enterprise: English Activities in Ireland, the Atlantic, and America 1480–1650* (Liverpool: Liverpool University Press, 1978); David B. Quinn, *Explorers and Colonies: America, 1500–1625* (London: Hambledon, 1991, esp. 421–23; J. H. Parry, *The Age of Reconnaissance* (Berkeley and Los Angeles: University of California Press, 1963, 1981), and *The Establishment of the European Hegemony: 1415–1715,* 3d ed. (New York: Harper Torchbooks, 1966); James Axtell, "The Invasion Within: The Contest of Cultures in Colonial North America," in *The European and the Indian: Essays in the Ethnohistory of Colonial North America* (Oxford: Oxford University Press, 1981), and Louis B. Wright, *Middle-Class Culture in Elizabethan England* (Chapel Hill: University of North Carolina Press, 1935; repr. Ithaca: Cornell University Press, 1958), 508–48.

9. Jonson, *Pleasure Reconciled to Virtue,* in *Ben Jonson,* ed. Hereford, Simpson, and Simpson, 7:221–23.

10. On "virgin land" as "blank page," see Louis Montrose, in "The Work of Gender in the Discourse of Discovery," *Representations* 33 (Winter 1991): 8.

11. On colonialist discourse, see Hulme, *Colonial Encounters;* Stephen Greenblatt, *Marvelous Possessions: The Wonder of the New World* (Chicago: University of Chicago Press, 1991); Ania Loomba, *Gender, Race, Renaissance Drama* (Manchester: Manchester University Press, 1989); and Tzvetan Todorov, *The Conquest of America: The Question of the Other,* trans. Richard Howard (New York: Harper and Row, 1984). On the dark-and-light imagery of the masques, see Hall, "Sexual Politics," Siddiqui, "Dark Incontinents," and Abdul R. JanMohammed, "The Economy of Manichean Allegory: The Function of Racial Difference in Colonialist Literature," in *"Race," Writing, and Difference,* ed. Henry Louis Gates Jr. (Chicago: University of Chicago Press, 1985), 83. On the transcoding of the body, see Peter Stallybrass, "Patriarchal Territories," and Stallybrass and Allon White, *The Politics and Poetics of Transgression* (Ithaca: Cornell University Press, 1986), 21–26; on over-flowing female bodies, see Parker, *Literary Fat Ladies,* Hall "Sexual Politics," and Siddiqui, "Dark Incontinents." Stephen J. Greenblatt, "Learning to Curse: Aspects of Linguistic Colonialism in the Sixteenth Century," in *First Images of America: The Impact of the New World on the Old,* vol. 2, ed. Ferdi Chiappelli, Michael J. B. Allen and Robert Benson (Berkeley and Los Angeles: University of California Press, 1976), and Terence Hawkes, "Swisser-Swatter: Making a Man of English Letters," in *Alternative Shakespeares,* ed. John Drakakis (London: Methuen, 1985), discuss the colonialism of "English Letters," and Jonathan Goldberg, *Writing Matter,* and Parker, *Literary Fat Ladies,* also emphasize the connections between writing, power, and self-definition.

12. Montrose discusses the conflation of discourses in "Work of Gender," 1, 8, and 19.

13. Stephen Mullaney, "Strange Things, Gross Terms, Curious Customs: The

Rehearsal of Cultures in the Late Renaissance," in *Representing the English Renaissance,* ed. Stephen Greenblatt (Berkeley and Los Angeles: University of California Press, 1988), 73, explains "cultural rehearsal" as "a period of free-play during which alternatives can be staged, unfamiliar roles tried out, the range of one's power to convince or persuade explored with some license; it is a period of performance, but one in which the customary demands of decorum are suspended, along with expectations of final and perfect form." Mullaney refers to events rather than representations; in the masque decorum is primary while the danger of actual exploration is suspended, but the mechanism is similar.

14. Thomas Smith, *De Republica Anglorum; A Discourse on the Commonwealth of England,* London, 1583, ed. L. Alston (Cambridge, 1906; New York: Barnes and Noble, 1974), chap. 24: "day laborers, poor husbandmen, merchants or retailers [who] have no free land, copyholders, and all artificers. These have no voice or authority in our commonwealth, and no account is made of them but only to be ruled."

15. Michel Foucault, "Of Other Spaces," *Diacritics* 16 (Spring 1986): 22–25.

16. On Renaissance maps and geography, see R. V. Tooley, *Maps and Map-Makers* (New York: Bonanza Books, 1949, 1961), 6–8; Parry, *Reconnaissance,* 195–213; J. R. Hale, *Renaissance Exploration* (New York: Norton, 1968), 14–15; and C. Raymond Beazley, in *The Dawn of Modern Geography: A History of Exploration and Geographical Science,* vol. 3, *1260–1420* (Oxford: Clarendon, 1906), 512. On the ideological significance of chorographic developments, Helgerson's *Forms of Nationhood,* and John Gillies, *Shakespeare and the Geography of Difference* (Cambridge: Cambridge University Press, 1994).

17. J. R. Hale, *Renaissance Europe* (Berkeley and Los Angeles: University of California Press, 1977), 51.

18. See Parry, *Reconnaissance,* 34, and Hale, *Renaissance Europe,* 53.

19. Strong, *Art and Power,* 33.

20. Hale, *Renaissance Europe,* 51–52.

21. E. H. Gombrich, *Norm and Form* (London: Phaidon, 1966), 108–9.

22. Crooke, *Microcosmographia,* 6, explains that man's navel is the center of a perfect circle and a perfect square (a compass set upon it passes through thumbs and toes, which also mark the corners of a perfect quadrant, and "if in any part this proportion fails, you may imagine a defect in this part."

23. Foucault, "Other Spaces," 23, not written of the measures, but applicable.

24. Joan Wildeblood, Introduction, *Apologie de la Danse by F. de Lauze,* 1623 (London: Frederich Muller, 1952) 25, cites Marin Mersenne, *Harmonie Universelle* (1636), on the French dances of his time: *passamezzas, pavanes, allemands, sarabands, voltes, courantes, canaries, bransles,* and *ballets;* his description of the *sarabande,* 31; and the Duchess's letter, 20.

25. Arbeau, *Orchesography,* 179–80. The lengthy conflict between Portugal and Spain for Madeira and the Canary Islands, long the outer border of the Mediterranean world, was finally settled in 1478, when as Hulme observes (*Colonial Encounters,* 37), in a "significant precedent" of Spain's later expansion in the America the Canaries were ceded to Castile. However, as Parry, *Age of Reconnaissance* 20 and

137, and Hulme (*Colonial Encounters,* 37) observe, the native Guanches were an intractable people, so uncooperative in support of European economic interests as to necessitate another "significant precedent," the importation of African labor to establish a profitable sugar trade.

26. See Montrose, "Work of Gender," especially 2–4; Parker, *Literary Fat Ladies,* 2; and Loomba, *Gender,* 78. Hulme (*Colonial Encounters,* 8–9) and many others observe that "America" is the feminine form of Amerigo Vespucci. The *canary* enacted obliteration as well as domination: Arbeau writes (*Orchesography,* 80) that the *tappements* were varied with a movement that finished "by scraping the foot backwards along the ground as if one were treading down spittle or killing a spider."

27. Helgerson, "The Land Speaks," 327.

28. All dances changed over time, as in the case of the *pavane,* which started as a slow, stately processional but consonant with changing tastes grew livelier as faster dances became more popular, so it is difficult to generalize about any dance. In the sixteenth century, the *coranto* was characterized by a vertical "springing" step later supplemented by the *pas chassé,* in which one leg "chased" the other across the floor, writes Arbeau (*Orchesography,* 123–25); on the seventeenth-century *coranto,* see Caroso, *Nobilità di Dame* and de Lauze, *Apologie de la Danse* 89–99. Later in century, the *coranto* became a slow, stately dance performed by one couple at a time, writes Wildeblood in the introduction, 25. See also Andrew Sabol on the *coranto* and its music in "The Original Music for the French King's Masque in *Love's Labour Lost,*" in *Shakespeare's Universe: Renaissance Ideas and Conventions. Essays in Honour of W. R. Elton,* ed. John M. Mucciolo with Stephen J. Doloff and Edward A. Rauchet (Brookfield, Vt.: Scolar, 1996), 207–23.

29. Davies, "*Orchestra,*" stanza 69.

30. Balthezar de Beaujoyeulx, *Le Balet Comique de la Royne,* facsimile with introduction and translation by Margaret McGowan (Binghamton, N.Y.: Center for Medieval and Early Renaissance Texts and Studies, 1982). On figured dancing and its ideological work in the French court masque, see Mark Franko, *Dance as Text,* 15–31.

31. Strong, *Art and Power,* 120.

32. As in the case of the "Druid alphabet" in the *Ballet de M. de Vendosme* (1610); see Margaret McGowan, *L'Art de Ballet de Cour en France, 1581–1643* (Paris: Edition du Centre National de la Recherche Scientifique, 1963), 74–75, and Meagher, *Method and Meaning,* 96–97.

33. Dedication to the Countess of Bedford, *The Complete Works of Samuel Daniel,* edited by Alexander B. Grosart (New York: Russell and Russell, 1963), 194–95.

34. Lindley, *Court Masque,* 5.

35. Franko, *Dance as Text,* 30–31.

36. See Hall, "Sexual Politics" 15 and Siddiqui, "Dark Incontinents," 141. The masques are printed as companion pieces in the Quarto, though three years separate their performances. As Wynne-Davies notes ("Queen's Masque," 89), this was not the first use of black paint in court masque: Hall, *Chronicle,* records an instance in 1510. Wynne-Davies, "Queen's Masque," 88–89, and Lewalski, *Writing Women,* 31–33, read the two masques as subverting, not authorizing, patriarchal power, observing that Jonson credits the queen with the idea, and reporting that the

blackened nymphs were regarded with distaste by the courtiers. "Representing herself and her ladies as black African beauties, the Queen associates them with alien cultural practices and primitive energies, with the feared and desired 'others' as imagined by contemporary explorers," writes Lewalski (*Writing Women,* 32).

37. Siddiqui asserts ("Dark Incontinents," 144), based on the spoken text, that "miscegenation" is forestalled, but the image of dancing couples implies the opposite.

38. Once again, Jonson credits the inclusion of female darkness to the Queen: "Her Majesty . . . had commanded me to think on some dance or show that might precede hers and have the place of a foil," in *Ben Jonson,* ed. Herford, Simpson, and Simpson, 7:282. The masque is recognized as a "tribute" to James's *Demonologie* (Edinburgh, 1597, London, 1603), though as Orgel observes ("Jonson and the Amazons"), one qualified by misattribution (124). Orgel links James's interest in witchcraft with his anxieties over political conspiracies (124–25), and the powerful women who made him king, Mary and Elizabeth (125–26); also see Deborah Willis, *Malevolent Nurture: Witch-Hunting and Maternal Power In Early Modern England,* (Ithaca: Cornell University Press, 1995), "James Among the Witch-Hunters." However, Margaret Maurer, "Reading Ben Jonson's *Queens,*" in *Seeking the Woman in Late Medieval and Renaissance Writings: Essays in Feminist Contextual Criticism,* ed. Sheila Fisher and Janet E. Halley (Knoxville: University of Tennessee Press, 1989), speculates that the antimasque, as an energetic, physical performance by males, might have appealed to James "as much for what it was as for what it represented" (255).

39. See Axtell, "Invasion Within," 49–52, on European attitudes toward North American Indians.

40. Jonson's marginalia cites James's *Demonologie,* but Orgel notes that the source rather seems to be Reginal Scot's *The Discoverie of Witches,* which James attacks ("Amazons" 124).

41. Orgel, *Jonsonian Masque,* 159, observes a similar heaviness in the verse of Comus in *Pleasure Reconciled to Virtue,* and Todorov equates barbarism with bad pronunciation (*Conquest of America,* 190).

42. Orgel, *Jonsonian Masque,* 46.

43. Jonson's stage directions for the reader doubly contain this spectacle of feminine unruliness with the frame of masculine mimesis: the dance was "excellently imitated by the maker of the dance, Mr. Hierome Herne, whose right it is here to be named" (351–53).

44. Davies, "*Orchestra,*" stanza 64.

45. Orgel, "Amazons," 124, observes that "the transition from witches to queens comes . . . without even a confrontation. Hulme (*Colonial Encounters,* 8) and many others note the "speed and scale" of the destruction of indigenous societies.

46. See Orgel, "Amazons," on the literary, mythological, and pictorial traditions from which Jonson draws (126–32), in a way that "subverts the queen's interests" but "fully supports the king's" (130).

47. On "militant female virtue," see Orgel, "Amazons," 123. Sir Walter Raleigh. *The History of the World* (London, 1652), book 4, chap. 2, part 15, "Of Thalestris, Queen of the Amazons, where, by way of digression, it is showed that

such Amazons have been, and are" affirms their existance in the New World, and Celeste Turner Wright, "The Amazons in Elizabethan Literature," *Studies in Philology* 37, no. 3 (July 1940): 433–56, compiles the references. Also see Montrose's discussion in "Work of Gender," 25–27, where he notes that the "Amazonian anticulture precisely inverts European norms of political authority, sexual license, marriage and child-rearing practices, and inheritance rules" (26).

48. Gossett, "Man-Maid, Begone!" 101.

49. John Bulwer, *A View of the People of the Whole World* (*Man Transformed: Or, the Artificial Changeling*) (London, 1654), earlier titled *Anthropometamorphosis,* offers a view of both Amazonian possibilities, 332.

50. Davies, "*Orchestra,*" stanza 112.

51. "Their free movement and challenging speech—their very actions and language—are constrained and denied in a final reassertion of the containment of women," writes Wynne-Davies ("Queen's Masque," 84).

52. Hulme, *Colonial Encounters,* 99.

53. In a provocative essay that diverges from both political and feminist critical traditions, Margaret Maurer ("Reading") argues that the *Masque of Queens* "is the occasion of a particularly belabored struggle . . . to represent women . . . meaningfully" (235), women of the court who are best "known for their trivialized version of manly pursuits" (246); she sees the figures at the end of the masque as an emblem of female triviality: "it is hard to imagine less consequential action than a dance graphically disposing letters spelling out the name of Prince Charles" (256).

54. Richard Braithwait, *Natures Embassie; or, the Wilde-Man's Measures* (London, printed for Richard Whittaker, 1621), STC 3571, Folger Shakespeare Library. I thank Kim Hall for the reference.

55. The Morris was believed to have been of Moorish origin and imported from Spain; see E. K. Chambers, *Mediaeval Stage,* 1:195–98, entries on the Morris in Robert Chambers, *Book of Days* and Brand, *Popular Antiquities,* and Arbeau, *Orchesography,* 177–79. Darkness and femininity were both linked with unrestrained sexuality; Barthelemy (*Black Face*) emphasizes that "African licentiousness" was a commonplace (6, 92–93, and 121–23). The spectacle of masculine vitality that Maruer ("Reading") sees as a possible allure of the antimasque (255), may also operate here: Bruce Smith, *Homosexual Desire,* 122–25, suggests that a homoerotic element was encoded in the pantomime version of the Morris dance, a suggestion that may also apply to the Satyrs' dance.

56. Michael Neill, "Broken English and Broken Irish: Nation, Language, and the Optic of Power in Shakespeare's Histories," *Shakespeare Quarterly* 45, no. 1 (Spring 1994): 1–32, discusses the "barbarity" of Irish utterance as defining sign of bestial otherness (7 and 15). Also see Philip Edwards, *Threshold of a Nation: A Study in English and Irish Drama* (Cambridge: Cambridge University Press, 1979), and David Lindley, "Embarrassing Ben: The Masques for Frances Howard," in *Renaissance Historicism,* ed. Arthur F. Kinney and Dan S. Collins (Amherst: University of Massachusetts Press, 1986), 248–64.

57. Historical material from Nicholas Canny, "The Permissive Frontier: Social Control in English Settlements in Ireland and Virginia, 1550–1650," 23–27; Karl S. Bottigheimer, "Kingdom and Colony: Ireland in the Westward Enterprise,

1536–1660," in *The Westward Enterprise,* ed. Andrews, Canny, and Hair; Quinn, *Explorers and Colonies,* especially 101; and Parry, *Reconnaissance,* 208–9 and 286; and Neill, "Broken English."

58. Sir John Davies, *A Discoverie of the True Causes why Ireland was never entirely Subdued, nor brought under Obedience of the Crowne of England until the Beginning of His Majesties happy Reigne* (London: 1612), ed. James P. Myers Jr. (Washington: Catholic University Press, 1988).

59. Ibid., 24–30.

60. Ibid., 49.

61. By James's time a wave of Scottish immigration to Ireland had resulted in a rather thick-speaking settling class.

62. See Edwards, *Threshold,* 8–13, on the absurd fantasy that an Irish bard, as a high-status poet of Irish nationalism, would serve the English.

63. Neill, "Broken English," 25, quotes Fynes Moryson's warning that the mantle could serve "as a cabin for an outlaw in the woods, a bed for a rebel, and a cloak for a thief."

64. Marcus observes, *Politics of Mirth* 120, that Comus's Cupbearer wore red and Virtue white, and relates this scheme to Anglican symbolism of the via media, which James enlisted in his program for the "measurement" of popular pastimes.

65. Marcus, *Politics of Mirth,* 114.

66. Certainly, masque characters signified in many ways; Marcus, *Politics of Mirth,* persuasively links Comus and his bottles with unregulated pro-sport Catholics, Hercules' actions with James's regulation of sport, and the Pygmies with spoil-sport Puritans (112–15).

67. The crown that Virtue weaves, Penelope-like, to circle Hercules' immortal head (129–30) is a productive containment that repairs Comus's bursting girdles and restores femininity to Virtue that serves patriarchal "measure."

68. See Vigarello, "Upward Training," 179–81 and 150, and Meagher, *Method and Meaning,* 100.

69. Marcus, *Politics of Mirth,* 113 and 115, notes the transformation of Atlas, who is first seen covered with frost and snow (2–3), later with "choicest herbiage" (126).

70. Marcus, *Politics of Mirth,* 124, observes that the pattern of the verse suggests the act of climbing a mountain, to convey the "rigorous responsibility" of the courtier; Whigham suggests, however, that such a "trope of self-sacrifice" served to mystify the power of the gentle and conceal the exploitation of the base (*Ambition and Privilege,* 112).

SIX. MISCHIEFS MASKING IN EXPECTED PLEASURES

1. Relevant discussions of the body are those of Stallybrass, "Patriarchal Tendencies" and "Reading the Body"; Paster, "Leaky Vessels" and *Body Embarrassed;* Parker, *Literary Fat Ladies;* and Jonathan Dollimore, "Subjectivity, Sexuality, and Transgression: The Jacobean Connection," in *Renaissance Drama as Cultural History,* ed. Mary Beth Rose (Evanston: Northwestern University Press, 1990).

2. See Margot Heinemann, *Puritanism and Theatre: Thomas Middleton and Oppo-*

sition Drama under the Early Stuarts (Cambridge: Cambridge University Press, 1980), and "'God Help the Poor: The Rich Can Shift: The World Upside Down and the Popular Tradition in the Theatre, in *The Politics of Tragicomedy,* ed. Gordon McMullen and Jonathan Hope (London: Routledge, 1992); Walter Cohen, "Prerevolutionary Drama" in the same volume; Lawrence Venuti, *Our Halcyon Dayes: English Prerevolutionary Texts and Postmodern Culture* (Madison: University of Wisconsin Press, 1989); Martin Butler, *Theatre and Crisis, 1632–1642* (Cambridge: Cambridge University Press, 1984); Albert Tricomi, *Anticourt Drama in England, 1603–1642* (Charlottesville: University of Virginia Press, 1989); and Theodore Leinwand, *The City Staged: Jacobean Comedy, 1603–1613* (Madison: University of Wisconsin Press, 1986). Pennino-Baskerville, "Terpsichore Reviled," 493, asserts that antidance writing "anticipat[ed] an England under Cromwell and the Puritans."

3. Citations to *The Works of Thomas Middleton,* ed. A. H. Bullen (New York: AMS Press, 1964), except for *Women Beware Women,* ed. Roma Gill (New York: Norton, 1968, 1983). Middleton's only city masque with a dance is *The Triumph of Honor and Industry* (1617), in which antimasque-like Indians cavort around trees as they grow spices for export (7:298), and generally, dancing played little part in these celebrations.

4. On Middleton's life, works, and politics, see Heinemann, *Puritanism* especially 49–55, 76–77, and 126–33; Dorothy M. Farr, *Thomas Middleton and the Drama of Realism* (New York: Harper and Row, 1973), 1–8; and R. H. Barker, *Thomas Middleton* (New York: Columbia University Press, 1958). On the city comedies, see Brian Gibbons, *Jacobean City Comedy: A Study of Satiric Plays by Jonson, Marston, and Middleton,* 2d ed. (London: Methuen, 1980), and on dating the plays, David J. Lake, *The Canon of Thomas Middleton's Plays: Internal Evidence for the Major Problems of Authorship* (London: Cambridge University Press, 1975).

5. Heinemann, *Puritanism,* 14. On social instability, see Lawrence Stone, *The Causes of the English Revolution 1529–1642* (New York: Harper and Row, 1972), "Social Mobility in England, and *The Crisis of the Aristocracy,* 21–64 and 724; Christopher Hill, *Puritanism and Revolution: Studies in the Interpretation of the English Revolution of the Seventeenth Century* (London: Secker and Warburg, 1958), and *The World Turned Upside Down: Radical Ideas During The English Revolution* (Middlesex: Penguin, 1972, 1985); A. L. Beier, "Vagrants and the Social Order in Elizabethan England," *Past and Present* 64 (1974), and *Masterless Men: The Vagrancy Problem in England, 1560–1640* (London: Methuen, 1985); Wrightson, *English Society;* Underdown, *Revel, Riot, and Rebellion;* and Heinemann, *Puritanism,* 3–12 and 31. However, this picture has been challenged, notably by Steve Rappaport, *Worlds Within Worlds: Structures of Life in Sixteenth-Century London* (Cambridge and New York: Cambridge University Press, 1989), who emphasizes London's fundamental stability, even in the troubled 1590s.

6. Heinemann, "Upside-Down," 151, and *Puritanism,* 36–39, asserts that censorship tightened during the Jacobean era, and shows how gesture could supplement the written word. The role of the Spaniard in *The Triumphs of Honor and Industry,* she observes (28–29), "looks quite unremarkable in the text, but according to [the] report [of the Venetian Ambassador Horatio Busoni] he kissed his hand to

the ladies and the Spanish ambassador, and behaved with a ridiculous affected gallantry, which delighted the crowds." Janet Clare, *"Art Made Tongue-Tied by Authority": Elizabethan and Jacobean Dramatic Censorship* (Manchester: Manchester University Press, 1990), suggests that "reading techniques had indeed developed in response to writing strategies constructed so as to evade censorship. Readers were familiar with codes of reference that enabled the writer to comment on prohibited matters" (21), some of which were certainly visual. Martin Butler (*Theatre and Crisis,* 6) also refers to these devices. However, Philip J. Finkelpearl, "'The Comedians' Liberty': Censorship of the Jacobean Stage Reconsidered," in *Renaissance Historicism,* ed. Arthur F. Kinney and Dan. S. Collins (Amherst: University of Massachusetts Press, 1987), argues that Jacobean censorship was not so efficient as has been assumed.

7. Frontispiece to Francis Kirkman, *The Wits, or, Sport Upon Sport* (London, 1632); a variety of national, social, and sexual anxieties were no doubt displaced upon the figure of the French Dancing Master, as a male cultural authority of a "feminizing" practice, and a "stranger" of low social status.

8. John Webster, *The Duchess of Malfi,* 4.11, in *Drama of the English Renaissance,* vol. 2, ed. Russell A. Fraser and Norman Rabkin (New York: Macmillan, 1976). See Frank W. Wadworth, "'Rough Music' in *The Duchess of Malfi*: Webster's Dance of Madmen and the Charivari Tradition," in *Rite, Drama, Festival, Spectacle: Rehearsals Toward a Theory of Cultural Performance,* ed. John A. MacAloon (Philadelphia: Institute for the Study of Human Issues, 1984), on Webster's use of popular rituals in the play.

9. On paradigms of gender and exchange in the play, see Lisa Jardine, *Still Harping on Daughters;* Loomba, *Gender,* 94–103; Heinemann, *Puritanism,* 180–86; and Gill's introduction to Middleton, *Women Beware Women.* And see Coppélia Kahn, "Whores and Wives in Jacobean Drama," and Margaret Lael Mikesell, "The Formative Power of Marriage in Stuart Tragedy," in *In Another Country: Feminist Perspectives on Renaissance Drama,* ed. Dorothea Kehler and Susan Baker (Metuchen, N.J.: Scarecrow, 1991); Catherine Belsey, *Subject of Tragedy;* and Dympna Callaghan, *Women and Gender.*

10. Loomba, *Gender,* 101.

11. Ibid., 102.

12. See Kahn's discussion of these misogynist icons of femininity, "Whores and Wives," 250–51.

13. Middleton, *Works,* ed. Bullen, vol. 7.

14. Middleton, *Women Beware Women,* ed. Gill, xxv.

15. Since neither play has a stage history, they cannot be accurately dated, but *Women Beware Women* is often dated 1621 because of the age of the Duke: James, too, was fifty-five in 1621, and *More Dissemblers Besides Women,* licensed as "an old play" in 1623, has been dated 1615–17; see Middleton, *Works,* ed. Bullen, 6:375.

16. George E. Rowe Jr., *Thomas Middleton and the New Comedy Tradition* (Lincoln: University of Nebraska Press, 1979), 156.

17. Jean E. Howard, "Sex and Social Conflict: The Erotics of *The Roaring Girl,*" in *Erotic Politics: The Dynamics of Desire on the English Renaissance Stage,* ed. Susan

Zimmerman (London: Routledge, 1992), suggests that the disruptive sexuality of the Roaring Girl functions this way.

18. Kahn, "Whores and Wives," 250–51.

19. On homoerotic master-servant relations, see Bruce Smith, *Homosexual Desire,* esp. 192–95, and Mario DiGangi, "Asses and Wits: The Homoerotics of Mastery in Satiric Comedy," *English Literary Renaissance* 25 (1995): 179–208. The cross-dressed boy player underneath the cross-dressed Page further complicates the sexual charge of the scene.

20. See Arthur F. Kinney, *Rogues, Vagabonds, and Sturdy Beggars* (Amherst: University of Massachusetts Press, 1990), and Gibbons, *Jacobean City Comedy,* 11–12 and app. A, on city comedy and the cony-catching pamphlets.

21. Rowe, *Thomas Middleton,* 162.

22. The cornet is associated with military endeavors, writes Arbeau (*Orchesography,* 18), and notes that there is "no workman so humble that he does wish to have hautboys and sackbuts at his wedding," 51.

23. As Rowe points out (*Thomas Middleton,* 172), both "crochet" and "cliffs" were used in relation to female anatomy: a "crochet" was an obstetrical instrument, and "cliffs" referred to female genitalia.

24. See Paster, *Body Embarrassed,* on the "conventional construction of female appetite as greedy at both ends" (60).

25. Rowe cites the *OED* (*Thomas Middleton,* 172).

26. In her discussion of the erotics of *The Roaring Girl* ("Sex and Social Conflict," 22–24), Jean Howard notes that the viol was both gendered—a man's instrument—and eroticized as a variety of "fiddle."

27. de Lauze, *Apologie de la Danse,* 69–71.

28. By the late sixteenth century, good form in dancing demanded the outward rotation of the leg, notes Arbeau (*Orchesography,* 83)—accomplished by means of firm buttocks that provided the patriarchal body with some of its "closure."

29. In performing his "honor," the gentleman transferred the weight of the body to the right leg, freeing the left to extend sharply toward those to whom he wished to honor, in a not-very-subtle phallic gesture politely ignored by dance historians and literary critics alike.

30. Callaghan discusses the tendency in Jacobean tragedy for gender, marriage, and family to be reduced to universal, heterosexual "love" (*Women and Gender,* 35).

31. Walter Cohen suggests, "Prerevolutionary Drama," 122–27, that between 1610 and 1642, the tragicomedy was a "prerevolutionary" genre in which social anxieties were displaced onto gender conflict, and the improbability of the resolution subvert it.

32. Callaghan, *Women and Gender,* 38.

Bibliography

PRIMARY SOURCES

Arbeau, Toinot [Jehan Tabourot]. *Orchésographie.* Langres: Jehan de Preyz, 1588. Translated as *Orchesography* by Mary Stewart Evans, with introduction and notes by Julia Sutton. New York: Dover, 1967.

Arena, Antonius. *. . . ad suos compagnones studiantes qui sunt de persona friantes, bassas dansas in gallanti stilo bisognatas. . . .* Avignon, 1517, Lyon: Benoist Rigaud, 1572. Translated as *Rules of Dancing* by John Guthrie and Mario Zorzi. *Dance Research* 4, no. 2 (1986): 3–52.

Ascham, Roger. *The Scholemaster, or plaine and perfite way of teachyng children the Latin Tong.* London: John Daye, 1570. Edited by Edward Arber. Westminster: A. Constable and Co., 1895.

Barrough, Philip. *The Method of Physick, Containing the Causes, Signs, and Cures of inward Diseases in man's bodie.* 7th ed. London: George Miller, 1634. STC 1515.

Beaujoyeulx, Balthasar de. *Le Balet Comique de la Royne.* Facsimile, translated and with an introduction by Margaret McGowan. Binghamton, N.Y.: Center for Medieval and Early Renaissance Texts and Studies, 1982.

Braithwait, Richard. *Natures Embassie: or, the Wilde-Mans Measures.* London: Richard Whittaker, 1621. STC 3571.

Bullein, William. *Bullein's Bulwarke of Defense against all Sicknesse, Soreness, and Wounds that doe dayly assault mankinde.* 1562, printed 1569. STC 4034.

Bulwer, John. *A View of the People of the Whole World (Man Transformed: Or, the Artificiall Changeling),* formerly titled *Anthropometamorphosis.* London, William Hunt, 1654.

Caroso, Fabritio. *Nobilità di Dame.* Venice, 1600. Translated and introduction by Julia Sutton. Music transcribed and edited by F. Marian Walker. Oxford: Oxford University Press, 1986.

Castiglione, Baldesar. *Il Cortegiano.* 1528. Translated as *The Booke of the Courtyer* by Thomas Hoby, 1561. London: David Nutt, 1900.

Closson, Ernest. *Le Manuscrit des Basses Danses de la Bibliothèque de Bourgogne.* 1912. Reprint, Brussels: Société des Bibliophiles et Iconophiles de Belgiques, 1975.

Coplande, Robert. *The maner of dauncynge of bace daunces after the use of fraunce & other places.* 1521. Facsimile. Sussex: Pear Tree Press, 1937.

Cornazano, Antonio. *Libro dell'arte del danzare.* c. 1455. Translated as *The Art of Dancing* by Madeleine Inglehearn and Peggy Forsyth. London: Dance Books, 1981.

Crooke, Helkiah. *Microcosmographia.* London, 1615.

Davies, John. *The Muses Sacrifice or Divine Meditations.* London: George Norton, 1612. STC 6338.

Davies, Sir John. *A Discoverie of the True Causes why Ireland was never entirely Subdued, nor brought under Obedience of the Crowne of England untill the Beginning of His Majesties happy Reigne.* London, 1612. STC 6348. Edited by James P. Meyers Jr. Washington, D.C.: Catholic University Press, 1988.

———. "*Orchestra,* or a Poeme of Dauncing." 1596. In *The Poems of Sir John Davies,* edited by Robert Krueger. Oxford: Clarendon, 1971.

de Lauze, F. *Apologie de la Danse.* 1623. Translated by Joan Wildeblood. London: Frederick Muller, 1952.

de Maisse, Andre Hurault. *A Journal of All That Was Accomplished by Monsieur de Maisse Ambassador in England from Henri IV to Queen Elizabeth, anno Domini, 1597.* Translated by G. B. Harrison and R. A. Jones. London: Nonesuch, 1931.

Dod, John, and Robert Cleaver. *A Godly Forme of Houshold Government, for the ordering of private families according to the direction of God's Word.* London, 1598. STC 5388.

Domenico da Piacenza. *De arte saltanj & choreas ducendj.* Paris.

Dorat, Jean. *Magnificentissimi spectaculi.* Paris: Frederick Morel, 1573.

Ebreo, Guglielmo. *Guglielmo hebraei pisaurensis de practica seu arte tripudii vulghare opusculum.* Milan: Paganus Rhaudensis, scribe, 1463.

Elyot, Sir Thomas. *The Boke named the Governour.* London: Thomas Bertheleti, 1531, 1564. Facsimile Reprint, English Linguistics, 1500–1800, No. 246. Edited by R. C. Alston. Menston, England: Scholar, 1970.

Fanshawe, Ann, Lady. *The Memoires of Lady Ann Fanshawe, 1600–1672.* 1676. London: John Lane, 1907.

Fetherstone, Christopher. *A dialogue against light, lewd, and lascivious dancing.* London, 1582.

Gosson, Stephen. *The Shoole of Abuse, containing a pleasaunt invective against poets, pipers, plaiers, jesters, and such like caterpillars of a commonwealth.* London, 1579. Edited by Arthur Freeman. New York: Garland, 1973.

Greville, Fulke, Baron Brooke. *Mustapha.* In *Poems and Dramas of Fulke Greville first lord Brooke.* Edited with introduction and notes by Geoffrey Bullough. Edinburgh: Oliver and Boyd, 1939.

Hall[e], Edward. *The Union of the Two Noble and Illustre Families of Lancastre & Yorke.* 1548. Reprint as *Hall's Chronicle.* London, 1809; New York: AMS Press, 1965.

Harrison, William. *The Description of England.* London, 1577. Edited by F. J. Furnivall. 4 Parts. London: New Shakespeare Society, 1877–1908.

"An Homily of Obedience." In *Certain Sermons, or Homilies appointed to be read in Churches in the time of the late Queene Elizabeth of famous memory.* Bishop Edmund Bonner et al. London, 1547; reprinted, London: John Bill, 1623.

"An Homily of the State of Matrimonie." In *The Second Tome of Homilies, of Such Matters as were Promised and Entytled in the former parte of Homilies.* Archbishop Matthew Parker et al. London, 1563.

Jones, John. *The Arte and Science of preserving Bodie and Soule in al Health, Wisdome, and Catholicke Religion: Physically, Philosophically, and Divinely.* London: Ralph Newberie, 1579. STC 14724a.

Josephus. *Jewish Antiquities.* Vol. 8. Books 15–17. Translated by Ralph Marcus. Cambridge: Harvard University Press, 1953.

Kempe, William. *Kempes nine daies wonder, performed in a dance from London to Norwich.* London, 1600. STC 14923.

Lemnius, Levinus. *The Touchstone of Complexions.* London, 1576. STC 15456.

Le Livre dit les Basses Danses. Brussels Bibliothèque Royale Ms. 9085.

Machyn, Henry. *Diary of Henry Machyn, Citizen of London, 1550–1563.* Edited by John Gough Nichols. Camden Society. Vol. 42. London, 1848.

Manningham, John. *Diary of John Manningham.* 1601–3. Edited by John Bruce. Westminster: Nichols, 1868.

Morley, Thomas. *A Plaine and Easie Introduction to Practicall Musicke.* London: Peter Short, 1597. Shakespeare Association Facsimile 14. London: Oxford University Press, 1937.

Mulcaster, Richard. *Positions Wherein Those Primitive Circumstances Be Examined, Which Are necessarie for the Training up of children, either for skill in their booke, or health in their bodie.* London, 1581. New York: Da Capo, 1971.

Negri, Cesare. *Le Gratie d'Amore.* Milan, 1602. Monuments of Music and Music Literature in Facsimile, 141. New York: Bronde Bros, 1969.

Northbrooke, John. *A treatise wherein dicing, dauncing, vaine playes or enterluds . . . are reproved.* 1577. Shakespeare Society. London, 1843.

Playford, John. *The English Dancing Master, or Plaine and easie Rules for the Dancing of Country Dances, with the Tune to each Dance.* London, 1651.

Sherry, Richard. *A Treatise of Schemes and Tropes.* London, 1550.

Smith, Thomas. *De Republica Anglorum; A Discourse on the Commonwealth of England.* London, 1583. Edited by L. Alston. Cambridge, 1906; New York: Barnes and Noble, 1974.

Stow, John. *Survey of London.* 1598, 1603. Edited by Valerie Pearl. London: J. M. Dent, 1987.

Stubbes, Phillip. *The Anatomie of Abuses.* London, 1583. Edited by Frederick J. Furnivall as *Phillip Stubbes's Anatomy of Abuses in England in Shakspere's Youth.* New Shakespeare Society. London: N. Trubner & Co., 1877–79.

Toulouze, Michel. *Lart and instruction de bien dancer.* Paris, c. 1488. Facsimile with notes by Victor Scholderer, music transcribed by Richard Rastell. London: Royal College of Physicians, 1936.

A Treatise of Daunces, wherin it is shewed, that they are as it were accessories and dependants . . . to whoredom, where also by the way is touched and proved, that Playes are joined and knit together in a rancke or rowe with them. London, 1581. Facsimile edited by Arthur Freeman. New York: Garland, 1974.

Vaughn, William. *Approved Directions for Health.* 4th ed. London, 1612. STC 24615.

Vives, Juan Luis. *De institutio feominae christianae.* 1523. Translated as *The Instruction of a Christian Woman* by Richard Hyrde. London, 1540.

SECONDARY SOURCES

Agnew, Jean-Christophe. *Worlds Apart: The Market and the Theatre in Anglo-American Thought, 1550–1750.* Cambridge: Cambridge University Press, 1986.

Althusser, Louis. "Ideology and Ideological State Apparatuses (Notes towards an Investigation)." In *Lenin and Philosophy, and Other Essays,* translated by Ben Brewster. London: New Left Books, 1971.

Amussen, Susan Dwyer. "Gender, Family, and the Social Order, 1560–1725." In *Order and Disorder in Early Modern England,* edited by Anthony Fletcher and John Stevenson. Cambridge: Cambridge University Press, 1985.

————. *An Ordered Society: Gender and Class in Early Modern England.* London: Basil Blackwell, 1988.

Anderson, Perry. *Lineages of the Absolutist State.* London: New Left Books, 1974.

Andrews, K. R., N. P. Canny, and P. E. H. Hair, eds. *The Westward Enterprise: English Activities in Ireland, the Atlantic, and America, 1480–1650.* Liverpool: Liverpool University Press, 1978.

Anglo, Sidney. *Spectacle, Pageantry, and Early Tudor Policy.* Oxford: Clarendon, 1969.

Archer, Ian W. "The Nostalgia of John Snow." In *The Theatrical City: Culture, Theatre, and Politics in London, 1576–1649,* edited by David L. Smith, Richard Strier, and David Bevington. Cambridge: Cambridge University Press, 1995.

————. *The Pursuit of Stability: Social Relations in Elizabethan London.* Cambridge: Cambridge University Press, 1991.

Avril, François. *Manuscript Painting at the Court of France: The Fourteenth Century.* Translated by Ursule Molinaro and Bruce Benderson. New York: Braziller, 1976.

Axtell, James. "The Invasion Within: The Contest of Cultures in Colonial North America." In his *The European and the Indian: Essays in the Ethnohistory of Colonial North America.* Oxford: Oxford University Press, 1981.

Axton, Marie. *The Queen's Two Bodies: Drama and the Elizabethan Succession.* London: Royal Historical Society, 1977.

Bakhtin, Mikhail. *Rabelais and his World.* Translated by Helene Iswolsky. Bloomington: Indiana University Press, 1984.

Barber, C. L. *Shakespeare's Festive Comedy: A Study of Dramatic Form and Its Relation to Social Custom.* Princeton: Princeton University Press, 1959, 1972.

Barish, Jonas. *The Antitheatrical Prejudice.* Berkeley and Los Angeles: University of California Press, 1981.

Barthelemy, Anthony Gerard. *Black Face, Maligned Race.* Baton Rouge: Louisiana State University Press, 1987.

Barker, R. H. *Thomas Middleton.* New York: Columbia University Press, 1958.

Baskervill, Charles Read. *The Elizabethan Jig and Related Song Dramas.* Chicago: University of Chicago Press, 1929.

Beazley, C. Raymond. *The Dawn of Modern Geography: A History of Exploration and Geographical Science.* Vol. 3, *1260–1420.* Oxford: Clarendon, 1906.

Beier, A. L. *Masterless Men: The Vagrancy Problem in England, 1560–1640.* London: Methuen, 1985.

————. "Vagrants and the Social Order in Elizabethan England." *Past and Present* 64 (1974):

Beilin, Elaine V. "Elizabeth Cary and *The Tragedie of Mariam*." *Papers on Language and Literature* 16, no. 1 (1980): 45–64.

————. *Redeeming Eve: Women Writers of the English Renaissance.* Princeton: Princeton University Press, 1987.

Belsey, Catherine. "Disrupting Sexual Difference: Meaning and Gender in the Comedies." In *Alternative Shakespeares,* edited by John Drakakis. London Methuen, 1985.

————. *The Subject of Tragedy: Identity and Difference in Renaissance Tragedy.* London: Methuen, 1985.

Berger, Harry, Jr. "Against the Sink-a-Pace: Sexual and Family Politics in *Much Ado About Nothing*." *Shakespeare Quarterly* 33 (1982): 302–13.

Bergeron, David. *English Civic Pageantry, 1558–1642.* London: Arnold, 1971.

Bordo, Susan R. "The Body and the Reproduction of Femininity: A Feminist Appropriation of Foucault." In *Gender/Body/Knowledge: Feminist Reconstructions of Being and Knowing,* edited by Alison M. Jaggar and Susan R. Bordo. New Brunswick: Rutgers University Press, 1989.

Bottigheimer, Karl S. "Kingdom and Colony: Ireland in the Westward Enterprise, 1536–1660." In *The Westward Enterprise: English Activities in Ireland, the Atlantic, and America, 1480–1650,* edited by K. R. Andrews, N. P. Canny, and P. E. H. Hair. Detroit: Wayne State University Press, 1979.

Bowers, Rick. "John Lowin's Conclusions Upon Dances: Puritan Conclusions of a Godly Player." *Renaissance and Reformation/Renaissance et Réforme,* n.s., 11, no. 2 (1987): 163–73.

Brainard, Ingrid. *The Art of Courtly Dancing in the Early Renaissance.* Part 2, *The Practice of Courtly Dances.* West Newton, Mass., 1981.

————. "Modes, Manners, Movement: The Interaction of Dance and Dress from the Late Middle Ages to the Present." In *Proceedings of Dance History Scholars' Sixth Annual Conference.* 1983.

Brand, John. *Observations on Popular Antiquities.* Edited by Henry Ellis. London, 1841–42.

Brink, J. R. "Sir John Davies's Orchestra: Political Symbolism and Textual Revisions." *Durham University Journal* 72 (1980): 195–202.

————. "The 1622 Edition of John Davies's Orchestra." *The Library: A Quarterly Journal of Bibliography* 30 (1975): 25–33.

Brink, Jean R., ed. *Privileging Gender in Early Modern England.* Kirksville, Mo.: Sixteenth Century Journal, 1993.

Brissenden, Alan. *Shakespeare and the Dance.* Atlantic Highlands, N.J.: Humanities Press, 1981.

Bristol, Michael D. *Carnival and Theatre: Plebean Culture and the Structure of Authority in Renaissance England.* New York: Methuen, 1985.

Brooks, Harold F., ed. *A Midsummer Night's Dream.* Arden ed. London: Methuen, 1979.

Burke, Peter. *Popular Culture in Early Modern Europe.* New York: Harper and Row, 1978.

————. "Popular Culture in Seventeenth-Century London." In *Popular Culture in*

Seventeenth-Century England, edited by Barry Reay. London: Croom Helm, 1985.

Butler, Judith. *Gender Trouble: Feminism and the Subversion of Identity.* London: Routledge, 1991.

———. "Performative Acts and Gender Constitution: An Essay on Phenomenology and Feminist Theory." In *Performing Feminisms: Feminist Critical Theory and Theatre,* edited by Sue-Ellen Case. Baltimore: Johns Hopkins University Press, 1990.

Butler, Martin. *Theatre and Crisis, 1632–1642.* Cambridge: Cambridge University Press, 1984.

Byrne, Muriel St. Claire, ed. *The Lisle Letters.* 6 vols. Chicago: University of Chicago Press, 1981.

Callaghan, Dympna. *Women and Gender in Renaissance Tragedy A Study of King Lear, Othello, The Duchess of Malfi, and The White Devil.* Atlantic Highlands, N.J.: Humanities Press, 1989.

Canny, Nicholas. "The Permissive Frontier: Social Control in English Settlements in Ireland and Virginia, 1550–1650." In *The Westward Enterprise: English Activities in Ireland, the Atlantic, and America, 1480–1650,* edited by K. R. Andrews, N. P. Canny, and P. E. H. Hair. Detroit: Wayne State University Press, 1979.

Cary, Elizabeth. *The Tragedy of Mariam, the Fair Queen of Jewry, with The Lady Falkland: Her Life.* 1613. Edited by Barry Weller and Margaret W. Ferguson. Berkeley and Los Angeles: University of California Press, 1994.

———. *The Tragedy of Mariam, the Faire Queen of Jewry.* Malone Society Reprints. Edited by A. C. Dunstan and W. W. Greg. Oxford: Oxford University Press, 1914.

Chambers, E. K. *The Elizabethan Stage.* 4 vols. Oxford: Oxford University Press, 1928.

———. *The Mediaeval Stage.* 2 vols. Oxford: Oxford University Press, 1903, 1951.

Chambers, Robert, ed. *The Book of Days, A Miscellany of Popular Antiquities in Connection with the Calendar, Including Anecdote, Biography, & History, Curiosities of Literature, and Oddities of Human Life and Character.* London: W. & R. Chambers, 1863, 1967.

Chapman, George. *Bussy D'Ambois.* Edited by Nicholas Brooke. Revels Plays. Cambridge: Harvard University Press, 1964.

Clare, Janet. *"Art Made Tongue-Tied by Authority": Elizabethan and Jacobean Dramatic Censorship.* Manchester: Manchester University Press, 1990.

Cohen, Walter. *Drama of a Nation: Public Theater in Renaissance England and Spain.* Ithaca: Cornell University Press, 1985.

———. "Prerevolutionary Drama." In *The Politics of Tragicomedy,* edited by Gordon McMullen and Jonathan Hope. London: Routledge, 1992.

Cook, Carol. "The Sign and Semblance of Her Honor." *PMLA* 101 (1986): 186–202.

———. "Unbodied Figures of Desire." In *Performing Feminism: Feminist Critical Theory and Theater,* edited by Sue-Ellen Case. Baltimore: Johns Hopkins University Press, 1990.

Cressy, David. "Describing the Social Order in Elizabethan and Stuart England." *Literature and History,* no. 3 (March 1976): 29–34.

Davidson, Clifford. "What hempen home-spuns have we swaggering here? Amateur Actors in *A Midsummer Night's Dream* and the Coventry City Plays and Pageants." In *Shakespeare Studies* 19, edited by Leeds Barroll and Barry Gaines. New York: Burt Franklin, 1987.

DiGangi, Mario. "Asses and Wits: The Homoerotics of Mastery in Satiric Comedy." *English Literary Renaissance* 25 (1995): 179–208.

Dollimore, Jonathan. "Subjectivity, Sexuality and Transgression: The Jacobean Connection." In *Renaissance Drama as Cultural History,* edited by Mary Beth Rose. Evanston: Northwestern University Press, 1990.

Dolmetsch, Mabel. *Dances of England and France from 1450 to 1600, with Their Music and Authentic Manner of Performance.* London: Routledge and Kegan Paul, 1949; New York: Da Capo, 1976.

———. *Dances of Spain and Italy from 1400 to 1600.* London: Routledge and Kegan Paul, 1954.

Edwards, Philip. *Threshold of a Nation: A Study in English and Irish Drama.* Cambridge: Cambridge University Press, 1979.

Elam, Keir. *Shakespeare's Universe of Discourse.* Cambridge: Cambridge University Press, 1984.

Elias, Norbert. *The Civilizing Process.* Vol. 1, *The History of Manners.* Vol. 2, *Power and Civility.* Translated by Edmund Jephcott. New York: Pantheon, 1978, 1982.

Ellis, Henry. *Original Letters Illustrative of English History.* 5 vols. London, 1824.

Elton, G. R. *England Under the Tudors.* 3d ed. London: Routledge, 1991.

———. *Reform and Reformation: England, 1509–1558.* Cambridge: Harvard University Press, 1977.

Evans, G. Blakemore, ed. *The Riverside Shakespeare.* Boston: Houghton Mifflin, 1974.

Ezell, Margaret J. M. *The Patriarch's Wife: Literary Evidence and the History of the Family.* Chapel Hill: University of North Carolina Press, 1987.

Farr, Dorothy M. *Thomas Middleton and the Drama of Realism.* New York: Harper and Row, 1973.

Ferguson, Margaret W. "A Room Not Their Own: Renaissance Women as Readers and Writers." In *The Comparative Perspective on Literary Approaches to Theory and Practice,* edited by Clayton Koelb and Susan Noakes. Ithaca: Cornell University Press, 1985.

———. "Running On with Almost Public Voice: The Case of 'E.C.'" In *Tradition and the Talents of Women,* edited by Florence Howe. Urbana: University of Illinois Press, 1991.

———. "The Spectre of Resistance." In *Staging the Renaissance: Reinterpretations of Elizabethan and Jacobean Drama,* edited by David Scott Kastan and Peter Stallybrass. London: Routledge, 1991.

Ferguson, Margaret W., Maureen Quilligan, and Nancy J. Vickers, eds. *Rewriting the Renaissance: The Discourses of Sexual Difference in Early Modern Europe.* Chicago: University of Chicago Press, 1986.

Fetterly, Judith. *The Resisting Reader: A Feminist Approach to American Fiction.* Bloomington: Indiana University Press, 1978.

Finkelpearl, Philip J. "'The Comedians' Liberty': Censorship of the Jacobean Stage Reconsidered." In *Renaissance Historicism,* edited by Arthur F. Kinney and Dan S. Collins. Amherst: University of Massachusetts Press, 1987.

———. *John Marston of the Middle Temple: An Elizabethan Dramatist in His Social Setting.* Cambridge: Harvard University Press, 1969.

Fischer, Sandra K. "Elizabeth Cary and Tyranny, Domestic and Religious." In *Silent But for the Word,* edited by Margaret Patterson Hannay. Kent: Kent State University Press, 1985.

Foley, Stephen Merriam. "Coming to Terms: Thomas Elyot's Definitions and the Particularity of Human Letters." *English Literary Renaissance* 61 (1994): 211–30.

Foster, Donald W. "Resurrecting the Author: Elizabeth Tanfield Cary." In *Privileging Gender in Early Modern England,* edited by Jean R. Brink. Kirksville, Mo.: Sixteenth Century Journal, 1993.

Foster, R. F. *Modern Ireland.* London: Allan Lane, 1988.

Foucault, Michel. *Discipline and Punish: The Birth of the Prison.* Translated by Alan Sheridan. New York: Vintage, 1980.

———. *The History of Sexuality.* Vol. 1, *An Introduction.* Translated by Robert Hurley. New York: Vintage, 1980.

———. "Of Other Spaces." *Diacritics* 16 (1986): 22–27.

———. *Power/Knowledge.* Edited by Colin Gordon. New York: Pantheon, 1972.

Franko, Mark. *Dance as Text: Ideologies of the Baroque Body.* Cambridge: Cambridge University Press, 1993.

———. *The Dancing Body in Renaissance Choreography (1416–1589).* Birmingham, Ala.: Summa Publications, 1986.

———. "Renaissance Conduct Literature and the Kinesis of *Bonne Grace.*" In *Persons in Groups: Social Behavior as Identity Formation in Medieval and Renaissance Europe,* edited by Richard C. Trexler. Binghamton, N.Y.: Medieval and Renaissance Texts and Studies, 1985.

Frye, Susan. *Elizabeth I: The Competition for Representation.* Oxford: Oxford University Press, 1993.

Gates, Henry Louis, ed. *"Race," Writing, and Difference.* Chicago: University of Chicago Press, 1985.

Gibbons, Brian. *Jacobean City Comedy: A Study of Satiric Plays by Jonson, Marston, and Middleton.* 2d ed. London: Methuen, 1980.

Gillies, John. *Shakespeare and the Geography of Difference.* Cambridge: Cambridge University Press, 1994.

Ginzburg, Carlo. *The Cheese and the Worms: The Cosmos of a Sixteenth-Century Miller.* Translated by John Tedeschi and Anne Tedeschi. Baltimore: Johns Hopkins University Press, 1980.

Goldberg, Jonathan. *James I and the Politics of Literature: Jonson, Shakespeare, Donne, and Their Contemporaries.* Stanford: Stanford University Press, 1989.

———. *Writing Matter: From the Hands of the English Renaissance.* Stanford: Stanford University Press, 1990.

Gombrich, E. H. *Norm and Form*. London: Phaidon, 1966.

Gordon, D. J. *The Renaissance Imagination: Essays and Lectures*. Collected and edited by Stephen Orgel. Berkeley and Los Angeles: University of California Press, 1975.

Gossett, Suzanne. "'Man-Maid, Begone!': Women in Masques." *English Literary Renaissance* 18 (Winter 1988): 96–113.

Greenblatt, Stephen J. "Learning to Curse: Aspects of Linguistic Colonialism in the Sixteenth Century." In *First Images of America: The Impact of the New World on the Old,* vol. 2, edited by Ferdi Chiappelli, Michael J. B. Allen, and Robert Benson. Berkeley and Los Angeles: University of California Press, 1976.

———. *Marvelous Possessions: The Wonder of the New World*. Chicago: University of Chicago Press, 1991.

———. *Renaissance Self-Fashioning: From More to Shakespeare*. Chicago: University of Chicago Press, 1980.

———. *Shakespearean Negotiations: The Circulation of Social Energy in Renaissance England*. Berkeley and Los Angeles: University of California Press, 1988.

Greene, Gayle, and Coppélia Kahn, eds. *Making a Difference: Feminist Literary Criticism*. London: Methuen, 1985.

Grosart, Alexander B., ed. *The Complete Works of Samuel Daniel*. New York: Russell and Russell, 1963.

Guy, John. *Tudor England*. Oxford: Oxford University Press, 1988.

Hale, J. R. *Renaissance Europe: Individual and Society, 1480–1520*. Berkeley and Los Angeles: University of California Press, 1971.

———. *Renaissance Exploration*. New York: Norton, 1968.

Hall, Kim F. "Sexual Politics and Cultural Identity in *The Masque of Blackness*." In *The Performance of Power: Theatrical Discourse and Politics,* edited by Sue-Ellen Case and Janelle Reinelt. Iowa City: University of Iowa Press, 1991.

———. *Things of Darkness: Economies of Race and Gender in Early Modern England*. Ithaca: Cornell University Press, 1995.

Hanna, Judith Lynne. *Dance, Sex, and Gender: Signs of Identity, Dominance, Defiance, and Desire*. Chicago: University of Chicago Press, 1988.

———. *To Dance Is Human: A Theory of Non-Verbal Communication*. Chicago: University of Chicago Press, 1979.

Havelock, Eric A. *Preface to Plato*. Cambridge: Belknap Press of Harvard University Press, 1963.

Hawkes, Terence. "Swisser-Swatter Making a Man of English Letters." In *Alternative Shakespeares,* edited by John Drakakis. London: Methuen, 1985.

Hays, Janice. "Those 'Soft and Delicate Desires': *Much Ado* and the Distrust of Women." In *The Woman's Part: Feminist Criticism of Shakespeare,* edited by Carolyn Ruth Swift Lenz, Gayle Greene, and Carol Thomas Neely. Urbana: University of Illinois Press, 1980.

Heinemann, Margot. "'God Help the Poor: The Rich Can Shift': The World Upside Down and the Popular Tradition in the Theatre." In *The Politics of*

Tragicomedy, edited by Gordon McMullen and Jonathan Hope. London: Routledge, 1992.

————. *Puritanism and Theatre: Thomas Middleton and Opposition Drama under the Early Stuarts.* Cambridge: Cambridge University Press, 1980.

Helgerson, Richard. *Forms of Nationhood: The Elizabethan Writing of England.* Chicago: University of Chicago Press, 1992, 1994.

————. "The Land Speaks: Cartography, Choreography, and Subversion in Renaissance England." In *Representing the English Renaissance,* edited by Stephen J. Greenblatt. Berkeley and Los Angeles: University of California Press, 1988.

Herman, Peter C. *Rethinking the Henrician Era: Essays on Early Tudor Texts and Contexts.* Urbana: University of Illinois Press, 1994.

————. *Squitter-wits and Muse Haters: Sidney, Spenser, Milton and Renaissance Antipoetic Sentiment.* Detroit: Wayne State University Press, 1996.

Hill, Christopher. *Puritanism and Revolution: Studies in Interpretation of the English Revolution of the Seventeenth Century.* London: Secker and Warburg, 1958.

————. *The World Turned Upside Down: Radical Ideas During the English Revolution.* Harmondsworth: Penguin, 1972, 1985.

Holstein, F. W. H. *Dutch and Flemish Etchings, Engravings, and Woodcuts, c. 1450–1700.* 25 vols. Amsterdam, 1949–.

Hooper, Wilfrid. "The Tudor Sumptuary Laws." *English Historical Review* 30 (1915):433–49.

Howard, Jean E. "Crossdressing, The Theatre, and Gender Struggle in Early Modern England." *Shakespeare Quarterly* 39, no. 4 (Winter 1988): 418–40.

————. "The Difficulties of Closure: An Approach to the Problematic in Shakespearean Comedy." In *Comedy from Shakespeare to Sheridan: Change and Continuity in the English and European Dramatic Tradition. Essays in Honor of Eugene M. Waith,* edited by A. R. Braunmuller and J. C. Bulman. Newark: University of Delaware Press, 1986.

————. "Renaissance Antitheatricality and the Politics of Gender and Rank in *Much Ado About Nothing.*" In *Shakespeare Reproduced: The Text in History and Ideology,* edited by Jean E. Howard and Marian F. O'Connor. London: Methuen, 1987.

————. "Scripts and/versus Playhouses: Ideological Production and the Renaissance Public Stage." In *Renaissance Drama as Cultural History,* edited by Mary Beth Rose. Evanston: Northwestern University Press, 1989.

————. "Sex and Social Conflict: The Erotics of The Roaring Girl." In *Erotic Politics: The Dynamics of Desire on the English Renaissance Stage,* edited by Susan Zimmerman. London: Routledge, 1992.

————. *The Stage and Social Struggle in Early Modern England.* London: Routledge, 1994.

Hulme, Peter. *Colonial Encounters: Europe and the Native Caribbean, 1492–1797.* London: Methuen, 1986.

Ingram, R. W., ed. *Records of Early English Drama: Coventry.* Toronto: University of Toronto Press, 1981.

Ingram, William. "Minstrels in Elizabethan London: Who Were They, What Did They Do?" *English Literary Renaissance* 14 (1984): 29–54.

Irigaray, Luce. *This Sex Which Is Not One.* Translated by Catherine Porter. Ithaca: Cornell University Press, 1977, 1985.

Jackman, James L. *Fifteenth-Century Basse Dances.* Wellesley: Wellesley College, 1964.

James, Mervyn. *Society, Politics, and Culture: Studies in Early Modern England.* Cambridge: Cambridge University Press, 1986.

JanMohammed, Abdul R. "The Economy of Manichean Allegory: The Function of Racial Difference in Colonialist Literature." In *"Race," Writing, and Difference,* edited by Henry Louis Gates Jr. Chicago: University of Chicago Press, 1985.

Jardine, Alice. "Death Sentences: Writing Couples and Ideology." In *The Female Body in Western Culture: Contemporary Perspectives,* edited by Susan Robin Suleiman. Cambridge: Harvard University Press, 1986.

Jardine, Lisa. *Still Harping on Daughters: Women and Drama in the Age of Shakespeare.* New York: Columbia University Press, 1983.

Javitch, Daniel. *Poetry and Courtliness in Renaissance England.* Princeton: Princeton University Press, 1978.

Jenkins, Harold. "The Ball Scene in *Much Ado About Nothing.*" In *Shakespeare: Text, Language, Criticism,* edited by Bernard Fabian and Kurt Tetzeli von Rosador. Hildesheim: Olms, 1987.

Jones, Ann Rosalind. "Nets and Bridles: Early Modern Conduct Books and Sixteenth-Century Women's Lyrics." In *The Ideology of Conduct: Essays on Literature and the History of Sexuality,* edited by Nancy Armstrong and Leonard Tennenhouse. London: Methuen, 1987.

Jonson, Ben. *Masques.* Vol. 7 of *Ben Jonson,* 11 vols., edited by C. H. Hereford, Percy Simpson, and Evelyn Simpson. Oxford: Clarendon, 1925–52.

Jordan, Constance. *Renaissance Feminism: Literary Texts and Political Models.* Ithaca: Cornell University Press, 1990.

Josten, C. H., ed. *Elias Ashmole (1617–1692).* 5 vols. Oxford: Clarendon, 1966.

Kahn, Coppélia. "Whores and Wives in Jacobean Drama." In *In Another Country: Feminist Perspectives on Renaissance Drama,* edited by Dorothea Kehler and Susan Baker. Metuchen, N.J.: Scarecrow, 1991.

Kastan, David Scott. "Proud Majesty Made a Subject: Shakespeare and the Spectacle of Rule." *Shakespeare Quarterly* 37, no. 4 (Winter 1986): 458–75.

Kegl, Rosemary. *The Rhetoric of Concealment: Figuring Gender and Class in Renaissance Literature.* Ithaca: Cornell University Press, 1994.

Kelly, Joan. "Did Women Have a Renaissance?" In *Women, History, and Theory: The Essays of Joan Kelly.* Chicago: University of Chicago Press, 1984.

King, John N. "Queen Elizabeth I: Representations of the Virgin Queen." *Renaissance Quarterly* 43, no. 1 (Spring 1990): 30–74.

Kinkeldy, Otto. *A Jewish Dancing Master of the Renaissance: Guglielmo Ebreo.* New York: Dance Horizons, 1966.

Kinney, Arthur F. *Rogues, Vagabonds, and Sturdy Beggars: A New Gallery of Tudor and*

Early Stuart Rogue Literature Exposing the Lives, Times, and Cozening Tricks of the Elizabethan Underworld. Amherst: University of Massachusetts Press, 1991.

Kipling, Gordon. *The Triumph of Honour: Burgundian Origins of the Elizabethan Renaissance.* The Hague: Leyden University Press, 1977.

Kirk, R. E. G., and Ernest Kirk. *Returns of Aliens Dwelling in the City and Suburbs of London from the Reign of Henry VIII to that of James I.* 3 vols. Aberdeen: Huguenot Society, 1902.

Klausner, David N., ed. *Records of Early English Drama: Herefordshire/Worcestershire.* Toronto: University of Toronto Press, 1990.

Krueger, Robert, ed. *The Poems of Sir John Davies.* Oxford: Clarendon, 1971.

Lake, David J. *The Canon of Thomas Middleton's Plays: Internal Evidence for the Major Problems of Authorship.* London: Cambridge University Press, 1975.

Landes, David. *Revolution in Time: Clocks and the Making of the Modern World.* Cambridge: Harvard University Press, 1984.

Leimberg, Inge. "'Give me thy hand': Some Notes on the Phrase in Shakespeare's Comedies and Tragedies." In *Shakespeare: Text, Language, Criticism,* edited by Bernard Fabian and Kurt Tetzeli von Rosador. Hildesheim: Olms, 1987.

Leinwand, Theodore. *The City Staged: Jacobean Comedy, 1603–1613.* Madison: University of Wisconsin Press, 1986.

———. "'I believe we must leave the killing out': Deference and Accomodation in *A Midsummer Night's Dream.*" *Renaissance Papers* 1986, 11–30. Edited by Dale B. J. Randall and Joseph A. Parker. Southeastern Renaissance.

———. "Shakespeare and the Middling Sort." *Shakespeare Quarterly* 4, no. 3 (1993): 284–304.

Levin, Carole, and Jeanie Watson, eds. *Ambiguous Realities: Women in the Middle Ages and Renaissance.* Detroit: Wayne State University Press, 1987.

Levine, Laura. *Men in Women's Clothing: Anti-theatricality and Effeminization, 1579–1642.* Cambridge: Cambridge University Press, 1994.

Lewalski, Barbara Kiefer. *Writing Women in Jacobean England.* Cambridge: Harvard University Press, 1993.

Lindley, David, ed. *The Court Masque.* Manchester: Manchester University Press, 1984.

———. "Embarrassing Ben: The Masques for Frances Howard." In *Renaissance Historicism,* edited by Arthur F. Kinney and Dan S. Collins. Amherst: University of Massachusetts Press, 1986.

Loewenstein, Joseph. *Responsive Readings: Versions of Echo in Pastoral, Epic, and the Jonsonian Masque.* New Haven: Yale University Press, 1984.

Loomba, Ania. *Gender, Race, Renaissance Drama.* Manchester: Manchester University Press, 1989.

Luborsky, Ruth Samson. "Connections and Disconnections Netween Images and Text: The Case of Secular Book Illustration." *Word and Image* 3, no. 1 (January–March 1987): 74–85.

MacCaffrey, Wallace. "Place and Patronage in Elizabethan Politics." In *Elizabethan*

Government and Society: Essays Presented to Sir John Neale, edited by S. T. Bindoff, Joel Hurstfield, and C. H. Williams. London: Athlone, 1961.

Macdonell, Diane. *Theories of Discourse: An Introduction.* Oxford: Basil Blackwell, 1986.

Maclean, Ian. *The Renaissance Notion of Woman: A Study in the Fortunes of Scholasticism and Medical Science in European Intellectual Life.* Cambridge: Cambridge University Press, 1980.

Major, John M. "The Moralization of the Dance in Elyot's Governor." *Studies in the Renaissance* 5 (1958): 26–36.

Marcus, Leah Sinanoglou. "Masquing Occasions and Masque Structure." *Research Opportunities in Renaissance Drama* 24 (1981): 7–16.

———. *The Politics of Mirth: Jonson, Herrick, Milton, Marvell, and the Defense of Old Holiday Pastimes.* Chicago: University of Chicago Press, 1978.

———. "'Present Occasions' and the Shaping of Ben Jonson's Masques." *ELH* 45 (1978): 201–25.

Maurer, Margaret. "Reading Ben Jonson's *Queens.*" In *Seeking the Woman in Late Medieval and Renaissance Writings: Essays in Feminist Contextual Criticism,* edited by Sheila Fisher and Janet E. Halley. Knoxville: University of Tennessee Press, 1989.

McGowan, Margaret. *L'Art de Ballet de Cour en France, 1581–1643.* Paris: Edition du Centre National de la Recherche Scientifique, 1963.

Meagher, John C. *Method and Madness in Jonson's Masques.* Notre Dame: University of Notre Dame Press, 1966.

Mellor, Hugh, and Leslie Bridgewater, eds. *The English Dancing Master; or, Plain and Easy Rules for the Dancing of Country Dances, with the Tunes to each Dance.* London: Dance Books, 1984. (Originally published 1651.)

Meyland, Raymond. *L'Enigme de la musique des basses danses du quinzième siècle.* Bern: Paul Haupt, 1968.

Middleton, Thomas. *Women Beware Women.* Edited by Roma Gill. New York: Norton, 1968, 1983.

———. *The Works of Thomas Middleton.* Edited by A. H. Bullen. 8 vols. New York: AMS Press, 1964.

Mikesell, Margaret Lael. "The Formative Power of Marriage in Stuart Tragedy." In *In Another Country: Feminist Perspectives on Renaissance Drama,* edited by Dorothy Kehler and Susan Baker. Metuchen, N.J.: Scarecrow, 1991.

Miller, James. *Measures of Wisdom: The Cosmic Dance in Classical and Christian Antiquity.* Toronto: University of Toronto Press, 1986.

Molen, Richard L. "Richard Mulcaster and Elizabethan Pageantry." *Studies in English Literature* 14 (1974): 209–21.

Montrose, Louis Adrian. "'Eliza, Queene of Shepherdes,' and the Pastoral of Power." In *Renaissance Historicism,* edited by Arthur F. Kinney and Dan S. Collins. Amherst: University of Massachusetts Press, 1987.

———. "A Kingdom of Shadows." In *The Theatrical City: Culture, Theatre, and Politics in London, 1576–1649,* edited by David L. Smith, Richard Strier, and David Bevington. Cambridge: Cambridge University Press, 1995.

211

————. *The Purpose of Playing: Shakespeare and the Cultural Politics of the Elizabethan Theatre.* Chicago: University of Chicago Press, 1996.

————. "'Shaping Fantasies': Figurations of Gender and Power in Elizabethan Culture." In *Representing the English Renaissance,* edited by Stephen Greenblatt. Berkeley and Los Angeles: University of California Press, 1988.

————. "The Work of Gender in the Discourse of Discovery." *Representations* 33 (Winter 1991): 1–41.

Moxey, Keith. *Peasants, Warriors, and Wives: Popular Imagery in the Reformation.* Chicago: University of Chicago Press, 1989.

Mullaney, Stephen. "Strange Things, Gross Terms, Curious Customs: The Rehearsal of Cultures in the Late Renaissance." In *Representing the English Renaissance,* edited by Stephen Greenblatt. Berkeley and Los Angeles: University of California Press, 1988.

Neely, Carol Thomas. *Broken Nuptials in Shakespeare's Plays.* New Haven: Yale University Press, 1985.

Neill, Michael. "Broken English and Broken Irish: Nation, Language, and the Optic of Power in Shakespeare's Histories." *Shakespeare Quarterly* 45, no. 1 (1994): 1–32.

Nethercot, Arthur H., Charles R. Baskerville, and Virgil B. Heltzel, eds. *Elizabethan Plays.* Revised by Arthur H. Nethercott. New York: Holt, Rinehart and Winston, 1971.

Orgel, Stephen. *Illusion of Power: Political Theater in the English Renaissance.* Berkeley and Los Angeles: University of California Press, 1975.

————. "Jonson and the Amazons." In *Soliciting Interpretation: Literary Theory and Seventeenth-Century Poetry,* edited by Elizabeth D. Harvey and Katherine Eisaman Maus. Chicago: University of Chicago Press, 1991.

————. *The Jonsonian Masque.* New York: Columbia University Press, 1965.

————. "Nobody's Perfect: Or, Why Did the English Stage Take Boys for Women?" *South Atlantic Quarterly* 88 (1989): 7–30.

————. "The Spectacles of State." In *Persons in Groups: Social Behaviors as Identity Formation in Medieval and Renaissance Europe,* edited by Richard C. Trexler. Binghamton, N.Y.: Medieval and Renaissance Texts and Studies, 1985.

Palliser, D. M. *The Age of Elizabeth: England Under the Late Tudors, 1547–1603.* London: Longman, 1983.

Parker, Patricia. *Literary Fat Ladies: Rhetoric, Gender, Property.* London: Methuen, 1987.

————. *Shakespeare from the Margins: Language, Culture, Context.* Chicago: University of Chicago Press, 1995.

Parry, J. H. *The Age of Reconnaisance: Discovery, Exploration, and Settlement, 1450 to 1650.* Berkeley and Los Angeles: University of California Press, 1963, 1981.

————. *The Establishment of the European Hegemony: 1415–1715.* 3d ed. New York: Harper Torchbooks, 1966.

Paster, Gail Kern. *The Body Embarrassed: Drama and the Disciplines of Shame in Early Modern England.* Ithaca: Cornell University Press, 1993.

———. "Leaky Vessels: The Incontinent Women of City Comedy." In *Renaissance Drama as Cultural History,* edited by Mary Beth Rose. Evanston: Northwestern University Press, 1990.

Patterson, Annabel M. *Shakespeare and the Popular Voice.* Oxford: Basil Blackwell, 1989.

Pearse, Nancy Cotton. "Elizabeth Cary, Renaissance Playwright." *Texas Studies in Literature and Language* 18, no. 4 (1977): 601–8.

Pennino-Baskerville, Mary. "Terpsichore Reviled: Antidance Tracts in Elizabethan England." *Sixteenth Century Journal* 22, no. 3 (1991): 475–93.

Perry, Donna. "Procne's Song." In *Gender/Body/Knowledge: Feminist Reconstructions of Being and Knowing,* edited by Alison M. Jaggar and Susan R. Bordo. New Brunswick: Rutgers University Press, 1989.

Pollard, A. W., ed. *The Queen's Majesty: Entertainment at Woodstock, 1575.* Oxford: H. Dorrell and H. Hart, 1903, 1910.

Prior, Roger. "Jewish Musicians at the Tudor Court." *Musical Quarterly* 69, no. 2 (1983): 253–65.

Quinn, David B. *Explorers and Colonies: America, 1500–1625.* London: Hambledon, 1991.

Rackin, Phyllis. "Androgyny, Mimesis, and the Marriage of the Boy Heroine on the English Renaissance Stage." *PMLA* 102 (1987): 29–41.

———. "Historical Difference/Sexual Difference." In *Privileging Gender in Early Modern England,* edited by Jean R. Brink. Kirksville, Mo.: Sixteenth Century Journal, 1993.

———. *Stages of History: Shakespeare's English Chronicles.* Ithaca: Cornell University Press, 1990.

Raffe, W. G., comp., writer, and ed., assisted by M. E. Purdom. *Dictionary of the Dance.* New York: A. S. Barnes, 1964.

Reay, Barry. *Popular Culture in Seventeenth-Century England.* London: Croom Helm, 1985.

Rees, Joan, ed. *The Writings of Fulke Greville.* London: Athlone, 1973.

Reyher, Paul. *Les Masques Anglais.* New York: Benjamin Blom, 1909, 1964.

Ringler, William A., Jr. "The Number of Actors in Shakespeare's Early Plays." In *The Seventeenth-Century Stage: A Collection of Critical Essays,* edited and with an Introduction by Gerald Eades Bentley. Chicago: University of Chicago Press, 1968.

Rowe, George E. *Thomas Middleton and the New Comedy Tradition.* Lincoln: University of Nebraska Press, 1979.

Russell, Conrad. *The Crisis of Parliaments: English History, 1509–1660.* Oxford: Oxford University Press, 1971.

Rust, Frances. *Dance in Society.* London: Routledge and Kegan Paul, 1969.

Sabol, Andrew J., ed. *Four Hundred Songs and Dances from the Stuart Masque.* Providence: Brown University Press, 1978, 1982.

———. "The Original Music for the French King's Masque in *Love's Labour's Lost.*" In *Shakespeare's Universe: Renaissance Ideas and Conventions. Essays in Honour of W. R. Elton,* edited by John M. Mucciolo, with the assistance of Stephen J. Doloff and Edward A. Rauchat. Brookfield, Vt.: Scholar, 1996.

Sachs, Curt. *World History of the Dance.* Translated by Bessie Schoenberg. New York: Norton, 1937.

Sanderson, James. *Sir John Davies.* Boston: Twayne, 1975.

Schweikart, Patrocinio P. "Reading Ourselves." In *Speaking of Gender,* edited by Elaine Showalter. New York: Routledge, Chapman and Hall, 1989.

Sedinger, Tracey. "'If Sight and Shape be True': The Epistemology of Cross-Dressing on the London Stage." *Shakespeare Quarterly* 48, no. 1 (Spring 1997): 63–79.

Shapiro, James S. *Shakespeare and the Jews.* New York: Columbia University Press, 1996.

Sharp, Cecil. *The Morris Book.* 1912–24. Yorkshire: EP Publishing, 1974.

Siddiqui, Yumna. "Dark Incontinents: The Discourses of Race and Gender in Three Renaissance Masques." In *Renaissance Drama* 23, edited by Mary Beth Rose. Evanston: Northwestern University Press, 1993.

Smith, Bruce. *Homosexual Desire in Shakespeare's England: A Cultural Poetics.* Chicago: University of Chicago Press, 1991.

———. "Landscape with Figures: The Three Realms of Queen Elizabeth's Country-house Revels." *Renaissance Drama,* n.s., 8 (1997): 57–109.

Smith, David L., Richard Strier, and David Bevington, eds. *The Theatrical City: Culture, Theatre, and Politics in London, 1576–1649.* Cambridge: Cambridge University Press, 1995.

Sorell, Walter. *Dance in Its Time.* New York: Doubleday, 1981.

———. "Shakespeare and the Dance." *Shakespeare Quarterly* 8 (1957): 367–71.

Stallybrass, Peter. "Patriarchal Tendencies: The Body Enclosed." In *Rewriting the Renaissance: The Discourses of Sexual Difference in Early Modern Europe,* edited by Margaret W. Ferguson, Maureen Quilligan, and Nancy J. Vickers. Chicago: University of Chicago Press, 1986.

———. "Reading the Body: *The Revenger's Tragedy* and the Jacobean Theater of Consumption." In *Renaissance Drama* 18, edited by Mary Beth Rose. Evanston: Northwestern University Press, 1987.

Stallybrass, Peter, and Allon White. *The Politics and Poetics of Transgression.* Ithaca: Cornell University Press, 1986.

Starkey, David, ed. *Henry VIII: A European Court in England.* London: Collins and Brown, 1991.

Stone, Lawrence. *The Causes of the English Revolution, 1529–1642.* New York: Harper and Row, 1972.

———. *The Crisis of the Aristocracy, 1558–1641.* Oxford: Oxford University Press, 1965.

———. *The Family, Sex and Marriage in England, 1500–1800.* London: Weidenfeld and Nicolson, 1977.

———. "Social Mobility in England, 1500–1700." *Past and Present* 33 (1966): 16–55.

Strong, Roy C. *Art and Power: Renaissance Festivals, 1450–1650.* Woodbridge, Suffolk: Boydell, 1973.

———. *The Cult of Elizabeth: Elizabethan Portraiture and Pageantry.* Berkeley and Los Angeles: University of California Press, 1977.

Strutt, Joseph. *Sports and Pastimes of the People of England: Including the Rural and Domestic Recreations, May Games, Mummeries, Shows, Processions, Pageants, and Pompous Spectacles, From the Earliest Period to the Present Time.* Edited by William Howe. London: Chatto and Windus, 1876.

Sutherland, Sarah P. *Masques in Jacobean Tragedy.* New York: AMS Press, 1983.

Tennenhouse, Leonard. *Power on Display: The Politics of Shakespearean Genres.* London: Methuen, 1986.

Thesiger, Sarah. "The Orchestra of Sir John Davies and the Image of the Dance." *Journal of the Warburg and Courtauld Institutes* 36 (1973): 277–304.

Tillyard, E. M. W. *The Elizabethan World Picture.* New York: Macmillan, 1943.

Todorov, Tzvetan. *The Conquest of America: The Question of the Other.* Translated by Richard Howard. New York: Harper and Row, 1984.

Tooley, R. V. *Maps and Map-Makers.* New York: Bonanza Books, 1949, 1961.

Travitsky, Betty S. "The *Feme Covert* in Elizabeth Cary's *Mariam.*" In *Ambiguous Realities: Women in the Middle Ages and Renaissance,* edited by Carole Levin and Jeanie Watson. Detroit: Wayne State University Press, 1987.

Trexler, Richard C. *Persons in Groups: Social Behavior as Identity Formation in Medieval and Renaissance Europe.* Binghamton, N.Y.: Medieval and Renaissance Texts and Studies, 1985.

Tricomi, Albert. *Anticourt Drama in England, 1603–1642.* Charlottesville: University Press of Virginia, 1989.

Underdown, David. *Fire from Heaven: Life in an English Town in the Seventeenth Century.* New Haven: Yale University Press, 1992.

———. *Revel, Riot, and Rebellion: Popular Politics and Culture in England, 1603–1660.* Oxford: Clarendon, 1985.

Venuti, Lawrence. *Our Halcyon Dayes: English Prerevolutionary Texts and Postmodern Culture.* Madison: University of Wisconsin Press, 1989.

Vigarello, Georges. "The Upward Training of the Body from the Age of Chivalry to Courtly Civility." In *Fragments for a History of the Human Body, Part Two,* edited by Michel Feher, with Ramona Naddaff and Nadia Tazi. New York: Zone, 1989.

Wadworth, Frank W. "'Rough Music' in *The Duchess of Malfi:* Webster's Dance of Madmen and the Charivari Tradition." In *Rite, Drama, Festival, Spectacle: Rehearsals Toward a Theory of Cultural Performance,* edited by John A. MacAloon. Philadelphia: Institute for the Study of Human Issues, 1984.

Weimann, Robert. *Shakespeare and the Popular Tradition in the Theater: Studies in the Social Dimension of Dramatic Form and Function.* Edited by Robert Schwartz. Baltimore: Johns Hopkins University Press, 1978.

———. "Towards a Literary Theory of Ideology: Mimesis, Representation, Authority." In *Shakespeare Reproduced: The Text in History and Ideology,* edited by Jean E. Howard and Marion F. O'Connor. New York: Methuen, 1987.

Welch, Charles, ed. *Register of Freeman of the City of London in the Reigns of Henry VIII and Edward IV.* London: Archeological Society, 1908.

Welsford, Enid. *The Court Masque: A Study in the Relationship between Poetry and the Revels.* New York: Russell and Russell, 1927.

Whigham, Frank. *Ambition and Privilege: The Social Tropes of Elizabethan Courtesy Theory.* Berkeley and Los Angeles: University of California Press, 1984.

White, Hayden. *Tropics of Discourse: Essays in Cultural Criticism.* Baltimore: Johns Hopkins University Press, 1978.

Wickham, Glynne William Gladstone. *Early English Stages, Vol. 1 1300 to 1660.* London: Routledge, 1959.

———. *The Medieval Theatre.* Cambridge: Cambridge University Press, 1974.

Wildeblood, Joan. *Apologie de la Danse by F. De Lauze 1623: A Treatise of Instruction in Dancing and Deportment given in the Original French with a Translation, Introduction, and Notes by Joan Wildeblood.* Music transcribed by Eduardo M. Torner. London: Frederick Muller, 1952.

Wilding, Michael. "Milton's 'A Masque Presented at Ludlow Castle, 1634': Theatre and Politics at the Border." *Trivium* 29 (May 1985): 147–79.

Wiles, David. *Shakespeare's Almanac: A Midsummer Night's Dream, Marriage, and the Elizabethan Calendar.* Cambridge: D. S. Brewer, 1993.

Williams, Raymond. *Marxism and Literature.* Oxford: Oxford University Press, 1977.

Williamson, G. C. *George, Third Earl of Cumberland (1558–1605), His Life and Voyages.* Cambridge: Cambridge University Press, 1920.

———. *Lady Anne Clifford, Countess of Dorset, Pembroke, and Montgomery, 1590–1676.* London: S. R. Publishers, 1867, 1922.

Willis, Deborah. *Malevolent Nurture: Witch-Hunting and Maternal Power in Early Modern England.* Ithaca: Cornell University Press, 1995.

Wilshire, Donna. "The Uses of Myth, Image, and the Female Body in Re-visioning Knowledge." In *Gender/Body/Knowledge: Feminist Reconstructions of Being and Knowing,* edited by Alison M. Jaggar and Susan R. Bordo. New Brunswick: Rutgers University Press, 1989.

Wilson, Jean. *Entertainments for Elizabeth I.* Woodbridge, U.K.: D. S. Brewer, 1980.

Wright, Celeste Turner. "The Amazons in Elizabethan Literature." *Studies in Philology* 37, no. 3 (July 1940): 433–56.

Wright, Louis B. *Middle-Class Culture in Elizabethan England.* Chapel Hill: University of North Carolina Press, 1935. Ithaca: Published for the Folger Shakespeare Library by Cornell University Press, 1958.

Wright, Pam. "A Change in Direction: The Ramifications of a Female Household, 1558–1603." In *The English Court: From the Wars of the Roses to the Civil War,* edited by David Starkey et al. London: Longman, 1987.

Wrightson, Keith. *English Society, 1580–1680.* New Brunswick: Rutgers University Press, 1982.

Wynne-Davies, Marion. "The Queen's Masque: Renaissance Women and the Seventeenth-Century Court Masque." In *Gloriana's Face: Public and Private, in the English Renaissance,* edited by S. P. Cerasano and Marion Wynne-Davies. Detroit: Wayne State University Press, 1992.

Yates, Frances. *Astraea: The Imperial Theme in the Sixteenth Century.* London: Routledge and Kegan Paul, 1975.

Index

217